Dear Reader,

If you've bought this book, I know you're interested in your customers and how to improve your service to them.

I know that you can't give excellent service 100 percent of the time. Let's face it, mistakes happen. And I want to know about them. This is my first Nationwide "Worst" Customer Service Contest! Positively Outrageous, I know. But I want you to tell me your absolutely worst customer service story from you, your company, or about your own business, if you're lucky enough to own one. In 300 words or less, tell me all the gory details. You have until Feb. 1, 1994 to send me your tale of customer woe. I'll personally select the "winner,"or should I say "loser"? My reward? I will come and visit you, your company, or your business, and conduct a personal, free seminar on how to improve your customer service and how to create that essential Positively Outrageous Service, which will WOW your customers and keep them coming back to your company.

So don't be shy. I'm darned sure those bad word-of-mouth customer experiences are already floating around inside your company, so just send them on down to Uncle Scott:

T. Scott Gross
HCR 1, Box 561
Center Point, TX 78010

D1316278

I'll select the best of the toughest by March of 1994. For the runners-up, you'll receive a free copy of *How to Get What You Want from Almost Anybody.*

"The number-one perceived value is a good time. So show 'em a good time!"

— Stan Clark, Eskimo Joe's

"If I didn't do the things that people told me not to do, I wouldn't be where I am today."

— Phil Romano, entrepreneur

"Some people who have a rigid sense of what is and isn't management, don't accommodate this well. They don't seem to grasp that the world is lining up into two camps. . .the devalued commodity and the valued experience."

— Paul Meunier, Signature Flight Support

"I have a good time. When people ask, 'Who are you playing to?' I tell them, 'myself.' Because if you are enjoying yourself, they enjoy you!"

— Emmett Kelly, Jr., clown

"Rule number one is to love your audience. Whether or not they love you is immaterial. You love them. And when that happens...it's real hard not to love somebody who loves you."

— Herb Henson, Fiesta Texas

POSITIVELY OUTRAGEOUS SERVICE and SHOWMANSHIP

*Industrial Strength Fun
Makes Sales Sizzle!!!*

T. SCOTT GROSS

MASTERMEDIA LIMITED • NEW YORK

ISBN # 0-942361-82-2
Production services by Martin Cook Associates, Ltd., New York.
Manufactured in the United States of America

10 9 8 7 6 5 4 3 2 1

Table of Contents

Preface

There is one thing that I have learned since writing *Positively Outrageous Service:* The product or service you sell is almost not relevant. It is only an excuse to connect with the customer.

How you handle that connection earns you the right to take up space on the planet.

Giving Positively Outrageous Service, dazzling folks with small acts of showmanship and truly loving on your customers is easier said than done. Our biggest concern should be that we do more than talk our talk, we want to make the promise...and then keep it.

Saint Francis of Assisi said, "It is of no use walking anywhere to preach unless our walking is our preaching."

Serve well.

Have fun.

Make a difference.

Don't forget to love one another.

Positively Outrageous Service and Showmanship

Scott Gross's book proves that breaking the standards and doing things people told you not to do is the essence of showmanship.

— *Philip Romano, entrepreneur*

CHAPTER ONE

POS, Again

Life seems filled with those awkward moments.

Sometimes after hours of careful rehearsal, you say your piece only to discover — as the door slams behind you — that there was one clever line you forgot to add. It was oh, so-clever, and you have blown the opportunity. It would have made all the difference, you think.

The idea you tried to sell would have been accepted in a roar of applause. Your pitch would have been received warmly because you had been so brilliant at making the point.

But all the would-haves, could-haves and should-haves in the end don't amount to a hill of beans.

Fortunately, you've invited me in again and now we can share the ideas that you have taught me about Positively Outrageous Service over the past several years.

Positively Outrageous Service is the service story you cannot wait to tell. It's the surprise that made your customer say WOW!

The long definition is: A random, unexpected service event that is so out of proportion to the circumstance and so involving of the customer that it results in compelling, positive word-of-mouth.

What makes that definition so interesting? When you substitute the word "negative" for the word "positive," you have the definition of the *worst* service ever.

It turns out that the difference between great service and awful service is purely a matter of expectation. In fact, it is the difference between the expectation and the reality that causes that fabled marketing concept that we call word-of-mouth. Customers talk about service when they have been surprised. When we deliver service outside their expectations, customers feel compelled to talk about it.

Perhaps it's not surprising that customers do not easily talk about good service. They rarely make a point of calling a friend or butting into a conversation to tell something good. But they shout from the mountaintops when they have been cheated of the service experience they expected.

There is no point in moaning about the fact that humans by nature do not take marketing your product or service to be their personal mission in life. What we can do is take advantage of human nature. If we understand that people are most likely to talk when they have been surprised, then we can surprise them and collect our leverage on that surprise in positive word-of-mouth and increased customer loyalty.

Promise good customer service in a clean, safe environment at reasonable prices. Deliver on that promise and what's there to talk about? You promised...you delivered. Big deal.

Customers will talk when they perceive that they got something they didn't expect, or perhaps pay for, or if they think that somehow they have been cheated out of the service they deserve. There is rarely a price component listed for customer service. But don't think for a moment that customers are not aware that they pay for quality service.

On the other hand, if customers arrive not expecting much and you keep that promise, it's not likely that they will complain. Think of some of those "plastic places," the fast feeders that make no more promise than that the food will be served quickly and that the price will be cheap, cheap, cheap. Ever wonder how they can remain in business serving mediocre food year after year? Simple. They promise mediocre food, they deliver mediocre food, no surprises.

Beware the Nordstrom Curse!

Customers only talk when the expectation is different from the reality. Nordstrom, a predominantly west coast department store, famous for incredible customer service, is cursed with a "crisis of expectation."

The problem for Nordstrom seems to have developed when the media began to report on their fabulous customer service. Nordstrom employees are highly empowered to do pretty much whatever it takes to keep their customers happy. That's not a problem. What is a problem is that customers began to *expect* that someone would jump through a hoop every time they visited a Nordstrom.

There is one widely told story about a woman who ran out of gas as she was driving by a Nordstrom. The concierge (yes, they have a concierge!) rushed into the street, pushed the woman's car to the curb, and immediately proceeded to get her a tank of gas. Of course, this was all at no charge.

All by itself this is definitely an example of Positively Outrageous Service. The problem comes only when people begin to expect this kind of treatment on a regular basis.

I like to embellish the story by saying, "Now when people in the neighborhood get low on gas, they circle Nordstrom!"

When your reputation gets ahead of reality, you have created a problem, not necessarily of not good enough service but of too high a service expectation. Often when people leave Nordstrom, they leave disappointed...not because the service wasn't good because it almost always is, but because the service did not achieve the level of the fables that Nordstrom customers have come to believe.

We happened to share a limousine with a Nordstrom's manager while on a trip to San Francisco.

"Oh, Nordstrom! You guys really have a reputation!"

"Too good, I'm afraid," came the surprise answer. "We would be a lot better off if people expected less. Then when we had an opportunity to step out of the box, we could knock their socks off. Now they just expect the moon and the stars and are disappointed if we don't deliver them wrapped in foil at no charge."

Positively Outrageous Service really is a matter of surprise. Remove the element of surprise and you are back to everyday service. Whatever your level of service is, hold something in reserve to use when the occasion is right for making a customer say WOW!

People discover that an act that would be Positively Outrageous Service at one place is simply an expected part of the routine somewhere else. The element of surprise makes the difference. Hold back something for a surprise. Do it only on a random basis. And, for goodness sake, don't tell half the world. It will only raise the level of expectation and make satisfying customers with your ordinarily good service all the more difficult.

True students of Positively Outrageous Service understand that the element of surprise creates compelling, positive word-of-mouth. Random. Random. Random.

The principle of the slot machine best explains why POS works.

Why do people play the slots? Because, most of the time, they deposit their hard-earned money and get absolutely nothing in return. Actually, it is because occasionally they get more than they put into the machine. And because they never know just exactly when that miraculous event will occur.

The payoff on slot machines is about 95 percent. Theoretically, if you put $100 into a slot machine, the odds are that you'll get $95 in return.

Theoretically, that is. My friend, Paul Russell, explained to me that slot machines have little built-in discouragement detectors. About belly button high, these discouragement detectors go off just at the moment when you have decided that the machine you are playing is not going to get another dollar.

You make the decision that if this machine doesn't pay on the very next bet, you're going to move on and fill up the rest of the machines! Boom! The discouragement detector goes off and as you walk away to try another machine, you hear the chink, chink, chink of three of your hard earned dollars returning to you via the pan at the base of the machine. You now have had returned to you three of the $40 that you dumped into this turkey and being the intelligent, savvy human being that you are, you turn around and say these immortal words: "I'm on a roll now!"

Back you go to fill that machine until either you run out of dollars or the little detector goes off again.

That is how Positively Outrageous Service works. Occasionally you do something that is so unexpected that the customer comes back again and again, waiting for the surprise to hit again.

Surprises that happen on a too frequent or regular basis cease to be surprises. They become expectations. And expectations that are not fulfilled become the subject of compelling, albeit negative, word-of-mouth. Careful!

Out of Proportion

A Positively Outrageous Service event must be big. Big enough to break through the clutter of the ordinary and stand out in the mind of the customer.

Too often we fail in our promotions because we failed to dare and take our idea to a higher level. A typical example: The restauranteur who offers half-price desserts on Tuesday nights. Have you ever been sitting at home in your Jockey's, watching the tube when you remembered that it was a half-price dessert night? Did you jump up and yell, "Honey, get dressed quick...it's half-price dessert night!"

NOT!

That is the point. What may have been just another ordinary event missed becoming a POS classic simply because someone failed to think big enough.

Instead of routine...make that "boring and expected" special offer, give me a chance to be surprised or rewarded beyond the expected.

While exploring the principles behind Positively Outrageous Service, we created a promotion that came to be known as the Great Ping Pong Pour, when we dropped ping pong balls by the thousands on the parking lot at our restaurant. Each ball was numbered and good for a prize from a local merchant.

The results were fabulous. Thousands of people came to the event and it had a tremendous, positive impact on our sales. But we blew it. We had already set our customers for a surprise. They knew that the ping pong balls were each good for a prize, but what if we had focused our resources on one or two really incredible prizes? Like the lottery when the pot gets really big.

If we had put more bucks into a truly out-of-proportion prize, we would have had a turnout that would have been more than huge. It would have been incredible!

Positively Outrageous Service does not require some unbelievable prize or expense to create compelling, positive word-of-mouth. But...the velocity and the quantity of what word-of-mouth results increases geometrically as the act itself exceeds the expected. Get it? Bigger surprises create geometrically greater word-of-mouth advertising.

Meet Me in Fun

We like to say that Positively Outrageous Service invites the customer to play or otherwise become highly involved. What we did not fully appreciate the first time around is the importance of carefully selecting your customer or target before you begin anything that may smack of playfulness. Though POS may be both borderline-bizarre and sweetly elegant, if you intend to serve up a dose of the former, you had better pick your mark with care.

It isn't any different than a nightclub act that features a magician or hypnotist. The call goes out for volunteers and immediately 100 people look into their lap, playing the game that made us laugh as two-year-olds who, when playing "peek-a-boo," assume that if they cover their eyes, they cannot be seen.

So what do we do? We look into our laps, working on that same distorted principle that by looking there, we cannot be seen. Except, of course, for your weird Uncle Norbert, who is nearly jumping out of his skin in an effort to be selected.

And what are you doing once you see that the magician isn't interested in you but weird ol' Uncle Norbert? We point to Norb and suggest that he would make a perfect dummy.

Point: Not everyone wants to play at every game every time.

The answer: Look for someone who is "in fun," a term that we apply to people who are ready to play.

It's easy to spot folks who are ready to play. They look like your Uncle

Norbert. Actually, they just look like fun people. The most noticeable features of these people: The smile, the willingness to speak up, and the body language that announces there is enough energy to handle a little extra attention. (You might want to use these same clues to spot potential new hires!)

In the hands of a pro show-off, even the hard-core, non-fun folks can be brought around. Here's my story:

At the drive-through of our small restaurant, folks who have OD'd on too much pushy selling at other fast-food operations often respond to our request for their order by listing their desires followed by a very definite "and that's ALL!"

"Yes, sir! That's one two-piece mixed order of chicken and biscuits...and that's absolutely all. I won't even mention our fresh-brewed iced tea or our sweet, buttery corn on the cob. Please drive through and we'll have you out of here in a New York minute."

At the drive-through window, we let them wait just long enough for them to see us package an order of that sweet, buttery corn on the cob that we promised not to even mention.

"What kind of corn did you say you have?"

"Oh, that was sweet, buttery corn on the cob. USDA grade-A fancy, just about to burst with flavor."

Now, here is the cue to walking away with the rest of the order.

"Here you go, sir. Two pieces of the hottest, freshest fried chicken you ever wrapped your gums around...and, as promised, that's ALL."

"I think I'll try some of that corn you've been talking about."

"Gee, I'm sorry. But you've already driven across the I-can't-sell-you-corn-line. I can make an exception this time, but next time you'll have to drive all the way around and start over again."

Get it? If the approach is right, even Scrooge himself can be sucked in with a little charm and pizazz.

One Man's...

It is amazing that the definition of the worst service you have ever received is identical to the definition of the best service you ever experienced. As Bill Oncken, management thinker and trainer extraordinaire, used to point out, the definition of comedy is exactly the same as the definition of tragedy. The difference is little more than a matter of perspective.

The same holds true for service that is Positively Outrageous or simply outrageous. Either way, it is unexpected, out of proportion to the circumstance, and the customer is highly involved. And in both instances, the result is compelling word-of-mouth, positive on the one hand, negative on the other.

What accounts for the swing is all in the expectation. It is true that if you expect mediocre, even awful service and you get it, you are not likely to complain. After all, that's what you expected. It is only when *reality is different from the expectation* that people begin to talk.

Poor service, fair service, wonderful service. Like beauty, it lies in the eye of the beholder.

Trends Revisited

Several trends seem to control the modern consumer. These are not the only trends impacting society, but they are the most important trends influencing consumer behavior.

An aging population. Obviously we are all getting older. What may not be quite so obvious is that the average age of consumers in the developed western world is getting older. With the post-World War II baby boom, we see the increasing age and large numbers of the "Boomers" influencing the shape of the economy.

Older people have different needs based not solely on their age, but also on the cultural influences that shaped their development. In the early seventies, investors could build a restaurant or movie theater darned near anywhere and count on it to be a success. In those days, markets were not saturated with competitors and the baby boom provided a steadily growing population to gobble up whatever goods or services were offered. It was an "If you build it, we will come" kind of world.

Young consumers will buy nearly anything. They have much less expectation of quality and a considerable reliance on fad and style. Tell them that something is cool and they will buy it.

As the Boomers began to age, their tastes and needs began to change.

Now, much less influenced by style alone, Boomers look for quality and security. They want to know that they are getting the best for their money. They like guaranties. They want to avoid mistakes. Security is a key issue. Just for an example, notice how few older adults attend the movies. Do you think it's because they have lost an interest in all things Hollywood? Not at all. Older consumers do not want to face the insecurity of a 40-acre parking lot on a dark and threatening Friday night.

Along with this trend toward a net older population is the fact that older consumers for the most part are shopping fatigued. No longer are they likely to go gaga over a stroll through the mall. These consumers have shopped and they have dropped. They no longer have a need for stuff. They have stuff.

Older consumers have so much stuff that they have no room to put more stuff if they could be convinced to buy it. Perhaps the one exception might be when it comes to buying toys. As the baby boomlet begins to develop, as the yuppie-puppies begin to have little yuppies of their own, Grandma and Grandpa Boomer can be expected to jump back into the market for stuff. Otherwise, it doesn't make a lot of sense to expect wild consumer spending for stuff to drive the economy.

What the new consumer will want is an experience. After all, they won't be buying stuff. What will there be left to buy but experiences? This trend seems to point toward a new boom in travel. Not just any kind of travel, but travel that broadens horizons, that educates and perhaps has social value, such as a tour that might also include an archeological dig or a week spent building houses with the Habitat for Humanity of Jimmy Carter fame.

But people will still have to shop for household necessities and such. The trend simply says that those businesses that can make even such mundane chores a bit of an experience will have a distinct competitive advantage. What can you do to make the ordinary extraordinary?

Robert Blazer turned shopping for produce into an experience and wound up with a produce stand that grosses 50 million dollars a year. Blazer buys farm fresh produce directly from local farmers and stocks a wide variety of both common and exotic produce in his suburban Decatur, Georgia store. What he did was nothing that hadn't been done a dozen times over, except that he managed to make shopping for produce an experience.

He put more varieties under one roof than anyone would expect. He made a big deal out of a little deal. He made shopping fun. The bizarre-like atmosphere did more than attract a curious consumer. It also attracted a rather curious collection of foreign-born employees who felt comfortable working at a store that for all the world resembled the town square in their native country. Faced with a small army of employees who seemed to speak nearly every language but English, Blazer turned a potential liability into an asset and further added to the experience of shopping at Your DeKalb Farmers Market.

Name tags do more than announce names. They tell the customer what language is spoken by the employee behind the badge. Not only does this overcome resistance to dealing with folks who may struggle a bit with English, but it also heightens the experience and serves as a great conversation starter. Imagine being waited on by a clerk whose name tag proclaims, "Patel, I speak Gujarati and Hindi."

The question comes back to you. What can you create to make doing business with your company an experience?

Trend number two is declining leisure. The seventies promised that, with the advent of the computer, westerners would soon be struggling to fill their days with meaningful activity. The computer promised to do all our work both better and faster.

Whoever made that promise had yet to read the manuals that make software into an alien dialect! The surprise has been that, instead of helping us finish our work hours ahead of time, the computer allows us simply to do more work in the same amount of time.

And, somehow, we have found even more work to do. Since 1972, roughly the advent of the personal computer, Americans are working not fewer hours but more. Today, Americans work 158 more hours per year. This amounts to nearly a month's worth of 40-hour work weeks.

As you might expect, as leisure time shrinks, its value increases. If there is a single cry of the decade, it surely must be the consumers' constant questioning to discover is something "worth it?"

Worth it.

Today's consumers are so cautious that they constantly evaluate whether or not something is "worth it."

People no longer eat empty calories. They want all their calories to be good calories. If they are going to eat fat and cholesterol-laden foods, they had better be "worth it." Ice cream sandwiches are out because they just aren't "worth it." On the other hand, Dove bars are in because, even though they may have many times the fat and calories, they are so good that they are "worth it."

As leisure time continues to shrink, consumers will become even more critical as they evaluate whether a business has made their investment in time "worth it."

Faster service may be in, but also so is the trend toward quality service. People are telling us that they will not wait. What they are saying is that if we want to them to wait, we had better well make the wait "worth it."

Consumers faced with declining leisure can be expected to turn increasingly to shopping by catalogue. If you offer a product that can be easily distributed via catalogue, then it's time to ask what you have done to make shopping in person at your store worth the inconvenience of dragging halfway across town and fighting for a parking space.

The catalogue store is open 24-hours-per-day. Parking is no problem at all and waiting for the product has been made a problem of the past, thanks to a host of reliable, inexpensive overnight delivery services. (Did we say "inexpensive?" Perhaps we should just say that they are "worth it.")

Declining leisure simply means that customers will be increasingly critical when deciding how they will spend that precious commodity of time. Every buying decision will come under close scrutiny. Salvation will belong to those who have given that buying decision value in excess of the product itself. Service in the unfolding '90s will be seen as "adding value."

Adding value with service means getting the perceived cost of the service as low as possible. This cost of service could be called the "cost of convenience." Smart business thinkers understand that the difference between the cost of the raw materials and the cost of the delivered goods is the cost of convenience.

For example, if I could make a sandwich at home for 50 cents worth of ingredients, and that same sandwich can be purchased for a dollar from a local merchant, then the cost of the convenience for having someone else make the sandwich and clean up the mess is 50 cents. The lower the cost of convenience, the greater the perceived value of doing business with the provider of the service.

The problem gets complicated when I have to put a value on the time and effort I must spend to do business with you. Was it difficult to park? Did I have to wait a long time? Were your employees friendly? Or better yet, did you do something for me that I couldn't have done for myself that made the transaction an experience that was "worth it?"

The trend toward high-tech needing to be psychologically balanced by high-touch plays perfectly into the hands of an industrial showman. John Naisbett named the trend years ago in his book *Megatrends*. He was right on target then. If it's possible to be closer than on target, then that is exactly the case with high-tech/high-touch.

Simply stated, the trend tells us that as customers deal more and more in a high-tech world, they will need to put their lives into emotional balance through high-touch experiences. Apparently, the human psyche needs to be in touch with nature. We need to touch and be touched by other living beings. When we were created, there was a limit installed on our ability to tolerate plastic. Plastic cups, plastic food, and plastic relationships.

The industrial showman realizes that customers are crying for an experience. They want to touch and be touched. They can only tolerate so many conversations via a drive-through menu speaker. They can accommodate a finite number of conversations with their Automated Teller Machines.

We can take advantage of this need for human contact as well as the need to be in contact with nature and natural materials.

Customers are not seeking earth tones so much as they are seeking the Earth herself. There really is a need for fern bars as long as neither the ferns nor the waitstaff are plastic. Customers will kill for an opportunity to breathe unpolluted air just as they will seek to do business with those who live the natural lifestyle they envy.

L.L. Bean, for example, does not sell great boots as much as they sell the idea of needing to wear boots.

Move the customer service phones of Lands' End from its small, midwestern town to midtown New York City and you risk destroying the very reason why people call them in the first place. Those customers are buying a lifestyle fantasy. There is plenty of room for other entrepreneurs to sell the exact same product in a radically different package.

Over and over again, customers are telling us to reach out and touch someone...them! Look at most of the really successful businesses of today and, if they are not selling commodity items at a discount from a warehouse, they are selling an experience. Customers today are looking for an experience. That is what industrial-strength showmen are doing. They are inviting their customers to play.

The fourth trend that is shaping the way smart folks do business today: Polarized buying habits. Look at Sears. Quick!

Sears is targeted straight at the American middle class and failing miserably. It's not only the Wal-Marts of the world that are beating their pants off...everyone is beating their pants off! And it's probably not their fault.

They haven't offended or lost touch with their market. Their market simply discovered that there are alternative ways to shop. Sam Walton made them a different sort of offer and they didn't refuse.

Sears' customers discovered that there are some products for which sane people simply do not any longer pay full retail to purchase. Much as the fast feeders have pretty much destroyed their full price market, retailers are quickly following suit. Even the airlines have so many discount programs that passengers who are forced by short notice to pay full price are resentful as the Devil, and can't help feeling ripped off.

The Giant Stirs

What should make the little guy shake in his boots is the fact that the big discount houses are quickly discovering that providing quality customer service is not all that expensive.

A recent story in the *San Antonio Express-News* made the point very well. A reader wrote to cheer a Wal-Mart manager for service that can only be described as Positively Outrageous Service.

The manager had received a call from a hospital patient who was recovering from back surgery. Still not quite fully mobile, but needing shoes to cover the leg braces that would be required during her recovery, the patient inquired if a pair could be sent to the hospital by taxi.

"No way," said the manager. "We can do a lot better than that."

After work, he arrived at her bedside with an assortment of shoes in hand. There he assisted the patient with her purchase and, in the process, made a Wal-Mart customer for life.

Now who says that the discounters have only price as an advantage?

Sell it cheap or make it an experience. There seems to be little or no middle ground. At least, the middle ground is shrinking and those who insist on playing in the middle may find themselves stuck in exactly that spot. Customers today are looking for an experience. When the discounters discover how to make shopping with them an experience, the little guy had better watch out or sell out.

What are you doing to make doing business with you an experience? What are you doing to make doing business with you fun? If you fail to come up with an answer, be patient. Your competition will.

More Lessons

We learned from Positively Outrageous Service that there are thousands of heads-up business people who encourage their employees to play with the customers. Many wrote or called to say thank you for giving them permission to do the things they have been doing or wanted to do for years. Now they had a name for the funny things that they do with their customers.

But there is a middle ground between Positively Outrageous Service and ordinary get 'em in and get 'em out customer service. If Positively Outrageous Service is something that you do at random to your customers, what do you call that playful style of service that on a regular basis invites the customer to get involved with his or her service transaction?

When the old garden tractor, a 1977 16-HP Sears Ugly, bit the dust, we towed her up to C&C Air Cooled Engine Repair. "Fix this turkey," was all I said as I tossed the key onto the mechanic's bench. In a matter of hours, a polite voice called to give the prognosis. He told me what had already been done and made several recommendations.

"Whatever it takes," was my response. Still, it was hard not to be impressed with a mechanic who wanted me to be absolutely sure that not only would he fix the original complaint, but that he had anticipated the near-term problems as well.

When we stopped to check on the old horse, the mechanic was grinning from ear to ear. "I think I have this baby running like a top. You know, it's about the ugliest looking thing I've ever allowed in my garage, but I think it has lots of miles left on it if you will let me take care of it for you."

Then he insisted that I look under the hood so that I could learn where to find the model and serial numbers. That way, if there was a problem, I could call him with the information and he could order parts in advance of picking up my tractor.

"Can you deliver it for me? My hitch hasn't been installed yet."

"No problem. I'll call you just before I'm ready to leave."

My dog announced the arrival of the mechanic and his duelie truck, and we went out to help with the unloading.

"Here, I brought you a present!" This was accompanied by a smile that seemed more than a little out of place.

"What is it?" I tested.

"Go ahead. Open it."

It was a bag of dirt.

"Just what I've always wanted. How can I ever say thank you enough?"

"When I fired it up and engaged the mower deck, the whole thing stopped dead. I got all that dirt out of the pulley assembly. It should work like a charm now. I greased the blade shafts while I had it open."

By now I didn't care what the bill was. I had been involved from the very beginning. I didn't feel like I had been sold a bill of goods. I had been given a bag of dirt. But it was my dirt. It helped me understand how my mower was behaving and I had acquired a partner in keeping the world's ugliest lawn tractor going and going and going.

There are other ways to keep the customer involved besides inviting him to look under the hood or bringing him a bag of dirt. Perhaps the best way to look at the opportunity for involving the customer is to think of the process as a continuum. At one end is the too usual "thank you for shopping Acme" approach. At the other is that Positively Outrageous Service event.

It is the "somewhere in the middle" that we handle here.

We have a name for that middle ground between so-so service and Positively Outrageous Service. We call it "Flirting." It is so similar to the social dance we engaged in as teenagers to attract members of the opposite sex and make ourselves attractive to our peer group, that "flirting" just accurately describes how true lovers of people go about playing with their customers.

Flirting is that playful kidding that goes on between people who like each other. If you haven't done it, or worse, been invited to play along, then shame on you. Flirting occurs naturally. Perhaps that is why it is such a rarity when service workers deal with the public. It requires the suspension of anonymity.

Did you get that? The suspension of anonymity is the willingness to put aside the fact that you have not been formally introduced or, plainer, that you do not know the person you are about to serve.

Now you have a picture of the flirting personality. It is that Will Rogers persona who has never met a stranger.

Our neighbor's daughter was part of a group of high school seniors who were touring a nearby college. The goal was to help the young people become familiar with the campus and students, and ease their adjustment to campus living.

While waiting in the bus for the sponsors to return with directions, a group of about twenty young men happened by. They began an exercise program within sight of the bus.

"I bet you a dollar that you won't go out and say hello," dared the girls who were interested in flirting by proxy, but too bashful to make the first move on their own. They certainly could have saved their money because our neighbor was off the bus in a flash.

"Howdy!" And a smile was all she needed to break the ice. Within minutes, the fellows had turned the conversation to a favorite campus pastime, dancing.

"Can you two-step?"

"I'm a country girl and can two-step with the best of them."

"Can you jitterbug?"

"Sure!"

"But do you know the...."

When the sponsors returned to the bus, the noses pressed against the windows told them that something unusual was happening. Following the staring eyes, they saw our neighbor, Stacey, holding court and trading jitterbug steps in the parking lot.

Some folks are naturals at suspending anonymity. The rest of the world has to work at it.

We'll show you how to encourage ordinary people to suspend their own anonymity and engage your customers in a playful, Positively Outrageous Service experience.

Call Betty at (800) 635-7524, Monday–Friday between the hours of 9 AM–4 PM (Central) for a free copy of our IdeaLetter.

CHAPTER TWO

The Heart of
the Matter

"I've got it!" my customer said as she eased up to the table next to me, her lunch staring up from her tray.

"What have you got?" (Now it was my turn in the conversation. We've learned not to be surprised at anything our customers have to offer.)

"I've finally figured out what it is that makes your crew so special."

I didn't know if I should begin a small smile in anticipation of a joke or try to look serious as if I expected a great truth. It turned out to be a truth. And depending on how you personally view life, it could be considered a great truth all right.

"They love each other. They really love each other. Look at them play with each other and tease and anticipate as if they were connected."

Then she took a bite of her hot fried chicken as if to say that, now that truth had been dispensed, it was okay to eat lunch.

After studying showmen across the country and with apologies to my crew for failing to recognize truth in my own backyard, I've come to the conclusion that my customers have had it figured right all along.

What makes the difference between a great crew and a mediocre crew is whether or not they love one another. What makes the difference between great art, or great customer service (a form of art), and run-of-the-mill performance has not as much to do with the art as it has to do with the artist. The great ones are always thinking of their audience. The great ones are in love with those they serve. Interestingly enough, the great ones love unconditionally. And that means that they love first.

We spent a full day shooting one segment of a series on showman-.ship that we created for HNEN-TV (Hospitality, News, and Education Network), a network dedicated to improving the professionalism in the hospitality industry distributed by satellite to restauranteurs nationwide.

All day we hauled equipment from location to location, setting up and shooting, looking for tips from people who we recognized as great showmen. We wanted their input, their secrets for hiring and training employees who were willing to play with their customers.

They kept harping on the same cornball theme. No matter where we set up our cameras, no matter who we interviewed, the message was the same. It seems that for some reason, all of these supposedly sane, successful managers thought it was the culture of their organization that not only helped them to get their employees to extend a relationship to their customers, but also the culture that had considerable impact on the people who were attracted to apply in the first place.

Most of these folks used the word love like the rest of the world grunts "uhh!" to hold their place in conversation.

Love. What a strange concept to find holding court in a high-tech world. And it turned out that they were not talking about some new twist on an old idea. They were talking about the old fashioned, "I love you" kind of love. What an odd idea!

We had only one day free in our schedule to shoot our segments, and it turned out to be the Friday marking the official start of spring break. Not exactly the day you would expect to be received with welcome arms, especially if you arrived toting half a ton of video equipment and enough cable and lights to fire up a Super Bowl game.

But we were welcomed.

"Friday would be the perfect time for you to catch us at our best. We're incredibly busy on Fridays, so it will be a great time for us to show our stuff!"

Testing one, two. Had my hearing gone out? Was I really hearing an invitation to visit in the middle of the busiest day? Most of the time when we ask permission to shoot, we have to promise to show up in the dead of the night and evaporate before our hosts open for business.

Another of our hosts said, "Oh great! We'd be delighted to have you shoot Friday night. We really get clobbered on Friday nights, so we schedule our hammiest hams to work that shift. Come any time. You'll have a ball watching our people do their thing!"

Incredible. For this assignment, it seemed that not only were we welcomed to visit during a busy time, we were actually encouraged to wait until business was at its furious peak.

What was the difference? It was the people that we had selected to interview for our show. They were all showmen, the best of the best. They were not intimidated by the prospect of cameras, lights and microphones poking around their operation in the heat of a rush. In fact, they welcomed the opportunity to show off.

One characteristic of top operators...and showmen, is their ability to be calm in the middle of crises. Crises, it seems, only turn them on rather than frightening them away. These people have a certain presence that enables them to sort the important from the critical. They can concentrate on the task at hand without being pulled into the distractions of their surroundings.

One of our associates, Cindy Harris, was complimented for her attention to detail. She seemed to be juggling a million facts effortlessly. In spite of a full plate, she kept her cool and simply took one task at a time. Handling it as if it were the only thing she had to consider.

When we mentioned that her performance was really something special, she thanked us for noticing and then failed to resist adding that handling these "few" details was really no great trick. She had, after all, run a three-and-a-half-million dollar restaurant and done more than survive with her mind intact. She had thrived on the challenge.

Great show people are unflappable. Seek out the folks who have been able to thrive in the high pressure environment of public service and/or performance. They have the ability to remain calm in the heat of battle. They are the last in the world to be thrown off their stride by the small disasters that would stymie a mere mortal.

We started our shoot at the San Antonio airport. It was more than crowded. It was jammed with thousands of travelers getting an early jump on their spring vacation. We had asked Southwest Airlines for permission to shoot a few scenes to be used for the opening of our show, which is called "On the Road."

San Antonio Station Manager, Carl Warrell, broke away from his hectic day to be certain that we had everything we needed. Customer Service Supervisor, Gary Gerfers, had a cart brought out for our equipment, freeing a skycap to help us around. Gary took us personally to the gate area to be sure that we would get the shots that we needed.

In the gate area, everyone called Gary just plain old Gary. And why not? Gary is one of those instantly likeable people who is so easy to feel comfortable around. This is a trait that eerily haunts most of Southwest's crew whether they handle baggage or maintenance, ticketing, reservations or flight operations.

When we shot at the gate counter, a lovely young woman, named Bianca Sifuentes, served up a healthy sampling of Southwest hospitality. Shooting at the head of the jetway, we encountered a delightful flight attendant who, upon learning that she had read my first book, wasted no time in giving me a squeeze and a smile of encouragement.

Everywhere we went, people took time to be more than simply courteous; they gave us their 100 percent attention in the middle of a service hurricane. And it was clear that they loved what they were doing and the players on their team. It was the customers who benefited from this oddball set of values and feelings that consultants call "corporate culture."

Next stop was the theme park "Fiesta Texas," a playground extraordinaire that was less than 24-hours away from opening day of their second season. Not exactly the best time to request an interview, you would think, but when we called Anamaria Suescun, public relations representative, she did more than agree to go along. She noticed that our schedule was full and offered to help compensate by being flexible about when we could visit.

"Stop by whenever you are ready. I'll make certain that they are expecting you at the gate. We'll round up the people you want to talk to by radio when you arrive."

What's going on here? The day before opening, rehearsals going full tilt and some idiot wants an interview. You've got to be kidding.

But no, we weren't, and yes was their only response.

CHAPTER THREE

Cattle Call

I know how you hire.

It's the coroner's method.

Find a body. Check its references...maybe...and, if it's not overly offensive and you have a gaping hole on the schedule that needs filling, hire and hope for the best. Like the coroner, your biggest and sometimes only decision is whether or not it's dead or alive. Hold a chilled mirror under the nostril and if it fogs over, hire!

Too many managers think that their hiring responsibilities end when the schedule is full, or when there are enough employees to handle "no shows" and "quit without notices" without booting the payroll into overtime and risking ruining their shot at a weekend off.

In the seventies, we used to build new retail outlets like we were building the Field of Dreams. If we built it, they (customers) would come. And so would a raft of fairly well-qualified applicants wanting to make a career, or at least a summer, working just for us. Those were the days when people still called their boss "Mister." There were a few female supervisors but not all that many. (That was before women were acknowledged to be able to sweat. Then all they were allowed to do was "glow." My, but times have changed!)

In those days, we would hardly have a building framed before legions of eager applicants would begin dropping around to check on the progress and schmooze with the manager, in the hope of securing top name recognition when the hiring process got underway. It was not unusual to pick through the stack of applications, tossing aside any that failed to be neat and complete. A few would be typed!

"Don't bother with this one. He doesn't write very neatly."

Today we don't pick through a stack of applications because there isn't one. Today, if we are lucky enough to get an applicant, we may shout, "Oh, look! He *can* write! Let's make him the assistant manager!"

Okay, so maybe that is an exaggeration. But it's not far off the money in many industries.

What do you do in a tough labor market? And remember, please, that high unemployment only means that there are a lot of potential applicants. It does not mean that they will actually apply or that they will be qualified if they do.

The job of management is to hire...not just until the schedule is full, but until it is full with winners. Then, keep hiring! Keep hiring because:

Scott's Law of Expansion

A business will expand in direct proportion to the
number of winning employees that can be found. Hire
all the winners, get all the business!

Therefore, once the schedule is filled with world-class, winning service employees, keep hiring because as you find more winners, the business will expand to keep them busy. The only brake on this phenomenon is the ability of the boss/owner to create space, training and tools.

Not long ago, we hired a winner worrying about how we would pay her wages, but still committed to the principle. She had been an unexpected find, just too good to pass up. What foolish people we were! Nearly instantly she brought in so much new business that we found ourselves right back where we had started...looking for another winner!

Even in the tightest labor markets, management is wise to hire patiently. Body snatch if you have to; we all understand and can forgive. What is unforgivable is if you hire only to solve your short term problem, failing to continue to search for an even better selection.

As overworked as sports analogies tend to be, this one makes sense. Good coaches don't stop hiring just because they win the championship. They know that next year their competitors may have an even tougher team to beat. In fact, next season, it is entirely likely that you will be beaten by a team fielding players that wore *your* uniform this season.

Good coaches keep their eyes on the competition. not just to see how they coach and play, but to look for opportunities to pick up one of their key players. Notice, please, that the competition isn't going to try to steal your dogs; those are what they offer to you as a trade.

If you wake up some morning and discover that you have more winners than you need, you can always send them over to your competitor. Better yet, why not open another branch or even buy out your competition?

Don't Hire. Audition!

Disney says that they do it. Perhaps they do. The really sharp operators never hire. They hold auditions. Hiring is too much like body snatching.

Auditioning for new employees has a number of advantages, one of the biggest being the mindset it establishes for both you and the applicant.

A side comment here.

There are three key mindsets that good marketers attempt to establish. They want the customer to think that the product is:

- Believable
- Convenient
- Desirable/Exclusive

Believable means that the product does what it's supposed to do and does it so well that it is worth the price, whatever that may be be.

Convenient means that the product is easy to use. It doesn't require too much time, instruction or effort.

But it is the third mindset that has the most power, being *desirable* and/or *exclusive.* Exclusivity says that not everyone will be able to have this product. This makes the lucky few who are able to get their hands on one of these jobs, pretty special people.

And good managers don't hire because they are looking for just anybody. All they want is that proverbial "few good men/women."

Good managers audition because it tells the employee that getting this job won't be easy, and keeping it will be a badge of honor.

How to Conduct an Audition

Use a few tricks and a few more techniques to turn an ordinary interview into an extraordinary audition.

Schedule auditions. Because they are so important, they should never be held on the spur of the moment. And auditions or try-outs heighten the effect.

The best at hiring winners tend to make a big deal out of auditions. By extending an invitation to audition or to try-out, they let the applicant know right up front that the hiring decision is so very important that it is an honor to even be invited to try.

Even if you must commit the sin of body snatching, hire on a casual labor basis pending a later audition.

Auditions create a sense of competition. Whenever possible, applicants who are invited to audition should be made aware of the competition. They should see exactly who they are trying to beat out for the job. They could even be invited to audition simultaneously to further heighten the sense of competition as well as to drive home the point that the job is desirable, a factor that will ultimately impact turnover.

Best of all, simultaneous auditions let you see instantly who will fold in the heat of battle. This is very important for jobs that require high customer contact.

If this all sounds brutal, well, business is brutal. Besides, the ability to hire a team that stands out from the competition sometimes requires management to do things that the competition wouldn't bother to do. And don't forget that the competition would be only too happy to put you and your crew into another line of business, or even completely out of business. So being tough, and insisting on only hiring the best-and-brightest, is nothing more than the greatest insurance policy that you could buy to protect the investment of the owners and the jobs of the people who have already signed on as part of the team.

Have top management involved in the audition process. This makes the point that auditions are important — to current employees as well as the applicants. In fact, in addition to management and the applicants, current employees should also be a part of the audition process. It's good for them to see again that they are special to have made the cut. That, and a close look at the competition, goes a long way toward putting the value of their jobs into sharp perspective.

We let our employees vote on new hires. It certainly makes the point to applicants that they are not just taking a job, they are joining a team and the team has a vital interest in both their performance and their success.

Southwest Airlines invites selected customers from their frequent-flyer program, called The Company Club, to participate in hiring decisions. The theory behind it: Who should or would be most affected by hiring decisions? The customer, of course. And, at Southwest Airlines, the customer is definitely number one.

Think about it. We subject our customers to the hiring process, but only after it is too late. Why not include at least some of them right from the beginning? Pick a typical customer and ask, "What is it that makes a good employee?" Some will want playful servers. Others will want servers who are highly skilled or trained. It doesn't matter what kind of employee your customer would choose, so long as it's the kind of employee that you hire.

For example, Grandy's, the fried chicken and biscuit people, decided that their customers would respond to grandmotherly hostesses who would keep iced tea filled and the dining room tidy, while pinching babies and loving on kids of all ages. Hooters, another restaurant chain, made an entirely different set of decisions!

Whatever the case, the key is to hire employees that make your customers feel good.

Auditions are more than an interview; they are a performance.

In fact, a performance is exactly what is required to make an audition something truly special. Here are several ideas to help you create an audition format for your organization. They are exercises from the theater designed to quickly reveal whether or not a candidate has that special stage presence that puts audiences (or customers) into the palm of their hand.

(And don't miss the point that these exercises can be the basis for future training sessions to improve the contact skills of your crew.)

- Monologue
- Phone call
- Echo
- Mirror
- Simultaneous story

Monologue

Nearly every business requires employees to recite some type of monologue. It can be a simple greeting, a standardized sales pitch, or a canned telemarketing script. Most of the time it is just plain boring.

Like bus drivers who are required to rattle off street names in the event that one of the passengers is hearing impaired, monologues heard in business are about as interesting as watching paint dry on a humid day. Too many waiters torture too many diners with their "Hi! My name is Biff and I'll be your server" monologue.

Do you get the point? Or would you like to hear about the daily special and the soup of the hour?

Of course, when you start with the requirement of repeating a monologue that is deadly dull from the get-go, there isn't much that will make it a treat for either party. *That* we will handle in later chapters. For now, let's see how an enthusiastic, turned-on employee can make even the dullest of monologues brighter, if not down right entertaining.

Take pre-flight announcements...please. It is hard not to yawn at the very thought of yet another boring, make that aggravating, rendition of pre-flight safety announcements.

Basically there are two major offenders, not counting the ones that talk too loud, burp or sniffle in mid-sentence or have one of those voices that will peel paint from 30 yards. Monologue offender number one, the Hillbilly cracker. This delightful rendition comes complete with a voice full of such forced cheerfulness, that it cracks at the beginning of each sentence like a heart-breaking hillbilly singer after losing his job, his sweetheart, his mother and the pick-up.

There is no solution for the Hillbilly cracker other than to run.

Offender type two, the Drop-out. Drop-outs are so bored with their job and the monologue that they feel obligated to let you know by dropping their tone of voice at the end of each and every phrase and sentence. The result is not a monologue at all but an elongated whine. Can't you just hear it?

"Welcome to flight 77. We'll be leaving the gate in just a few minutes."

And at the end of each sentence, the pitch of the voice drops and drags all the way into depression, sucking the listener right along.

To protect you and your customer from the Crackers and the Drop-outs, why not make delivery of the monologue a part of the audition process? Monologues are not inherently bad; they are just inherently dangerous.

While new employees may need a standard patter to help make certain that they cover all the bases, the rest of us need to be protected not from beginners but from those folks who will never get it right.

Ask applicants to deliver a monologue that is your standard service patter or some variation on the theme. It could be as simple as "Hi! Welcome to Acme. My name is _____, and I'll be available to help you find anything you need and to answer questions about our products. What project are you working on today?"

Invite the applicant to deliver the lines straight or personalize them to suit. Better yet, do the entire routine with the applicant interacting with several types of customers. Your part: Observe how well the applicant senses the needs of the different "customers," and adapt the spiel to fit the situation.

As a side idea, it will also be helpful to throw in any related skills that may influence the hiring decision. If the job requires basic math or counting skills, then make them a part of the process.

For example, a worker in a lumber yard could be asked to estimate and calculate the number of board feet required to complete an order, or even give advice on a common do-it-yourself project.

A waitperson could be asked to make simple change. A flight attendant could be asked to deliver the lines while also using the demo safety equipment. And a nanny should be asked to do at least a dozen things at once!

The best addition to the monologue is the requirement to handle an angry or complaining customer. Role practice the situation and quickly discover the applicant's natural abilities for conflict resolution. Does he buckle under pressure? Does she attack, rather than hold steadfast to "the customer is always right" mentality?

This can be a revealing exercise as well as an opportunity to communicate key corporate service values even before the formal act of hiring.

Just be careful not to use the term "role play." To many, it communicates that the situation is much less serious than it is. Role "practice" indicates that, while humor may be appropriate, the exercise is not designed to screen for comedic ability.

Also, be careful that whatever you require as part of the audition is truly a required behavior on the job. See your local HRD professional if you would rather hear a thousand reasons why you cannot do anything out of the ordinary and why you are required by law to continue hiring people who haven't a prayer of being successful working for you.

Phone Call

Add a little more invention to Monologue and you get Phone Call. Give the applicant the challenge of creating one side of a phone call, you name the caller. It could be anyone from the President to an angry customer. How the call is handled will give you great insight into the ability to empathize with a "customer."

Echo

Echo is a great exercise that will really give you a close look at an individual's ability to listen and respond instantaneously. Plus, it's just plain fun.

Echo involves one person, you, telling a story while the applicant instantaneously tells the exact same story.

My brother Steve used to make me nuts by repeating everything I said just a millisecond after I said it. He would wait until I was thoroughly aggravated with him for pulling this stunt, usually in public where I couldn't really haul off and clobber him. But it actually was so much fun, we always ended up laughing so hard that I would forget about clobbering him...until we got home!

The next time your kids or your employees accuse you of not listening, try the echo routine. In less than 60 seconds, they'll think differently.

In a job audition, applicants asked to echo will quickly reveal their ability to listen, their ability to respond quickly and their sense of humor.

Mirror

The visual equivalent of Echo is Mirror. Ask the applicant to mirror *à la* monkey see, monkey do, the actions of another applicant. In a heartbeat, you will see who is capable of staying finely attuned to the presence of others.

Simultaneous Story

When you are ready to up the ante and really have some fun, try telling a simultaneous story. This can involve the interviewer and an applicant or two applicants. Pick two totally different subjects, say, "green frogs" and "Chevys." Each participant is instructed to tell a story about one of the subjects while listening to the other story and incorporating the other story.

If that sounds difficult, it is...for some people. But for really sharp communicators, simultaneous story is nothing more than an opportunity to show off.

"I had a terrific '57 Chevy...

"I had this wonderful green frog...born about '58, I think...

"This old Chevy was as green as green gets...

"Darned frog moved about like a Chevy...once you got him started...

"Starting a Chevy is a lot like starting a frog...

"Just turn 'em loose and those suckers will fly...

"Flying frogs...interesting idea, used to hit a few when we took the Chevy out...

"Makes you wonder which is fastest...

"Green frogs or green Chevys...

"As long as you don't say...'step on it!' "

Get the idea? Simultaneous story is a great way to double-check mental stamina. Anyone who, in the heat of the moment, can tell two stories without getting totally confused is perfect for service where there is high customer contact.

Truly great customer servers never get rattled. They can pick out the one or two stable factors in a confused environment and hold their mental position. Simultaneous story will help sort out the folks who are most likely to fall apart when the going gets tough. It will also help you discover those rare people who can find fun in any situation.

What to Watch

When you conduct an audition, you should remove yourself from the entertainment value of the moment, and view the proceedings as if you were a customer and this was more than a simple exercise. How does this person make you feel? And yes, this is a gut level kind of thing.

It's probably not a good idea to expect every applicant to be a performer. You are not casting for a Broadway play. But you are casting for a role that will played over and over, day-after-day, and often in front of your customer. So, whoever is selected should be ready to assume the role, even if it is a seemingly minor one that does not require intense customer contact.

And there is always the problem of recognizing your internal customers. Of course, employees are customers, aren't they? Since everyone serves someone, anyone selected should have a service-minded outlook that will also allow them to serve those oh-so important customers.

One of the best ways to kill a business is to fail to serve the servers. People just cannot resist kicking the cat when they have been kicked themselves. If the boss or the maintenance guy is rubbing away at sore spots, trust me, the customer will feel the pain.

During the audition—call it "assessment" if it makes you feel more businesslike—there are several things you want to see.

Is the voice strong and clear? Is the applicant easy to understand and able to use language appropriate for the circumstance? Does he tend to be physically shy, attempting to hide behind furniture or others in the group, or use concealing gestures? These are indicative of a person who just isn't comfortable performing.

Remember though, that while every employee should be expected to be a server, not everyone should be required to perform. If the person can sucessfully play the part of a maintenance staff member and you are hiring for that position, there is no need to hold out for a different set of abilities, simply because you find them more interesting.

We'll Let You Know

"Don't call us. We'll call you." That famous line that auditioners have been hearing for centuries still works. It illustrates the tension created by an audition. But think about it. How would you feel about a job that you won through hard work and quick thinking? It would seem like something special. You would feel as if you had won a prize of great value.

How do most applicants feel about the jobs they land? That they have won something valuable? I think not.

By calling the job interview an audition you create value.

Hire Provisionally

Even when the applicant has left you breathless with her skills and experience, no hire should be more than an extended trial period. Like bringing a player up from the minor leagues, the new hire should feel just slightly under the gun, aware that he/she made the team but is expected to produce.

This is an odd sensation for most service workers. In the real world— high unemployment notwithstanding—service workers often change jobs like city folk change their underwear. They know that, in too many cases, the manager hired them to fill a slot left vacant when another employee failed to report. The roster is short and any warm, breathing mammal will do just nicely.

So let the applicant know right up front that the job offer is provisional based on continued impressive performance.

Such a Character

At Disney and many other theme and amusement operations, employees are hired to play specific characters. They are asked not just to audition for their job, but uniforms are issued by the wardrobe department and employees are cautioned that, whenever they are "on stage," they must remain "in character."

Isn't that pretty much the way you want your employees to behave? Always "in character" whenever they are "on stage" in front of customers?

So often, managers complain that their employees have a bad "attitude." But really, do you care about your employee's attitude?

Absolutely not! All you are renting from your employees is their behavior. It matters not a whit whether or not your employees give a tinker's damn about your customers. The only thing that counts is whether or not they "act" like they care. It's all an act, and the quicker you start thinking in terms of the theater, the sooner you will realize this simple fact.

In our restaurant, the worst customer I can imagine is one of those chic-chic people who only eat white meat. Now I like well-bred people, just not at a fast-food fried chicken restaurant. They think that chickens come with all breasts. Invent one and you'll be a millionaire overnight. The simple fact is that chickens have about equal parts of white and dark meat.

Maybe at Wendy's "parts is parts" but at my place, chicken very definitely has several very different parts. And the last person you want to walk up to the counter is a high-borne with an overly groomed pooch, ordering a "Super Family, all breasts. Fifi only eats breasts."

"Right away," you hear yourself saying. "Would little Fifi like some of our delicious, sweet, buttery corn on the cob?"

All the while, you are smiling and wondering if Fifi is a puppy or the ugliest kid you've ever seen. That, and you are wondering what in the world you will do to move all the legs, thighs, and wings that are now left breastless, cooling under the lights, getting greasier by the minute.

But, here's the point. You don't care if your employees really like aristocrats. You only care that they *act* like they like them.

It's perfectly fine if inside they are thinking how neat it would be to see little Fifi swallow one of those bones sideways!

That brings me to my point: By starting with an audition, prospective employees understand that they are expected to stay in character and play their part.

CHAPTER FOUR

Great Customer Service, a Matter of Culture

Positively Outrageous Service is nothing more than a name for customer service that is surprising and involving. A step beyond good service, Positively Outrageous Service makes the customer say WOW! POS may be the service story you can't wait to tell, but telling great service stories is a heck of a lot easier than getting ordinary people to let go and actually deliver world class, Positively Outrageous Service.

The question of the day: "How do you create a corporate culture where POS is more than a series of isolated events?"

Since the principles of Positively Outrageous Service were first enumerated ("discovered" is far too important a word to describe the moment), it has become obvious that there must be other principles of management that explain how a few companies have managed to make POS something more than the slogan of the month.

These principles are:

- Passion-Charisma

- Flexibility
- Risk-taking
- Servant-Leadership

In the past few months, I have met hundreds of managers. Most are no different than the average corporate jock, which, I believe, explains why their companies do little to stand out from the competition. Fortunately, there are a few bright exceptions. My favorite examples, Kirk Lawrie of Richmond Savings in Vancouver, B.C., Herb Kelleher of Southwest Airlines headquartered in Dallas, Paul Meunier of Signature Flight Support headquartered in Orlando, and Bob Jones of the Lone Star Ice & Food Stores in San Antonio.

These men are leaders of a different stripe. Each has the passion-charisma, willingness to risk, flexibility and servant-leadership style that is required to put Positively Outrageous Service into action.

Passion-Charisma

It seems natural that a POS organization would require a dynamic, charismatic leadership style, dictated by the sometimes borderline, bizarre nature of Positively Outrageous Service. But, in fact, charisma is only an outward expression of an inwardly felt passion. The truly great service leaders may be charismatic; foremost they are passionate about serving their customers. They understand that their business has less to do with product than it does about their justification for taking up space on the planet.

POS leaders, above all, are interested in making the world a better place, and the fact that they sell financial instruments, transportation services, or ice cold six-packs is only incidental.

POS leaders are not always charismatic in the spirit of televangelists, but they are eloquent because of passion. Magic comes in words that pour from the heart. That adds a dimension that, individually defined, far exceeds a dictionary definition.

Listen, please, to the ordinary eloquence of people of passion. I frequently find myself on programs where I am asked to make my presentation following a few words by a clerk or server who has been singled out for special recognition. You cannot imagine the panic that I feel in such situations. I may be passionate about Positively Outrageous

Service, but nothing can compare to the passion of an employee who is truly turned on and dedicated to the success of his or her company.

Talk about eloquence! These souls can do more for language than a thousand journalism professors!

If there is a single word that describes a spellbinding speaker, that word must be "passion." If you have it, a stumble or stutter only enhances the power of the moment. If you do not, all the 50-cent words in Webster's fall flat and fail.

Flexibility

Flexibility. There's a word that is deserving of special attention. Think of two words: "flex" and "able."

An organization that can bend and flex is an organization that is able. Able to handle giant problems before lunch. Able to meet the challenge of change without self-destructing.

All POS organizations are flexible. Organizations driven by rules cannot by definition serve as a hospitable environment for Positively Outrageous Service. Acceptable service, perhaps. Good service, possibly. But Positively Outrageous Service, never. Why? Because POS is an affair of the heart and of the moment and cannot be mandated. It must be given freely and without the need to call the Puzzle Palace for permission.

Such freedom is anathema to a rules-driven organization.

Risk is a Four Letter Word

Organizations where POS finds a welcome home encourage—perhaps, even thrive on—risk. One definition of mental health is "the ability to take intelligent risk." Think about it. An individual or organization unwilling to take a calculated risk lies paralyzed with fear. Does that describe your organization? "That's the way we've always done things," is never heard at a POS organization.

Positively Outrageous Service is definitely a risky business. It requires management to stay relatively hands-off, turning the most valuable asset, the customer, into the hands of the employees without burdensome rules that discourage problem solving and creativity.

The movie "Indecent Proposal" sports a story line where a multimillionare offers a struggling young couple a million dollars in exchange for the pleasure of spending an evening alone with the wife. The media had a field day asking people on the street how they would respond to such a proposition. Most folks said that, even for a million dollars, they would refuse such an outrageous offer.

People profess, at least when the cameras are rolling, that their marital relationship is far too valuable to risk even for a million in cold, hard cash.

For business people, I offer this slightly less indecent proposal. "How much would it take to get you to put your most valuable asset, your customer, in the hands of a poorly hired, ill-trained employee?"

The answer is..."nothing. We do it every day."

Talk about risk-taking. Business people take the biggest risk of all nearly every day. Not only do we not bother to train our employees to make intelligent decisions, we make rules to prevent it!

God forbid that in a world where jobs have been "dummied down" to make them so idiot-proof that only idiots can do them, someone would actually encourage rampant decision-making!

Serve Someone, Stupid!

President Clinton had a sign placed squarely on his desk to remind him constantly of his top priorities. It read simply, "It's the Economy, Stupid."

If, as a leader, you need a sign to remind you of the path to corporate Heaven, then may I suggest that you, "Serve Someone, Stupid!"

The home to Positively Outrageous Service is also home to the corporate world's greatest servant-leaders, individuals who really care about the people who serve their customers. Servant-leaders are dedicated to serving the servers. They understand the term "support staff," and believe that serving those who serve is the highest calling.

Something More

There is one thing more that great leaders seem to know. They know that the product is only the bridge that connects them to their customers. The product for them is not all that relevant. Of course, on the surface, great leaders talk passionately about hamburgers or industrial adhesives or pre-popped popcorn. But it's all a ruse. For the greatest among us, the product is just the connection.

I borrow a story by a fellow named Pleasant DeSpain. In my version it's called "Bubba's Bridge." DeSpain's version is an old folk tale that he calls "Old Joe and the Carpenter."

"Across the road from us lies a huge hay field. What makes this field so unusual is that it is shared by the two ranchers who live on either side of this huge expanse of rolling pasture. Usually you expect that fields will be fenced, but in this case—and no one seems to know exactly why—there is no fence. The boundary, if there is one, is marked only by a small creek that runs occasionally across the field before slipping under the fence, sliding under the country road that runs beside the field, and finally into the woods on the other side of the road.

"On one side of the field is the large, brick house owned by the Webber family. Not as red as the big, metal barn that sits behind the house, the house is graced with wide porches from where you can sit and rock, looking across the field to the house that has been the birthplace for generations of the Higgens clan.

"Most days the barn doors are opened wide, spilling a quartet of huge, well-muscled workhorses into the field where they graze, not knowing or caring whether they are eating grass that belongs to a man named Webber or a man named Higgens.

"From the other side of the field come several huge longhorns that, like the horses, don't seem to respect on which side of the field their grass grows, caring little for the horses that share their table and hardly noticing the herd of disrespectful deer that joins the feast every day about sunset.

"Now the Webbers got the idea from a man who commanded a fleet of yellow earth-moving machines that he could help them get a better hay crop. All they had to do was hire him and his men to push their machines and the dirt before them across the field, smoothing away the swells that had grown over the years, making it more difficult at harvest time.

"And so they did.

"This story would have been stillborn had the Webbers thought to pick up the phone and call across the big, yellow field to let old man Higgens know of their plans.

"But they didn't.

"And when Higgens came home to find the earth movers gone and the creek that had previously meandered across the field on its own now following a different course, he was furious.

"Now the stream had not really been moved all that much. A few feet this way and a few more that. But net-net, it hadn't been moved enough to mention except that for Higgens, it was a surprise.

"About that time, a pick-up truck chugged to a stop in front of the electric fence near the Higgens ranch house, and out stepped the number-twelve boot of a local boy who had a real name but everyone just called 'Bubba.'"

" 'Bubba, I want you to go and get that wood from the old barn we tore down last month and drag it out into that field yonder. Then I want you to build me a big wall or something so I don't have to sit on my porch and see those Webber people. They've gone and maneuvered the creek that's been the property line between these ranches for years.

" 'I'm goin' into the feed store and when I get back I'll help you finish the chore. If they ask you what you're doin', just tell 'em, they've lost more than a few feet of pasture. They've lost a darned good neighbor.'

"With that, Higgens was soon heading down the long gravel road that connects his ranch with the rest of the world.

"Bubba started to work. But he did so with an eloquent yet unspoken understanding of human nature. Bubba, in his slow moving manner— britches drooping belly-over-belt, and a pinch of snuff tucked indelicately between his cheek and gum—started to work. He worked not so much with a pile of used lumber as he worked with the idea that people need to be connected, not estranged.

"When Higgens traveled his route in reverse, he was startled as he drove onto his property, spying Bubba putting the last nail into the handrail of an elegant, curved, little foot bridge, arching delicately over the creek. Bubba, in his simple wisdom, had set about the chore of connecting the neighbors in an afternoon as surely as a wall would have divided them forever.

"Higgens was furious. The symbolism of the bridge had, for him,

joined the shallow water of the creek and washed away under the fence
at the edge of the field. He stomped into the field fully intending to let
Bubba know in no uncertain terms just how stupid he was.

"But a curious thing happened to save the moment. At the same time,
the Webbers had looked across the acres and were drawn by the sight to
go for a closer look. Fate brought all four to the very center of the bridge.

"Higgens was furious. So furious that he was unable to choose just
the right words to spray his anger at the vile neighbors who appeared to
be mocking him, standing with odd grins right from the center of this
awful structure that he himself had paid to erect.

"It was a good thing that the cat held so tightly to Higgens' tongue.
Before he could speak, Buddy Webber reached out to Higgens, whose
own emotions caused him to flinch. Buddy's giant paw started to pump
the hand of a thoroughly surprised Higgens.

" 'I've never seen anything quite so beautiful. I can't thank you
enough. I'll be telling half the boys in town at tonight's Lion's club
meeting what a lucky fellow I am to have a neighbor like you!'

"The startled Higgens had no time to recover before his diminutive
frame was enveloped by the hulking Mrs. Webber. She wrapped herself
around the little man like white bread on a weenie, rocking him from
side to side, holding him close to her considerable breasts.

"Higgens thought for a moment that it was a diabolical plan to
smother him, leaving him to be discovered by the buzzards that made
their home in the woods across the road. Then an angel of mercy caused
the wild woman to release him from her death grip. As she turned him
loose, the Mrs. kissed the gasping fellow right smack on his bald spot, a
feat that required little accuracy for the follically-impaired Higgens.

" 'Mr. Higgens! You are such a dear! Whatever made you think to
build this wonderful bridge to connect our families? I hope we're
neighbors forever and ever.'

"Higgens got it.

"He smiled. Just a little, but he smiled.

"Then he turned to Bubba saying, 'Well, actually, it was Bubba's idea.
Bubba! You done good. I know you need more work..and, well, uh, I
don't have much that needs doing this early in the season, but if you stick
around, I think I can keep you occupied for a few more days.'

"With that, Bubba bent slowly, picked up his hammer and set it gently into his tool box. He hitched up his britches as if to say that he was about to say something important. And then he did.

" 'Thank you, sir. I'd like to stay and work for you fine people but I really can't. I have more bridges to build.' "

Service is the bridge that connects us to our customer, whether the customer is internal or external. Whether the product is as sophisticated as a computer or as simple as seating a guest for dinner. The truly great leaders know this. They are passionate about their product but only because, for them, it is their version of Bubba's elegant little bridge.

The four leaders mentioned above are certainly not the only leaders in the world who are creating corporate service cultures. They aren't the only leaders who regard customer service as more than a litany of slogans and posters. But they are great examples of service-leadership worthy of our admiration and emulation.

There will always be examples of Positively Outrageous Service, those random acts of exaggerated attention to customer care. But until there are more leaders, and fewer managers and bean-counters, POS will remain the exception rather than the rule.

Call Betty at (800) 635-7524, Monday–Friday between the hours of 9 AM–4 PM (Central) for information on how you can be invited to our ranch-based Positively Outrageous Service seminars.

CHAPTER FIVE

Opening Lines

His real name was James but everyone called him "Doc." Not that any sane human would have even considered asking him for directions to the corner store, much less asking him for medical advice. He was one of those strange people who wander into and out of your life, always looking for a way that he might fit into the rhythm that passes for just gettin' by.

You know the kind. No matter what they say or do, it never quite seems to be appropriate for the moment. Doc was slow. Everything about him was just off the mark. Not so that you would laugh out loud, but just enough to make you shake your head and resolve to point out the next time he does something borderline weird, so that he too could have the benefit of your judgment.

People with education and a degree of social sophistication think that the world of minimum-wage grunt work is totally devoid of intellect and meaning. The kid in the thick glasses with the awkward gait and near-terminal zits couldn't possibly have much to offer a world that moves faster than he can think.

The truth is that there is a remarkable native intelligence waiting, sometimes pleading, to be tapped and put to use. The folks who pontificate from the Puzzle Palace, who create the rules of work from the lofty perch of a high-rise office and four years of sponging off Mommy and Daddy's generosity, love to give the poor, huddled masses the benefit of their annointed view of the world of work.

Keep in mind that they may never have personally stocked a shelf or sold a shirt or worked well into the night hosing shortening down the drain in a quick-service restaurant so they could finally get home and attempt to complete a homework assignment in time for an early morning class.

Then again, they have never felt the love and support of a group of strangers that, for a few hours a day, work in a cramped environment for little or nothing to serve a public that sometimes just plain doesn't care.

Doc understood. He had found a place for himself with the others who, for whatever reason, were chipping away at their limited time on the planet shoveling food into cardboard boxes for minimum wage.

And so it was, as it is in a million little joints and dives, that Doc could learn a craft of sorts. He could fail a hundred times over without feeling a failure, and he would finally come to a win that the entire crew would celebrate.

Doc just couldn't quite get the hang of suggestion selling. Suggestion selling is often called "suggestive" selling, a term that seems to imply more than necessary. It is the technique of reminding a customer of a product or service that would enhance both the original order and the bottom line. Most businesses live and die over the ability of the crew to coax just a little more from each and every customer. If God hadn't invented cheese, McDonald's would have. But neither God nor the boss seemed to be having much luck teaching good ol' Doc the art of persuading customers to open their wallets just another dime or two.

"Doc," I pleaded, "can't you just think of a product, any product, that the customer hasn't ordered and then suggest it?"

Doc couldn't. Try as he might, Doc would politely greet the customer, ask if he could help them, and then dutifully put their order into a box. He was fast. He was friendly. But he never quite got the hang of figuring what not-ordered item might be a good addition to the items the customer requested.

"Doc! At least do this. Every time a customer orders, say these words: 'Would you like a large, ice cold Pepsi to wash that down?' We can write that sentence on the window for you or you can have it on a card if that will help."

Doc assured the crew that he too would soon be a suggestion selling king. He promised that, no matter what, he would suggest to every customer the benefits of a large, ice cold Pepsi. He liked the added phrase, "to wash that down." It seemed to be a good enough reason for someone to say "yes," and Doc is one of those people who hear far too few "yeses."

A few days later I walked into the restaurant expecting the usual unusual. And I got it!

"Mr. Scott! Mr. Scott!" was the first thing I heard inside the door.

"I finally got it! I figured out suggestion selling. And..." he paused here for effect, "and I'm good!"

"Well, okay, Doc, let's go right now and see you do your stuff!"

We went straight to the drive-through. Doc planted himself in front of the microphone, legs spread for better balance, ready to show off his new-found skills. It wasn't a minute before a late afternoon customer piloted his pick-up into the drive-through and docked himself next to the menuboard, where Doc was waiting to electronically spring into action.

"Thanks for choosing Church's!"

(That's an opening line that is pretty much a standard at our place.)

"Order whenever you're ready."

Doc issued this phrase almost as a challenge.

Then it happened. Bubba-in-the-pick-up blew away a week's worth of practice and a lifetime of confidence.

"I want a large, ice cold Pepsi."

You could have knocked Doc's bugged eyes off with a stick. For an instant time stood still. The crew members who had made themselves available to supply applause and adoration were instead looking for the quickest way to make themselves scarce.

Doc was in the worst shape. He looked for all the world like a deer caught in the headlights of a speeding eighteen-wheeler, wanting to disappear from the universe before being escorted out in a hail of humiliation.

But those who underestimate the eloquence and quick wit of folks that too often are underestimated, were once again about to get a comeuppance. Doc returned from his tour of the outer reaches of the solar system and, with great certainty, said these now immortal words:

"Yes, sir! That's one large, ice cold Pepsi! Now, how about some hot, fresh french fries to wash that down?"

There's only so much charity to go around, even among a crew that is normally as supportive and patient as Job!

"Hell, that could have been me," each must have been thinking. "And I would never have heard the end of it."

In the instant before the laughter could break out of the collective throat, Bubba-in-the-pick-up beat us all to the punch. He started with a chuckle that built quickly to a roar.

"French fries to wash that down!? Better give me a family-size order if they're that good!"

"Yes, sir!" Doc beamed into the microphone, turning just enough sideways for the rest of us to catch a hint of his "eat dirt and die" grin of triumph. Then he pivoted to his left, scooped up a cup of ice, and started the Pepsi as he popped a fry box with all the flare of a circus hawker. With a flourish and a smile, he finished the order, then took his place at the center of the next week's conversation.

In a heartbeat, he had traveled from thoughts of suicide to hero of sorts.

For most of us, the difference between hero and nobody is only a matter of a word or two. If you want to make heroes of your people, you may have to supply the words.

A Few Words from Our Sponsor

Getting ordinary employees to play with customers sometimes requires a boost in the form of a suggested line. Patter is the word used by the hawkers of old. If you listen to the truly gifted, professional bull throwers, their sales pitch has an easy cadence. One word serves as a trigger for the next. Much as a salesperson trying to unload an over-priced vacuum calls the device a "miracle" instead of a vacuum, a pro at customer play has a line or a word for every situation. And perhaps the best part is that, through it all, it never sounds canned.

But it does sound and feel comfortable. When a service pro is at work, you can almost sense the love of craft and the feeling that this person is absolutely comfortable with both his job and his product.

The idea behind a service patter is to build comfort, not conformity. Give the employee a few good lines, lines that seem to work almost every time. This helps remove the risk and encourages further effort on the part of the employee.

Too many companies make the mistake of providing a rigid sales patter. This rigidity takes away all the fun and eliminates any opportunity to be spontaneous. Avoid canned sales patter at all costs. Just for fun, the next time you receive one of those annoying, unsolicited telemarketing calls, try to interrupt by asking a question about the product or even agreeing with the caller. It kills them! They have no mechanism for dealing with anything out of the ordinary.

What we suggest is exactly the opposite. Employees need ideas, not handcuffs.

Playing with customers begins with the greeting. Demanding that employees greet every customer in exactly the same way invites boredom and eliminates any chance for play. Companies should go only so far as to set standards requiring that customers be greeted in a polite, professional manner. But the words used should be the choice of the employee. If you don't trust your employees to handle something as simple as saying hello, you have problems far larger than could ever be covered in a book!

"Good evening. Welcome to Acme. My name is Dawn. How may I serve you?" *might* be a perfectly acceptable greeting. But then again, "What's hap'nen, homeboy?" might be just as appropriate depending on the situation.

The greeting, like the rest of the interaction, is wholly dependent on the situation.

A Few Good Lines

What was the hardest part of dating? Simple, the opening line. And now here we are asking people to approach perfect strangers and engage them in conversation. Darn near the exact same level of tension caused by that pretty, red-haired girl. Will she think I'm being forward? Will she laugh at me? Hooboy! No wonder customer service is such a challenge. We are asking people to do something that they would probably love to do, if it weren't for the fact that they are terrified!

Compound the problem with the fact that the boss isn't all that comfortable either! Now what do we do?

One approach is to remove the risk. Think for just a moment and you will agree that our social bravery is inversely proportional to the probability of embarrassment. Remove or lower the likelihood for embarrassment and, suddenly, wallflowers become social butterflies.

The best example has to be Halloween. From the safety of a mask, normally shy and retiring individuals become heroes of theater, playing with strangers and offering up funny lines. Strip off the mask and bye-bye, Mr. Microphone.

It happened to me once when a friend asked me to substitute for him at work. It was mid-December, and he had taken a part-time job playing Santa Claus at a local department store. Everything was going just fine. My "ho-ho-hoing" was right there with the best. At the time, I was a teenager not more than a few months from acquiring my license to freedom and driving the car!

I couldn't help think that this Santa business was a pretty cushy job. My lap was holding up well and my ability to react to quick-handed beard pullers was definitely pro-grade.

What I hadn't expected was a visit from a larger kid, a very attractive young girl just my age. She was the kind of girl a kid like me had fantasies about. The thought of her sitting on my lap was too good to be true, but just as I slid a chocolate-covered kid off my lap, I looked up to see who or what was next, and there she was. A vision of loveliness. And it was clear as crystal that she was waiting in line to see old Santa himself!

And what would you like for Christmas, little girl? I heard myself rehearsing that stupid line and felt my throat beginning to tighten. I gripped the arms on my Santa chair and held on for dear life.

Then it hit me. I was Santa Claus. Mr. Smoke and Mirrors himself! And she didn't know the zit-faced kid under the polyester beard from Adam, or even Eve for that matter! I could go with the flow and, at worst, I would come out of this with a story to flaunt at school. At best,

I could end up with a story and a phone number to go with it.

It's amazing how, when you are really nervous, time will stand still long enough for you to have so many delicious thoughts.

She sat on my lap. I could describe the moment in much more exquisite detail. She smiled. Sweetly. And then it happened. Just as I was about to impress the world with my great opening line about what she would like for Christmas, she kissed me.

Here the story gets a little confusing just as it seems to be getting really, really good. She kissed me. I guess we covered that already, but it's a big point. So, she kissed me...not again, but this time is for emphasis. Then, just as quickly as my young life had taken a serious turn for the better, she screamed.

We're not talking about one of those dainty, *sotto voce* screams that announce delight. No, we're talking about one of those great big, full-bodied air raid siren, powerful, somebody's killing me screams! It scared the daylights out of me and half the shoppers on the floor, and most certainly put the fear of God into the already shy kids who felt marginal about seeing the bearded guy in the first place.

She screamed. This one isn't for emphasis. She let out another one of those God-awful, spine-chilling war whoops.

We both jumped up together. It was a good thing that she moved when she did, because at first I had no idea that it was me that was the problem. I thought we were under attack or who knows what, and was looking to bail out right behind the two-year-olds who were abandoning the line just ahead of me.

Then she completed the carnage.

"You're not Steve!"

No kidding? Who would she have been expecting at this time of the year? The Easter Bunny?

"You're not Steve at all!"

With that, she trampled the remaining two-year-olds and beat a hasty retreat to the stairwell.

"Guess old Steve didn't know that his girlfriend would be visiting him mid-shift."

Guess old Scott was a bit surprised as well.

But I learned a lesson. From behind the polyester beard, it's impossible to tell who is operating the rest of the suit.

That night a snowstorm put the traffic lights out at the corner of First and Wilkenson in downtown Dayton, Ohio. Santa himself ventured into the intersection and took over traffic control until a more appropriately uniformed official arrived.

Directing traffic to the absolute delight of holiday shoppers, I found myself having the time of my life. The incident with Steve's girlfriend had already faded as I made outrageous traffic-directing moves. I had power to halt a river of traffic with the wave of a gloved hand. I got honks and waves when I stretched into the Arabesque that even today I sometimes spring on audiences when a photographer interrupts. They think the speaker is a ham, but I know differently. He is Santa Claus.

If you want to teach people to play with customers, give them a costume from which they can play without risking their own fragile personality. A second option is to take them out of their element and assure them that no one that they know will be around to notice while they practice.

Sometimes simply giving an employee a title indicating that play is expected will be all the permission that they need to turn loose and turn on.

Sometimes you will need to offer a little more support. The best support of customer showmanship is a darned good example. We have an employee named Bubba (no kidding!), who delights in working with me. He hovers close so that he can hear me play with customers who call in their orders. He hasn't taken the lead yet, but it is only a matter of time.

Me: "Thanks for choosing Church's...we need the sales!"

Customer: "I'd like to take a delivery order, please."

Me: "If you insist! Bring me a ham sandwich and a chocolate shake."

Customer: "I mean I'd like to *place* an order!"

Me: "Well, that's more like it! We can't make a dime if you bring the food. That's our job! What would you like for lunch?"

Customer: "What's the smallest order of chicken tenders?"

Me: "That would be our four-piece tender snack. If that's not small enough, we can leave a couple out!"

Customer: "You're funny!"

Me: "No, Ma'am. I'm peculiar! But no matter what, I'm fixing you the best lunch in town. We'll have your lunch to you in a New York minute. Thanks for calling!"

Tip number two: Get employees started by playing on the telephone. It's almost as good as a costume.

One great way to sharpen your showmanship skills is to play when you originate the call. Most of the time people are so surprised and refreshed when someone takes time to play, whether by phone or in person, that they are more than willing to play right along.

Me: "Hi! This is Scott Gross calling for Dan, please."

She: "Hello, Scott. How are you?"

Me: "Well, by telephone, I'm 6'6" and good-looking. It's in person that I'm such a miserable disappointment! How about you?"

She: "By phone, I'm pretty good looking myself!"

Get it? Take your time. Watch for the opportunity and take a risk.

Playing with customers in person is a little more risky. But paying attention and being even slightly willing to take a risk can pay off big when it comes to playing with customers. In fact, there are three simple steps to follow toward developing a service patter that works for you. Look, listen, and test.

Watch Out!

Pay attention and opportunities to play will announce themselves. Specifically, you are looking to find customers who are what we call "in fun." "In fun" is the psychological state of being ready to play. Some industries have a built-in advantage because their customers arrive already "in fun," ready to play.

Customers at movie theaters, amusement parks, and nightclubs are "in fun" even before they leave the house. In fact, it is the very idea that they may be invited to play and have a good time that caused them to leave the house in the first place. Patrons of these businesses are easy hits. They are actually paying to have a good time. They may even be disappointed if no one takes advantage of their happy spirits.

But playing with customers should not be limited to the entertainment industry. Playing with customers when they least expect to have a good time, much less be invited to play, is even easier and more rewarding.

You don't expect to be invited to play when you board an airplane or visit the dentist. But that is precisely when many customers need to lighten up.

Needing to lighten up and being willing to play are still two different things. That's why it is so important to learn to recognize when a customer is in fun, ready to play.

Was it Yogi Berra who said that the best way to observe is to look? Even if we've credited the wrong philosopher, the point should hold true.

Too often we forget to look to the customer for tips about how he or she prefers to be served. Rarely does it take serious rocket science to discover what the customer really wants or needs. The solution is even simpler than asking. Most often, the customer's outward appearance reveals his or her mood and service requirements.

A customer who arrives in a jazzed-up version of a popular car has already announced that he is ready to be noticed. The safest topic of conversation in the world will be that car. If the car is no car at all, but a beat up pick-up truck full-up with a pack of good-looking hunting dogs, you can bet that a conversation about those dogs will be a sure-fire hit. Never mind the kids or politics, just don't forget those dogs. It is the dogs that have defined this customer's identity. And you'll be wide by a country mile if you fail to pick up on the scent.

We encountered a bright-eyed lass last St. Patrick's Day who wore a giant, green badge daring all who read it, "Kiss me, I'm Irish!" A handsome, young laddie would have to be blind and stupid to pass up such a blatant invitation for showmanship. Trust us. Pucker up, this gal is definitely "in fun!"

It is a bit more daring, but infinitely more human, to notice when a customer is at the opposite extreme of being "in fun."

Customers often bring their previous experience with them when they come in to shop. We think they are rotten, grouchy people who should have stayed home, but the truth is more than likely that they are only reacting to the way they were treated the last time they visited your place or even your competitor.

You can always tell when someone has been at a fast-food place where suggestion selling went a bit too far.

Me: "Hi! Thanks for choosing Church's. Order whenever you're ready."

He: "I want a two-piece mix and *that's all!*"

Me: "Yes, sir! That will be a two-piece mixed chicken and biscuit only. We won't even mention our delicious corn on the cob, and a fresh brewed, iced tea is absolutely out of the question. Pull through when you are ready and we'll have you out of here in a jiffy."

He (now at the window): "What kind of corn did you say you have?"

Me: "Oh, that's our sweet, juicy, buttery corn on the cob. Sorry to hear you don't want any (smiling)."

He: "Well...go ahead and give me one."

Me: "I'm sorry, sir, but you've already gone and pulled up over the 'I-can't-sell-you-anything-else-line'...well, okay. This time. But next time I'll have to ask you to pull all the way around and order again."

Customers who are "in the pits" also broadcast their service needs.

A woman walked into our restaurant wearing the saddest expression this side of the Wailing Wall. Stuart, the manager, recognized her plight and offered her more than our customary fast, friendly service.

"Pardon me, Ma'am." (Stuart can be the most gentle soul in the universe when he senses a downtrodden spirit.)

"Is there something that I can do for you besides fixing your lunch?"

As it turned out, the woman was going through a rather traumatic family illness. Stuart fixed her lunch and made it on the house. Then he took a few minutes to listen and console the woman, who has since become a regular customer. Point: We talk about involving the customer, but sometimes the better approach is to be involved *with* the customer.

It was a bitterly cold Denver morning. The weather had been unpredictable. First, a warming trend would give the snow a chance to melt and run away, slipping from sight into the storm drains or running silently along the curbs, across side yards and under fences to the low-lying areas where it could complete its vanishing act. Then the cold would return with a vengeance bringing yet another coat of the white powdered precipitation, freezing what little remained from winter's previous blast and hiding it, an icy trap for street people.

This was a day for staying home, for having a cold and waiting for Mom to bring a cup of soup. It was a day for listening to the all-news radio and imagining the possibility of being snowbound without being too inconvenienced. That was the way the day was supposed to be.

I had a job speaking at the Denver Convention Center to a couple of hundred other people who, like me, were unable to have the sniffles and stay home for Mom to bring us soup. Instead, we gathered in the fraternity of humans, unable to do more about the weather than to talk about it, by being at the convention center.

I needed a battery for my wireless mic. What a great time to have gotten lazy by failing to pack a spare. There was no choice really. I had to have a battery. So I headed into the wind, head bowed, collar up, shuffling in too-thin dress shoes. I tried to pick my feet up high, walking sort of like a two-year-old who is wearing a first pair of shoes. Perception wasn't so much the problem, as was the fact that dress shoes are never practical shoes. When faced with a choice, most of us opt to look good and freeze.

Each step brought my thin suit pants close to my backside. The material was cold and reminded me that my mother would have never let me out of the house had she known I would have dressed so foolishly.

Around the corner, I spotted a small sign announcing that a 7-Eleven convenience store was within sight. If I walked quickly and lengthened my stride, I could reach the front door and shelter from the brisk wind without drawing a breath of lung-burning air. People who live in Denver like to play with outsiders by telling them that winter in Denver means enduring a pleasant kind of cold. "It's a much drier kind of cold," report the folks who have moved to Denver, when their relatives ask how they like life in the Mile-High city. Drier, my foot! It's cold enough to give the famous brass monkey reason to move. And humidity, or the lack of it, doesn't seem all that important when gusts of 40-mile-an-hour Arctic reminders are shooting up your backside.

Inside the 7-Eleven were two souls. One was behind the counter. Her name badge said that she was Roberta. Judging by her appearance, Roberta probably wished that she were home bringing hot soup and soothing words to her own little one. Instead, she would spend her day manning an outpost for commerce in a nearly abandoned, downtown Denver. She would be a beacon, a refuge for the few who were foolish enough to be out and about on a day so cold that words like "bitter" and "dangerous" would apply without exaggeration.

The other refugee was a tall, elderly gentleman who seemed comfortable with his surroundings. He was in absolutely no hurry to step back through the front door and risk sailing through town at the mercy of the wind and ice-covered sidewalks. I couldn't help but think that the gentleman had lost his mind or his way. To be out on such a day, shuffling through the merchandise of a 7-Eleven, the man must be completely daft.

I didn't have time to be concerned with old men who had taken leave of their senses and moved their fragile bones and thin skins into the elements so unnecessarily. I needed a battery, and there were a couple of hundred important people who had things left to do with their lives waiting for me back at the convention center. We had a purpose.

The old man somehow found his way to the counter ahead of me. Roberta smiled. He said not a single word. Roberta picked up each of his meager purchases and entered each amount into the cash register. The old man had dragged himself into the Denver morning for a lousy muffin and a banana. What a sorry mistake that was!

For a muffin and a banana, a sane man could wait until spring and then enjoy perhaps the opportunity to saunter the streets when they had returned to reasonableness. Not this guy. He had sailed his old carcass into the morning as if there were no tomorrow.

Perhaps there would be no tomorrow. After all, he was pretty old.

When Roberta had figured the total, a tired, old hand fished deep into the trench coat pocket. "Come on," I thought, "You may have all day, but I have things to do!"

The fishing hand caught a change purse as old as the hand that coffered it. A few coins and a wrinkled dollar bill fell onto the counter. Roberta treated them as though she were about to receive a treasure.

When the meager purchases had been placed into a plastic bag, something remarkable happened. Although not a word had been spoken by her elderly friend, an old, tired hand slowly extended over the counter. The hand trembled, then steadied.

Roberta spread the plastic handles on the bag and gently slipped them over his wrist. The fingers that dangled into space were gnarled and spotted with the marks of age.

Roberta smiled larger.

She scooped up the other tired, old hand and in an instant, she was holding them both, gathered in front of her brown face.

She warmed them. Top and bottom. Then sides.

She reached and pulled the scarf that had flown nearly off the broad but stooped shoulders. She pulled it close around his neck. Still he had not spoken a single word. He stood as if to cement the moment in his memory. It would have to last at least until the morrow, when he would once again shuffle through the cold.

Roberta buttoned a button that had eluded the manipulation of the old hands.

She looked him in the eye and, with a slender finger, mockingly scolded him.

"Now, Mr. Johnson. I want you to be very careful." She then paused ever so slightly for emphasis and added sincerely, "I need to see you in here tomorrow."

With those last words ringing in his ears, the old man had his orders. He hesitated, then turned, and one tired foot shuffling barely in front of the other, he moved slowly into the bitter Denver morning.

I realized then that he had not come in search of a banana and a muffin. He came in to get warm. In his heart.

I said, "WOW, Roberta! That was really some customer service. Was that your uncle or a neighbor or someone special?"

She was almost offended that I would think that she only gave such wonderful service to special people. To Roberta, apparently, everyone is special.

"Why, no," she protested. "That was one of my customers!"

"Then double WOW!" I said. "You're really something!"

Roberta just rolled those big, brown eyes and smiled as she reminded me, "Oh, thank heaven for 7-Eleven!"

Don't always think in terms of humor and fun when you think of inviting a customer to become involved. Sometimes you will invite the customer to play. Sometimes the invitation can be simply to share who they are with who you are.

Look first for the visual clues that tell so much about a customer's willingness to play. People who are in fun can be spotted a mile away. The funny hat or other visual clue that draws attention is a sign posted by the wearer in the hope that someone will notice and respond.

Verbal clues are there for the hearing. Humans must work very hard to disguise their moods. The alert people person can identify the mental state of others with little or no trouble at all. In fact, there is so little science involved that perhaps Nike gives the best advice of all...Just Do It.

Someone who is laughing when they pick up the phone is an easy mark for a people pro. They are telegraphing that you have reached a fun person and that—if you are smart enough to pick up on the fact—you, too, can join the fun.

Other customers telegraph their mental condition by the manner in which they place their order.

"Give me giant size, anything cold and quick," for example, would be an immediate clue that it's perfectly acceptable to comment on the customer's thirst. There is a story behind this that obviously wants to be told.

Even the mood itself can be a starting point for conversation.

"You're in a happy mood today. What's the occasion?"

Still, there is no guarantee that you will always read the message correctly and that they are really ready to play. So the next best step is to test the water. Try a little funny. Do something to create a conversational opening and see if the customer will pick up on it. Most of the time they will pick up on your hint that it's okay to play, and the fun will be immediately joined. But occasionally, the invitation to play will be ignored. Don't panic. Nothing ventured, nothing gained.

Observe, listen, and test. That's the way to begin a conversation with a customer that invites them to play and become part of the fun.

The same three steps are those we go through when dating or flirting. In fact, this kind of customer interaction should be properly called flirting. Flirting is nothing more than the psychological maneuvers that we go through to attract members of the opposite sex. Good customer interaction is almost always a sensuous thing.

We didn't say sexy. We did not imply that there should be any off-color talk or any use of double-entendre. We did say that good customer interaction is a sensuous matter. Sensuousness is simply stepping slightly into the customer's personal space, implying that he or she is worth knowing better and worth our investment in emotional energy.

Customer service is emotional labor. Emotions are difficult to mandate and control. Only employees who have been given permission, and who are comfortable with both the customer and themselves, will be able to flirt with the customer.

Choice

Quality customer service has to be a matter of choice. There has never been a successful customer service program that mandates personal involvement with strangers. Only when employees have the freedom to choose when, and with whom they will be intimate, is there any chance of building an intimate relationship with the customer.

We walked into a major discount electronics superstore and were interested to see that every employee had been tagged with a large, bright yellow badge. "I Care," shouted the badge in bold letters.

"So, exactly, what do you care about?" I quizzed the young man behind the counter.

"I care that it's Friday," was the only response he offered.

"Anything else?" I couldn't quite let the experiment end.

"I care about rock-and-roll. I care about getting paid," came the response now delivered with a slight edge on it.

It was obvious that he would have rather died than to tell us that he cared about this airy-fairy concept of customer service.

When we pulled into the drive-through of a national fast-food restaurant chain, we were greeted by a young woman who, like ourselves, was wondering what kind of world would have sane people buying and selling iced tea through a drive-through window at five o'clock in the morning.

She was pinned with a badge the size of a Volkswagon. "We care" was the message that flew out along with our tea, straws, and change.

"What does the badge mean?" (I can't seem to avoid asking. Maybe it is just an innate desire to reinforce some hapless training director's brainchild.)

"Huh?"

"The badge. I notice that you are wearing a badge that says, 'We care.' What's that all about?"

"Oh! The badge!" It was almost as if she had been able to forget a badge that was so heavy, it nearly pulled her uniform shirt off.

"It means that we give a shit!"

It was five in the morning and we were buying tea and it didn't seem so unlikely that we may have 'misunderheard' our host. It was my turn to say, "Huh?"

"It's our new program," she answered without missing a beat. "It means that when you come here, someone will give a shit."

Couldn't have said it better myself.

In Boston, I walked into the rental car office to retrieve my car. It was early and it was Boston, so pardon me for not expecting breakthrough customer service. A clean car delivered with as little hassle as possible would have been sufficient. Instead, I got an education.

Inside the office, I was surprised to discover that the corporate gurus had declared this was national customer service week. Fine. That shouldn't interfere too much with the task of acquiring a car and directions.

Near the counter, there was an appealing display of danish rolls and juice.

"Nice touch!" was my reaction.

At the counter, I noticed a pleasant lady who, you guessed it, was wearing a badge. One of those huge, round, pull-your-shirt-off badges.

Who is it that decided that in the badge department bigger is better?

The badge read P-R-I-D-E which, to no surprise, turned out to be an acronym no doubt dreamed up by the high-powered brain trust at the Puzzle Palace. I read the acronym before mentioning it to its bearer, a word not chosen by accident.

Professionalism, Reliability, Integrity, Dependability, and Excellence. All the things you would hope for in a rental car company, although it would have been fine with me if at least somewhere they had mentioned cars.

"What's with the badge?" I asked the smiling lady behind the counter.

"Oh, that's just something they sent us from headquarters," she said as she slapped herself trying to quickly cover the offending billboard.

"You don't seem to be too enthusiastic about the program. How come?"

"Every time you turn around, it's another new badge. The badge is all right but, to be completely honest, it doesn't seem to describe this company and I hate having to defend it."

And that's the way it is when service workers are not invited to choose.

Emotional labor is a tricky issue. The best way to get people to love on their customers is to hire lovers, give them the time, training, and tools to do the job, and then get the heck out of their way.

A Few Good Lines

"Hi! It's great to see you again!"

Use this line anytime you recognize a customer and anytime you don't. The fun part is watching them try to figure out how they know you.

"That's what I've got!"

This line was the favorite of a hawker at the San Antonio Mission's baseball games. He also used it when hawking at the Battle of Flowers Parade at Fiesta time in San Antonio. What is so great about this line is that it makes you look. "That's what I've got!" makes heads turn, which happens to be the number-one goal of industrial strength showmanship.

"Hi! I'm Gladys Knight and these are the Pips."

Use this line anytime, whether or not you really are Gladys Knight. Anytime you can give yourself a funny introduction, do it. Well, not anytime. Introducing yourself as Jimmy Hoffa to someone in the witness protection program may not be all that cute. Then again....

"You guys must be rolling in the dough!"

Say that to the bread man. Believe it or not, he hasn't heard it before. Every profession is due for some kidding.

I once responded to an attorney's letter and closed by warning him to be careful, he could give attorneys a bad name. (As if that were possible!) I closed with this P.S.: "Did you hear about the two farmers who were arguing over a cow? While they were arguing over it, the attorney was milking it!"

He sued me. No sense of humor.

Think of an amusing way to help people remember your name. You won't believe how hard people will try to top your funny introduction with a funny introduction of their own. I tell people that my name is Scott Gross. Scott, as in Sir Walter, and Gross, as in, Eeew, that's gross!

Usually they jump into the act and cannot resist the temptation to say, Eew that's gross! Best of all is the fact that once someone has made rude remarks about your name, they seem almost obligated to go out of their way to help you out.

No matter how you come to decide your funny lines, they will lose their punch if you attempt to turn funny lines into policy.

Southwest Airlines is the best example of putting people lovers to work. It doesn't happen all of the time, but occasionally a flight attendant will give a humorous version of the safety announcements or other such data.

As the Boeing 737 lifted away from McCarran International Airport in Las Vegas, Nevada, the flight attendant took to the microphone to let us know that something special was about to happen.

"Ladies and gentlemen. The captain has informed us that this particular takeoff route is one that we seldom use. So, if you will look out the windows on the right side of the aircraft...."

Now, by this time there were nearly 100 sets of eyes straining for a glimpse of something special out those right side windows. She continued....

"If you'll look out about right...about right...about right... here, you'll see my apartment!"

Naturally the fight attendant, whose name is Jennifer, got a great big laugh and round of applause.

When we began our descent for landing, Jennifer hit the public-address system a second time. This announcement was sung to the tune of the old Beverly Hillbillies theme song.

"Well, it looks like the captain has turned on the light,

"I guess this means it's the end of our flight...."

Jennifer, it turns out, is one of America's finest flight attendants. On the other hand, she should definitely hang on to her day job. Singing is not what you'd call her strong suit. Still, her willingness to risk embarrassment in front of a planeload of strangers made for what had to be the most listened to rendition of in-flight announcements ever.

Opening Lines

Developing opening lines is a matter of observation, experimentation, and creativity. Don't expect that your crew will change from wallflower to high-power with a simple stroke of policy. It takes time. It takes practice.

Here are suggestions to get you started:

Develop a standard patter as a guide.

Watch for trigger words.

Encourage experimentation.

Provide masks and costumes, real or imaginary.

The best encouragement is a good example.

Start by playing on the phone...it's easier!

Watch for opportunities to play.

Watch for customers who are "in fun."

Positively Outrageous Showmanship begins with the willingness to gamble. It takes special people, not just those who actually play with the customer, but with their managers as well. Empowering employees to develop a relationship with your customers is a mighty risky thing to do. What if the customers refuse to play? Or worse, what if the customers actually like it and come to expect it?

CHAPTER SIX

Ownership

If there is a magic word for empowerment, it must be ownership. We are not talking about anything more sophisticated than "my idea is better than your idea."

Or, to add a bit of perspective, ideas that are forced upon people are rarely well received.

The trick to creating ownership is not learning to sell your ideas to employees.

The trick is to get employees to generate ideas all on their own.

Careful! You did not read a suggestion to throw all of your employees into a room and ask them to begin to brainstorm ideas. That's an okay approach, but not the best approach.

In the best of all worlds, employees feel so much ownership in the company itself that company problems are internalized...they become personal.

You know that you have problems when you overhear employees using the term "they" to describe goings-on in the company. "*They* have this policy that...."

Get it? When employees use the term "they," there really is a "them versus us" condition.

"They" is a certain sign that you have neither ownership nor buy-in.

It is a sign that, most likely, policies are either not being followed or, if followed, are followed reluctantly. It is a sign that the speaker has yet to become fully integrated into the team. Smart operators are quick to react when "they" rears its ugly head.

"They" signals that it is time to move immediately to build bridges of both knowledge and relationships.

When you hear "they" being used as described, it's way too early to be thinking about ownership and empowerment. When you hear the term "they" used frequently, you'll be lucky if the employees aren't simply stealing you blind!

A true sense of ownership takes a long time to develop. Owning the company is just too big a concept for many employees. It is difficult to embrace, and it certainly will not result from decisions to write more policy or fancier mission statements.

Ownership cannot be decreed. It must be earned.

At first blush, it seems odd that you would need to work at giving something away, but unless you intend to actually hand over shares of stock, gaining employee ownership—in the sense that they feel personally invested in the company—is neither an easy nor overnight task.

Of course, while actually allowing employees to participate in the success of the operation is perhaps the ideal situation, it is not necessary to create elaborate employee stock plans or profit-sharing plans to have employees who feel personally attached to the company.

The secret is to demonstrate to the employee that the company has personally invested in her!

As this page was being written, a perfect example of how not to build employee ownership was taking place only a few feet away. An older employee and his younger sales manager were having an interesting conversation while waiting in the DFW airport for their flight to Memphis. The salesman had been asked to apologize for failing to close a sale, under the veiled threat of his sales manager. The sales manager reminded the salesman that only those employees who demonstrate their loyalty through performance can expect to keep their jobs.

The salesman was kneeling into the seat next to his manager. The manager was reared back in his seat, a posture of arrogant control. As the conversation continued to unfold, the tone of the salesman's voice turned slowly from one of enthusiastic willingness to take his lumps and appease the boss to one of quiet, perhaps desperate, resignation. You could hear his years of experience and countless wins in other sales situations melt into a dark sense of self-doubt.

Now the manager dropped a mini bomblet. The Wal-Mart account would be given to another salesperson. The salesman nodded his coerced agreement, and the smug expression on the face of his young tormentor was one of easy victory.

The sales manager kept up the subtle innuendo that he was in absolute authority and that his older, perhaps wiser, subordinate was serving solely at his pleasure.

I would like to punch the jerk and type words that more accurately describe his abusive style.

If he sits behind me on the plane, I will lean my seat all the way back and crowd his skinny knees into his chest.

The sales manager thinks that he is in absolute control, that he owns the salesman. But he owns not a shred of personal respect or loyalty. Given half the chance, the salesman will jump ship. Only his personal sense of what constitutes a class act will keep him from taking his clients with him.

When it is all said and done, the employer-employee relationship is a two-way contract. Well-written contracts always benefit both the buyer and the seller. Well-written contracts meet the needs of both parties. An employee-employer relationship is, if not a legally binding contract, a socially engaging contract.

The problem with socially engaging contracts is that the employee can easily withhold a portion of his obligation, while the employer cannot.

The employer's obligation is too easily measured. The paycheck must be exact or everybody will quickly be aware that cheating has occurred. But who can determine, for certain, when an employee is giving 100 percent? No one!

That is why employers are smart to at least create the conditions for building a sense of ownership. For an employee to fully work for the company, the company must fully work for the employee...first.

Bubba stopped by the store on his way to school. At 16, Bubba was working his first job, peddling fried chicken at our restaurant. He left his truck running and stuck his head through the sliding front order window.

Stuart was the opening manager. He was not surprised to see Bubba. Our employees often stop by when they are in the neighborhood for whatever reason. Sometimes it's just to say hello. Sometimes it's to refill their drink mug. More infrequently, it is to eat. Humans can only look at so much fried chicken before their appetite for the breaded bird begins to wane. Every two or three months I have to skip a day or two before needing another charge.

What made this visit different was that, after Bubba inquired if the store had been left clean and well-stocked from his shift the night before, a rather unexpected apology began to take shape. Bubba, 16-year-old Bubba, revealed his hand when he admitted that he had stopped to say he felt bad because of the low sales of the day before. As if a 16-year-old had some sort of karmic influence over the eating habits of people in a small country town!

That was an example of ownership, plain, pure, and simple.

The question at hand is, from where did that feeling come?

It came from giving a kid a chance to work and take his place in the world. It came from taking care that a good worker was not abused and asked to work all of those important Friday nights, and by being flexible when the family wanted to schedule a special gathering or long weekend get-away.

It came from including a 16-year-old in the decision-making process of running the store, from expressing confidence in his ability to handle customers and solve their problems without undue supervision. It came from giving constant nonjudgmental feedback on the performance of the individual and his team.

And when the numbers did not look good, a 16-year-old stopped on his way to school to express his personal ownership. And that is worth a day or two of awful sales just for the privilege of seeing the true measure of the crew that makes the good days out-number the bad.

Ownership canot be forced. It must be nursed. You must wait in the bushes, ready to spring when an opportunity presents itself.

I walked into the store and was instantly greeted by Christian, a high

school student-employee who had shown much promise, especially after
we had him remove the earring and tuck his hair under a cap. He was
jittery with excitement, as if his dream date had descended from a passing
cloud and asked him to the prom.

"Scott! I have a magic trick! Hold out your hand!"

Christian was holding a fat, blue, felt-tipped marker. He grabbed my
hand and placed the gooey tip of the instrument squarely in the palm of
my hand.

"Pretend that this is a mouse and it's standing in the middle of the
house. A cat comes in the door, right here." At that, he tweaked the tip
of one finger as if to illustrate the location of the door. I jerked my hand
away, pleased that I was too quick to be hoodwinked by a high schooler.

"Christian, I was in the fourth grade once myself and I know what you
are planning to do. If you are going to tell me that the mouse is
frightened by the cat and then draw a big, fat, blue mark up my arm,
I'm going to show you what it feels like to be chopped into little pieces,
battered, and deep-fried!"

"But our customers love it! We've been doing it all day at the
drive-through."

What!? Oh great. All right, who ate lunch at Church's Chicken in
Kerrville today? All of you with the big, fat, blue stripe up your arm,
please raise your sorry hand and identify yourself!

"Christian, if you want to do magic, then do magic. But for goodness'
sake, please don't draw on our customers!"

I rummaged through my briefcase, unable to be angry with Christian.
After all, he was attempting to entertain and delight our customers, and
that's not exactly the feeling most people recall when they think of their
last experience eating at a fast-food joint.

I fished out a neat, little card trick called two-card Monte. I've always
been intrigued by the surprise of magic tricks, even simple, easy-to-per-
form novelties like two-card Monte. Sometimes I carry a trick or two
that I use to liven up a long wait while traveling. It's a great way to get
people involved, and that is sort of what I do in life.

I showed Christian the trick. He was, as they say, amazed, amused,
and mystified. He wanted my trick-card set. Of course, I gave it to him.
That was a given from the very beginning of our encounter. I just wanted

him to really want it so I made him work hard at getting me to give in. Even though I complained that he had beaten me out of something special, I was secretly pleased that he was excited over the prospect of developing his showmanship. Only this time, he would not be using my customers as scratch paper!

It wasn't thirty seconds before everyone in the store had lined up to ask for a tour through my briefcase in search of a magic trick that was perfect for them. Unfortunately, the well of tricks was a shallow one. But I could decree a "magic trick" budget, and we had the beginning of a magic summer.

Not everyone was willing to risk the embarrassment that is possible if a trickster isn't quite clever enough or if a customer happens along who is just a bit to clever. But most of our employees were soon hard at work learning to make small scarfs disappear or plastic boxes change color or coins magically pass through our stainless steel counter tops.

Customers would be offered a free lunch if they could guess the right card. Sometimes we would bet a larger size drink if they could beat us at our own game. I knew we had them when customers started to show up with tricks of their own.

One late spring day, I stopped at the store and commandeered my favorite position, working the drive-through. A customer in a pick-up truck drove to the window. When I announced the total for his order, he began to dig for change in the armrest on the driver side door. Suddenly he looked up and said, "Hey! Wait a minute! Where's my trick?"

"Sorry, no tricks from me today, just a terrific lunch. Will that do the job?"

"Well, I'll do the trick then," he replied with a Cheshire Cat, semi-toothless grin.

"Hold out your hand," he commanded.

There I stood, face to face with a big, fat, blue felt-tipped marker and a healthy dose of my own medicine.

Ownership has a number of interesting side-effects, not the least of which is reduced shrink (which is usually due to theft). Simply stated, people do not steal from themselves. Employees who feel a deep sense of ownership wouldn't imagine stealing from the business. It would be too much like stealing from themselves.

After a speaking engagement in a southern city, I found myself at my usual after-hours post, waiting patiently for the plane that would carry me to my next destination. I hadn't eaten anything more than a stingy, mouth-drying muffin, and that, not since early in the morning on the short flight to the hub in Dallas.

Water will only carry one so far, and with the nearest possibility of dinner two flights and several hundred miles away, I headed for the airport snack bar to browse.

The sign promised Columbo yogurt, completely fat-free. (Fat-free is how one day I would like to be described.) So I sidled up to the bar and gave in to a small twist in a cup.

"Two-seventeen," was the grunted response from the woman behind the counter.

I handed her two singles and a quarter and stared blankly at the sign plastered to the counter.

"If we fail to give you a correct receipt, your order is free." That was more or less the message. Being in the business, I knew that the purpose of the sign was not to insure that busy business travelers would arrive home able to document their expenses.

The real purpose of the sign was to enlist business travelers in policing the largely unsupervised food operations that are spread over acres of concourse concrete.

What the operators hope is that, because people will be anxious to receive a free meal, they will help police the correct handling of cash.

"Do you need your receipt?"

The question forced me from my stupor just long enough to mumble, "Nah, I don't think so."

She pulled a key ring from her waist and opened the register drawer, quickly slipping out my eight cents in change and laying the bills into their slot. Then she closed the drawer, made a mark on a sheet of paper next to the register and, as I walked away, took what appeared to be a five o'clock reading.

It looked for all the world like a classic example of under ringing. (The register is not rung, the money is deposited, and a record is made so that later the exact amount of the excess can be removed, yet the journal tape and the cash in the drawer will be in complete agreement.) Business people love cashiers who come out even.

Wonder why the yogurt machine seems to be using so much product?

I walked to the supervisor's office. He just looked up and stared, never offering to help me or questioning my presence.

"I bet you are wondering who I am and why I'm here." I thought that might stir him to life.

"Not really. It's after five o'clock," was an answer so lame I could not have invented it. I told him that I thought he had a problem and may wish to look into it. To tell you the truth, I think he just wanted me to go away. The last thing he wanted at five o'clock was another problem and a reason to miss his dinner at home.

Ownership and trustworthy employees are hand-in-glove concepts. You just don't have one without the other.

But to have trustworthy employees—in a world where ethics at least seem to be going to hell in a handcart—is not such an easy task. Just as the willing suspension of anonymity is the key to the ability to play with customers, the willing suspension of estrangement is the key to creating an environment where employees will feel like they really belong.

The "willing suspension of estrangement?" Admittedly, that's a weird term. Fortunately, it describes an incredibly basic concept. Employees who are separated from their supervisors by snobbish titles and awkward work rules and relationships are just not going to feel like they own the joint. Never have I witnessed a work team that was spontaneous with the customer, yet was unable to express that same sense of familial spontaneity with their supervisor.

One of our favorite clients is Frank Felicella, president and CEO of Builders Square, a two-and-a-half-billion-dollar subsidiary of K-Mart.

When Frank took over the reins, he took off the coats and ties, and other outward signs of pretension. Frank was, at first tentatively, then warmly called by the same name that his mother probably used, Frank. For many, it was an uncomfortable transition to calling the boss, the big kahuna, el Jefe, by such a personal moniker as plain ol', just the way Mom said it, Frank.

But as the layers of formality were stripped away, they were replaced by new layers of respect. Only this time, it was to be mutual respect.

Frank would probably have an executive drawn and quartered for failing to treat a Builders Square employee or customer with respect.

When doors begin to open and titles start to melt away, there is more room for ideas. Employees who are invited to share their ideas really turn on to a sense of ownership. The down side is that executives no longer have anything to hide behind, other than their own competence. Not a comfortable feeling for some.

Ownership requires that the whip and the chair be replaced with intelligent compassion, a sense of enlightened leadership, where management does more than talk about values. They live them; they model them within a high-profile example, where everyone can see and get the message through the reality channel.

Employees who think that they will be zapped for a small mistake will refuse to take even the smallest of risks. And it is risk-taking that challenges the status quo, and brings evolution if not revolution to an organization.

Walk into an organization that is ruled by fear and you will see...not much. If the boss isn't there to declare or devine each and every move, you will see employees doing absolutely nothing more than what is spelled out by policy. To do either more or less is to risk getting zapped.

In times when jobs of any kind are difficult to find, employees tend to take even fewer risks. Yet these are just the times when an economy needs even more innovation.

Innovation requires risk. Innovation means stepping away from the tried and the true, too often read "the tired and the true." Who will offer up a new procedure or product, if the boss is herding around enough sacred cows to stock the Ponderosa Ranch?

In organizations where employee ownership is high, sacred cows can only be found one place, the menu! What sacred cows live in your reputation? What suggestions would send you through the ceiling? There are some, you know. If they aren't obvious to you, ask your employees. Ask them to present them to you typed like a lunch menu. Ask them to take your order and see which of those cows will be the first to go.

Go ahead. Take a chance. You may discover that a little cow-rustling expedition was well worth the risk.

Risk is the key word to describe an organization poised for the creation of employee ownership. It is a risky business to trust an employee to treat the business as if it is his/her own. It is risky business to stand aside or in the other room, while an hourly employee handles your most precious asset, the customer. But risk is exactly what it takes to develop an atmosphere where employees feel comfortable taking over the controls, sliding behind the wheel and testing the accelerator.

One warning before you turn the inmates loose. They may need support.

Sending employees on a crusade to revolutionize the way you do business will certainly be doomed to a disastrous failure, if they are not first completely certain of both how and why things are done now. How can you change something you don't fully understand?

For revolution to succeed, the goal should not be to tear down the existing structure just to watch it fall.

Revolutions that succeed begin with a vision of the new order. Killing the king only to replace his benevolent rule with unbridled anarchy serves no one well.

Besides, employees who crash and burn on their first attempt to make a change are considerably less likely to make a second attempt. For a corporate revolution to succeed, employees must taste a win early in the the war. It can be a small win, but it must be a win.

Wins are harder to come by when you do not have the tools or the time or the training to do the job. The wise ruler doesn't give away the keys to the castle, but he does offer another way in.

Go ahead. Take a chance.

If you can handle the certainty of a few nicks and fender-benders and deal with the possibility of a gut-wrenching crash, you are in for an exciting race. Hang on! Let go!

Call Betty at (800) 635-7524, Monday–Friday between the hours of 9 AM– 4 PM (Central) to order a videotape of Scott's keynote, Positively Outrageous Service.

CHAPTER SEVEN

Signature Showmanship

"Showmanship? This is like a spelling bee. I should spell it and use it in a sentence? Well, showmanship is the ability to bring to life, and bring life to, the show."

— *Bobbi Candler*
singer, actress

Crash! Clunk! There isn't an elegant thing about the sound of a cowbell. And in the quiet, almost sedate surroundings of a beautiful Old San Francisco Restaurant, the noise seems even more out of place. Yet, it has been precisely this out-of-the-ordinary sound, plus a world-class dining experience, that has made the Old San Francisco Restaurants favored haunts for discriminating diners throughout Texas.

The cowbell marks the ascent of an attractive, young woman who is buckled safely into a red velvet swing arching its way over the bar. Much as the swing has been suspended over the bar, diners have suspended their conversation mid-sentence as they watch the hourly performance at the front of the dining room.

It would be a mistake to imagine that the success of the Old San

Francisco group was solely due to the gimmicky performance of a pretty girl in a red velvet swing. But it is the swinging that customers can talk about for days after the memory of their meal has faded.

The swing. Who would have thought to put a swing over the bar? Who would have thought to create a lavish routine that has a young woman swaying from one side of the restaurant to the other, climaxing in an arch so high that she can ring a cowbell hung at either end of her route. The bells hang from the ceiling. (Also on the ceiling are the marks of a few missed opportunities as well.)

When customers bring friends and visiting relatives to Old San Francisco, it is because they have in mind a special treat. They tell their guests about the food, but most save the girl in the red velvet swing as a surprise.

Surprise!

Surprise is the first element of industrial-strength showmanship. If you want to develop "signature showmanship," then surprise is the first element to consider. Surprise makes ordinary events special.

A cupcake isn't likely to create a lot of excitement. But deliver it with a lighted candle while singing "Happy Birthday," and you've got yourself the makings of a real surprise. It isn't what you do or how much you spend, it is the element of surprise that turns the ordinary into a show.

Years ago while working my way through college as a Denny's cook, I used to enjoy surprising my customers with messages written in strips of sliced cheese melted across the top of their cheese omelets. Simple messages like "Vote" on election day or just a short, yellow "Hello!" for customers that hadn't been in recently always got a laugh.

Once I even put my phone number on the omelet I thought had been ordered by an attractive woman. How was I to guess that she had ordered for her macho-looking boyfriend while he was looking for a parking place?

The fresh-baked cookies that we sometimes slip onto the trays of diners at our restaurant take on an added value because they are unexpected. Anything ordinary has the potential of becoming special if it is presented as a surprise. I can't resist mentioning the restaurants that cut off the neckties of guests who do not know their "no tie" rule. What makes it fun is the fact that the guest doesn't expect to have his tie attacked...he is surprised. Not to mention, of course, mad as all Hell!

Theme

If you are looking to develop signature showmanship, then it might be a good idea to consider your theme...or not. If your business has a logo, tagline or decor theme, then there may be a natural opportunity for showmanship. The folks at Menke Manufacturing, makers of duck tape, pretty much have an open book when it comes to opportunities for showmanship. When they have a great quarter in terms of sales and profits, they invite their best vendors and suppliers to join them for a group race to jump, clothes and all, into their duck pond. They are quick, or should we say "quack?" to tell you that things aren't all that they are quacked up to be, and a jillion other puns that just naturally follow a product called "Duck Tape."

Following your theme, tagline, or logo may be the most obvious way to create signature showmanship. Then again, the obvious may not be what you want. Think about the girl in the swing at Old San Francisco. She may match the theme, but really, when would you ever expect something like that? She fits the theme only because she dresses like a hostess in an 1890's saloon, the theme of the restaurant. Swinging would be a surprise no matter what the theme of the restaurant.

Do-able

Whatever you consider for your signature showmanship, it must be something that you can do. Better add the idea of repeatability to the list. Whatever you choose, make darn good and certain that you can do it again and again for years to come. Decide to make flame-swallowing your signature showmanship and you'll have to live with the fact that flame-swallowers are not found on every corner.

Smart folks go with things that are fun by nature and that require little more in terms of talent and props than a sense of adventure.

Remember, signature showmanship does not need to be an elaborate production. It can be something as simple as a funny business card, an engaging story, or a simple bar-quality stunt. It only needs to be different, and slightly out of context, to WOW.

There are dentists who visit schools dressed like the tooth fairy, there are nurses who tell funny bedtime stories, there are truckers who delight in giving perfect strangers a piece of sugar candy, and traffic cops who execute stunning ballet moves while directing you through the intersection. Nothing expensive. Nothing difficult. The emphasis is on different and unexpected and just plain fun.

Macaroni Restaurant near my home is one of my favorites because I enjoy the sense of showmanship that makes every visit more than a meal. It is an experience. When we called for permission to shoot a segment for a satellite network on showmanship, not only did the folks at Macaroni say yes, they asked us to wait until Friday night.

All right, folks. What's wrong with that picture?

Nobody in their right mind requests that a video crew wait until the busiest night of the week to drag through the dining room with lights, cables, equipment and a small army of techies. Then again, who said that they are in their right mind at Macaroni?

They are crazy. Crazy, as in "Come on Friday, that's when we schedule our hammiest hams and when the crowd is most in the mood to play." Also they are crazy, as in "Well, let's take another million to the bank!"

But the point we need to mention here is that the fun at Macaroni includes Italian opera, beautifully performed tableside. The risk and effort is in the need to recruit talented opera stars to work as servers.

Can't you imagine the classified ad? "Wanted. Waitpersons. Must be able to sing in Italian."

Better to stick to signature showmanship that is a bit less ambitious. While it's not likely that your average customer will either appreciate opera or be able to sing along, they can both appreciate and join in something more common. There's the choice. Something tending toward the common or the truly knock-your-socks-off unique.

Non-topical

Choose a signature showmanship that is not likely to go out of style before word gets around that you are doing it. Or pick something that is so far out of style that it has become nostalgic.

Hooters Restaurant is a great place for a Philly cheese steak and an ice cold brewski. It's also a great place to brush up on your hula-hoop ability.

While you are waiting, the hostess at Hooters is likely to entertain you by challenging you to a round of hula-hooping. Now, when was the last time that you dragged out the old hoop and hula'd to your heart's content? Been awhile, hasn't it? And that, of course, is the point. Hooters picked up on a bit of showmanship that was so far out, it's in!

Nordstrom has taken the higher road. Walk into a Nordstrom department store and you are likely to be greeted by the delightfully soothing sounds of a grand piano. Not of the recorded variety, either. A real, honest-to-goodness, grand piano whose ivories are being tickled by someone for whom the term "piano player" just does not apply. Say "pianist," please.

Elegant or mondo-bizzaro, choose a signature showmanship that is not going to be re-thought two weeks after you finally master the routine.

Careful About Core Values

Our banker friends are always cautious about Positively Outrageous Service. And it is fair that they would be careful about organized silliness in a financial institution. There isn't anyone who would like to have fun while doing business more than I. But when it comes to handling my money, even I, the clown prince of industrial foolishness, am willing to sacrifice entertainment for accuracy.

The point is simple, choosing a signature showmanship must take into account the nature of the business itself.

A mortuary that sponsors casket races can count on plenty of free media attention, but not many customers when it comes to icing a favorite Uncle Fred. Medical professionals can and do benefit from a little applied showmanship. But when it comes to their particular area of medical art, they need to be as serious as a heart attack.

Still, those who can successfully push the limits, and perhaps poke a little fun at themselves or their professions, have an opportunity to score big with the public.

Linda Wilkerson of the Dane County Credit Union is one such person. Her claim to industrial-strength showmanship may be found in a box of bright red, foam clown noses that she keeps stowed in her desk drawer.

Linda saves the clown noses for those touchy situations when a credit union member shows up with a cranky kid in tow. Rather than allow the disruptive little darling to tear the building to its foundation, Linda offers a clown nose to keep the little reprobate entertained. A clown nose you just don't expect at your credit union, and that is just what makes it such a special treat.

A clown nose would not seem out of place in an attorney's office. Neither would leather underwear.

Let Me Choose

Bill Behling, the master showman for PFM, the college contract feeders, believes in the idea of vicarious participation. Whether from sheer practicality or simply because not every customer will want to play, Behling says that you can leverage your corporate fun simply by performing your showmanship in the presence of a crowd, even though perhaps only a single customer or guest can participate directly.

The example of the nightclub magician may illustrate the concept best. Recall, if you will, the last time you were in an audience and one of the performers called for a volunteer. Maybe it was a magician looking for a sucker to saw in sections. You looked for your mother-in-law and came up empty-handed.

When they called for a volunteer, what happened? Most of the audience looked into their lap, working on the theory of a two-year-old playing "Peek-a-boo" that if you couldn't see the magician, then he couldn't see you. You, of course, realized that this was ridiculous, but did everything possible to avoid making eye contact on the long shot chance that your two-year-old knew something that you didn't.

But there, near the front of the room, was this hand.

It shot into the air almost the instant that the call went out. The hand was insistent, a jumping, waving billboard attached to an odd-looking bird who called "Me, me, me!" That is the person who wants to play.

Not that the rest of the audience doesn't want to be part of the fun, and not that they think that the goings-on are somehow undignified or too juvenile. The truth is that some people would rather participate vicariously. They like the concept. They will smile and hoot. They just would rather die than risk making a fool of themselves in public or otherwise.

Industrial-strength showmanship should never, ever make the customer uncomfortable.

Industrial-strength showmanship should allow the customer to choose whether or not to participate.

Flying into Oakland aboard Southwest, we were treated to the usual/unusual entertainment that has become legendary among folks lucky enough to be served by the Southwest route system. The flight attendants announced that there would be a scavenger hunt and the prize was something I don't remember, but it wasn't likely much more than a double ration of the famous Southwest breakfast peanuts. (Southwest is not known for foodservice. Their philosophy is that if you are after a good meal, you should stop at Denny's.) If you want to fly from point A to point B and you want a wide choice of flights at low, low prices, then Southwest might be a better choice than Denny's.

Frequent Southwest flyers joke about the availability of breakfast peanuts, lunch peanuts, or the ever-popular dinner peanuts! Then they laugh about the money they are saving by not trying to buy dinner at 35,000 feet.

The flight attendants must have been up half the night dreaming up their list of oddball items that were soon the object of an intense plane-wide search. We looked for a sock with a hole in it, a compromising photograph, foreign currency (easy) and even a small bottle of shampoo. The passengers were having a great time. Even the few conservative souls who were much too self-important to participate personally occasionally gave a look over their reading glasses...and one was even caught smiling.

But the point is important. No one was forced to play, and even those that did not, participated in their own way.

No Extra Charge

Showmanship that you have to pay for quickly loses its shine. It is much better if it is perceived as an extra, an unexpected goodie that was tossed in as both a surprise and an added value.

Without making too big a deal out of Southwest Airlines, they are experts at making even short flights at the end of a long day seem lighter and brighter as the result of a little organized on-board fun.

A favorite game that they play on Southwest is "guess the combined age of your flight attendants." There's nothing more amusing than to watch three flight attendants parade through the cabin trying to look as young as possible. The prize is always something inconsequential. It is the playing of the game that is the fun. Talk about cheap entertainment!

The following story is to remind you that even if you don't feel a need to develop a signature style of showmanship, perhaps being known for a variety of surprises is just as good. And all that requires is a sense of humor and the willingness to take a risk....

Doodee

Showmanship can result from the smallest inspiration. The secret is to learn to be open to possibilities. A chance remark, a dream, the odd juxtaposition of words in ordinary conversation. Anything and darned-near-everything can set off the creative mind. After all, a surprise is nothing more than the result of our insistence on viewing the world as a predictable place only to discover that somehow our predictions, our expectations, have been thwarted.

Jill Hicks is one of those easy-to-meet people who don't mind sitting on the front row of a seminar. She shows up ready to learn and hoping to play. She laughs easily, probably because she is able to find humor under every rock or turn in the conversation.

While managing her family's theater in tiny Florence, Oregon, Hicks spent a lazy afternoon previewing the film "Caddy Shack" on the day it was to open.

In the movie, there is a swimming pool scene where a Baby Ruth candy bar gets away from some kids and ends up floating in the pool...emptying the pool of swimmers when one of the kids surfaces beside it and screams "Doodee!"

That's rude and crude but you have to admit funny as the dickens. Most of us have a touch of sixth-grade scatological humor left in us, and this pretty much fills the bill. Well, the scene struck a twisted chord with Hicks who realized that she had a full box of Baby Ruths in stock at the concession stand. Perfect ammunition to set up a prank that would be the talk of Florence for years.

Before she climbed the long staircase to start the film, Hicks handed a Baby Ruth to each patron in the auditorium.

She said not a word to spoil the joke and since this was the premiere night for the film in Florence, no one was likely to anticipate the surprise. The audience was abuzz over the unexpected free candy as the film finally began to roll from one giant platter to the next, snaking its way past the film gate and megawatt xenon lamp.

"Caddy Shack," as a movie, is full of sight gags and surprises but none quite as hilarious as the looks on the candy bar munchers when the swimmer on the screen surfaced and did more than clear the pool. He, with the help of Hicks grinning from the back of the house, grossed out an entire auditorium by yelling "Doodee!"

What have you done lately to yell "Doodee" to your customers? Don't get hung up on the scatology. Think instead how much fun a little showmanship would be to your customers and employees alike.

Parallel Analysis

Good ideas for corporate fun, like good ideas for marketing and new products, don't have to come from the same industry. In fact, it is a fun excercise to look at other non-similar industries to see how they have handled similar problems or taken advantage of similar opportunities.

Looking for a good time? Then see what others outside your industry are doing to play with their customers and think about how those ideas might be adapted to your special needs. Don't be afraid to let your imagination and your research wander.

We looked at Fiesta Texas, the San Antonio-based amusement park, in search of ideas for showmanship in the casual dining segment of the restaurant industry.

Much to our surprise, we discovered that the acting skills required of Fiesta Texas' "Streetmosphere" performers were directly applicable to restaurant operations where they are serious about serving fun along with dinner.

What wasn't much of a surprise was the discovery that a few miles west along the freeway, Phillip Romano had beat us to the punch. He had the foresight to arrange for a university professor to present acting lessons to his waitstaff as part of the pre-opening training for both his Macaroni Grill and Nachomama's Restaurants.

Peters and Waterman wrote about the world's greatest idea scroungers in their book *In Search of Excellence*. Stew Leonard, owner-operator of what is billed as the world's largest dairy store, was reported to conduct intensive searches on a daily basis for new ideas. Leonard's policy is to require each of his top managers to find at least one good, new idea every day.

Leonard and his managers frequently pile into the "Idea" van and drive off in search of their next big idea. They have no problem borrowing any idea, so long as it is a good one that can be used as is or adjusted to fit the Stew Leonard operation.

Stories like this make for interesting legend but as any successful person will agree, it is easier to talk-the-talk than to walk-the-talk. I found out that the Leonard family is exactly as advertised, when I happened to share a lunch table with Stew Leonard, Jr. He was on the agenda to talk to what was then the Clarke Check company.

During the conversation, I mentioned our Southern Fried Sundays, a weekly event where we barricaded the parking lot and set out hay bale benches so that we could treat our customers to a free evening of country western music. Ah, now that was unusual, and if Stew Leonard's is anything at all, it's unusual.

Stew Junior perked up and leaned forward so as not to miss a word. Then he reached into his jacket pocket and retrieved a small notebook. He scribbled a few words, asked again the name of the promotion and followed with a few questions about procedure. Then he smiled. He had his idea for the day.

The message is simple: Good ideas don't have to come from you; they don't have to come from an industry guru. Good ideas can come from anywhere if you will only open your eyes—your mind—and look.

Stick to a Theme...or Not!

Consider adopting a theme for your operation or at least your signature showmanship. Then carry the theme throughout...or not. Restaurants are famous for following a theme, but there is definitely no law governing this area. So why can't a theme be useful in other areas, and why must a theme "fit" naturally?

For example, a new hardware store could easily follow the theme of a turn-of-the-century, old fashioned general store. That theme would be a natural. But why must a theme be obvious? A men's clothing store wouldn't suffer from the adoption of a railroad theme to make the decor more interesting. Even a dry cleaner could choose to adopt an old west theme.

The Yacht Club Resort at Disney World has successfully adopted a nautical theme based on the days of traveling aboard luxury steamships. This is a tightly focused theme, but there are others who follow theme, along more general lines.

The shops in the Pittsburgh Station Square follow the general theme of railroading but don't hesitate to stray if they happen to run across a piece of memorabilia that is interesting, even if it doesn't fit the theme exactly.

Speaking of railroads, treat yourself to a visit to the Holiday Inn in downtown Indianapolis. The historical district surrounding the old railroad terminal has become a tourist Mecca. Parked regally in the lobby of the Holiday Inn is an impressive array of refurbished Pullman sleepers that are available for overnight guests. The crowning touch: Delightful statuary depicting scenes from the days of the railroad heyday. A businessman in bronze waits patiently for a train that he will never board. A woman carries a baby who will never leave her arms, and small children marvel at a train that will carry them only in the realm of the imagined.

The works are so lifelike that it is difficult to resist the temptation to ask the time or comment on the weather. No doubt more than one over-indulgent conventioneer has made the mistake of engaging in innocent chitchat to bronze ears from a century nearly forgotten.

Holiday Inn has used a theme to enchant the jaded traveler and offer an environment that is both entertaining and educational.

Some cities have made themes the lifeblood of thriving tourist trade.

Old Williamsburg, Virginia; Fredericksburg, Texas; and New Orleans, Louisiana, with its intriguing French Quarter alive with visitors nearly 24-hours-a-day — each of these areas tenaciously protects the integrity of its historical themes, knowing full well that it is the theme itself that draws tourists by the thousands.

Disney is the master practitioner of theme. Inside a Disney park, visitors find one interesting theme after another curiously juxtaposed in a patchwork quilt of sights and sounds. What makes Disney such a worthy example is the attention they pay to even the smallest detail. Whether it is a park bench or wall clock, the trim around a shop window or the hardware on a door, Disney remains faithful to every important detail.

Better still is their insistence that each and every employee behaves as an actor on a stage. The stage may be as large-as-life and the audience may be closer than any on Broadway, but it is to an acting job that each employee is hired.

They are hired by the casting office and report to wardrobe for their costumes. And that, more than any detail, is what allows Disney to put the New Orleans area right next to Frontier Land without so much as scratching the thin veneer of make-believe, or without allowing an ugly flood of reality to spill into the fun.

Wherever a theme is used successfully, it is because of attention to detail, remaining true to the theme, and insisting that each employee adopt a character, not just a position on the schedule.

Decor is an important part of any theme. It is the visual cue that primes the customer's expectation.

Walk into Nachomama's, Romano's Mexican restaurant in Leon Springs, Texas. You enter through a simple, wooden screen door that swings shut by itself, pulled by a weighted bucket attached to the door via an ingenious rope-and-pulley-system. Fresh vegetables signal that you are in the kitchen where something delicious is about to happen.

A sign over the bar decrees, without apology to polite company, that farting will not be tolerated at the bar. Ready or not, Romano's decor ideas jump out, giving the diner something to talk about, to love or to hate They become part of the show by hanging on the wall, being piled in the center of the serving floor, or intruding like the sign over the urinal commanding flatly that patrons should "Piss on Drugs."

Romano puts a whole new spin on the idea of graphic.

Above and often unnoticed by the first time visitor, a billboard sits on its perch, plastered to the ceiling, as a well-trained waitstaff serves nacho chips in, believe-it-or-not, hubcaps! Romano carries theme to its illogical extreme and gets away with it.

Down the road at the Magic Time Machine, a San Antonio company, they do the original costumed dinner house one better with a salad bar meticulously created from the gleaming shell of a 1932 Dusenburg automobile. That's showmanship. That's following a theme to the hilt.

Play It to the Hilt

If you ride into town on the theme bandwagon, then plan on playing it to the hilt. If you have decided to operate under the theme of an old-fashioned hardware store, then do it completely. You'll need hardwood floors and nails sold in kegs. You'll need to provide snap brim caps for your employees and carry at least some merchandise that, even though you don't expect it to ever sell, will add to the decor. In fact, some merchandise should not be carried as inventory, but instead should be written off as decor.

Theme works best when it captures the imagination of your customers. Actually, a theme carried to its extreme approaches theater. A theme played well actually engages the customer.

A perfect example of theme-as-theater is the development of theme restaurants that present the guest with an evening of dining in an oversized medieval castle. Such operations exist in major tourist cities, such as Orlando, Dallas, and Las Vegas.

Once beyond the imposing facade, the customer becomes court supplicant—and is treated to an evening of daring horsemanship and skill—as knights joust in the arena below, vying for the attention of any and every fair, and not-so- fair, damsel in the house.

One fun part of the theme: Dinner is served with not a single piece of silverware in sight. Customers dig into their meal with both hands, exhibiting table manners that would get them into trouble at home and thrown out of most self-respecting restaurants. The joke is that here you have a restaurant that has made the lack of amenity part of the service. The price actually goes up as the service goes down. What a neat joke that people will pay to be inconvenienced as long as it is in keeping with the theme!

Whatever your theme, play it to the hilt.

In Mexico, we were invited to take a short dinner cruise to a nearby island. The theme was roughly stated as an evening of rowdiness aboard an anything-goes pirate ship. Our hosts made announcements as though they were speaking to their fellow swabbies, and the crowning touch—the pantaloons that each of the tourists-cum-pirates were invited to wear. The concept was good. If the passengers had looked anything like the attractive models featured in the brochure, and had they really worn the pantaloons and tops with the daring side splits as had the models, it could have been an awesome evening. They weren't; they didn't; it wasn't.

Play the theme, but be certain that it matches your product and your customers.

Consider Group Showmanship

Not far from our home is an anomaly. Actually, it is a small town. What makes it so special? The retail sales in this small town of 7,500 friendly folks are nearly eight times greater than what would be expected for a town of this size. Perhaps that is why the people of Fredericksburg, Texas are so friendly. They're making money in buckets.

The reason for their good fortune? They have agreed—as a group—to play the same theme. Fredericksburg has a wonderful historical district. To violate the integrity of its old German-Texas theme would be the death of the town. Tourists travel for miles to sample the art, handicrafts, and German-style food and baked goods featured in the quaint shops that line an always-crowded, never-hurried Main Street. Add a plastic fast-food operation, throw in a gas station convenience store, and stir in a steel-and-glass office building, and in less than the time that it would take to say the words "ghost town," you would have one.

Fredericksburg, Texas exists simply because of a theme that group consensus and city ordinance has declared will be the order of business. No one would claim that the food, art, and general merchandise offered by the casual, accommodating merchants of Fredericksburg are all that special. The presentation makes the difference. These savvy merchants have learned to sell both the sizzle and the steak. The sizzle allows them to sell at a premium.

The merchants of Fredericksburg may complain about the high rent in the historical district, but they know that it is exactly this access to civic decor that puts strudel on the table.

How could you work with other nearby businesses to create a group theme? It doesn't have to be a historical theme. It could be something as simple as baskets of flowers hanging from the lightposts that line the street in front of your business. Check out Tacoma, Washington. Tacoma is a small town that would otherwise be remarkably unremarkable, if it were not for the gorgeous hanging baskets of flowers that add color to every corner.

Check out Victoria, British Columbia. In addition to horse-drawn carriages, you'll see another theme that revolves around breathtaking landscape and lovingly restored architectural delights.

Or visit Mill Valley, California. A hidden valley across the bay from San Francisco, Mill Valley is home to an eclectic mix of shops that, either by design or pure dumb luck, mesh comfortably in a neighborhood where doors are propped open, music is a hallmark of nearly every shop, and steel and glass are noticeable only by their absence.

What could you do to rally merchants in your neighborhood? Whatever it may be, try to march, not in lock-step but at least in homage, to the same drummer. Imagine the impact you could have on a shopping, dining, even service experience.

Make It a Department

Showmanship can be so important that it deserves a department of its own.

One of America's best examples of both showmanship and dedication to showmanship can be found at Fiesta Texas in San Antonio. You will find an entire cast of characters, serious actors and entertainers, all working in a department appropriately named "Streetmosphere."

It doesn't require rocket science to instantly get what Streetmosphere is all about. Their sole responsibility is to add the "human decor" necessary to finish creating the mood and magic that craftspeople have already begun through their faithful rendition of an old German village, a western town, a small town Main Street from the American 1950's, and a beautiful re-creation of a Mexican town square.

But, beautiful or not, the buildings and landscape are, in the end, nothing more than brick and mortar. The multiple casts from the Streetmosphere department that add the crowning touch, drawing every visitor into the fantasy of another world.

If showmanship is really key to your guests' enjoyment, then it deserves a department of its own. A backup position might be to make at least one person in the operations or marketing department responsible for seeing that someone is always at least thinking about adding the human pizazz necessary to turn an ordinary event or transaction into an extraordinary happening.

Why do we only think to turn on the creativity in our retail and service environments when we are faced with a holiday? The sharpest, most aggressive operators know that decor, brick and mortar, or humans can set their operation ahead of the pack anytime of the year.

Call Betty at (800) 635-7524, Monday–Friday between the hours of 9 AM–4 PM (Central) to order an audio tape of Scott's Positively Outrageous Service and Showmanship.

CHAPTER EIGHT

Retail Theater

It's not the product that matters. That's not to say that issues of design and quality are not important. It's only to make the point that a great retailer, one with a bit of imagination and the guts to take an intelligent risk, will be successful no matter what the product is.

If there is anything to be learned from the best of the best, it is probably this short list of key principles:

1. Listen to the customer;
2. Dare to be different;
3. Take good ideas and run;
4. Be absolutely committed to being the best.

These characteristics will be required for anyone who wants to be more than a "me, too" or worse, an "also-ran."

Beyond paying close attention to the operating values of other successful operators, it will be doubly important to keep a steady eye on the operating values of today's consumer. Quality and value will no longer be worth any more than entry into the game.

There may have been a time when such values as "clean," "safe," and perhaps the idea of "value priced" were considered to be competitive advantages. This is no longer true. The consistency brought to the marketplace by franchising and chains has made what used to be significant points of difference no more than the price of admission, in a game where possessing such values does little more than keep you from being eliminated from consideration.

Meeting the minimum expectation is no longer equivalent to leading the pack. Today's consumers are too sophisticated, spoiled by equally sophisticated retailers, service providers, and even slicker media campaigns.

The winners in the shakeout among retailers will be those who keep in mind the three "E's" of the '90s...Entertainment, Education, and Environment. These watchwords capture today's consumer, who is increasingly looking for value in the purchase experience that transcends the product itself.

Magnificent, Miracle Merchandising Mile

Take a walk along Chicago's Miracle Mile, the stretch of high-priced real estate that stretches along Michigan Avenue, just north of the loop, and you will see America's most innovative retailers showing off their products in an orgy of razzle dazzle that would have made P.T. Barnum proud.

If you really do walk this street and dare to wander into the highest profile show-offs, you won't be by yourself. The customer traffic in the busiest of stores will easily rival that of the mega-sized discount stores that today mark the borders of any self-respecting suburb.

The three anchors of this frenzy of merchandising are the Sony Gallery, Nike Town and FAO Schwarz.

Sony the Way to Go Home

Trying to locate the phone number for the Sony Gallery turned out to be a surprise opportunity to put the Sony system to an impromptu test. The information operator mistakenly gave us the phone number to the Sony Customer Service department, also located in the Chicago area code.

The call was a textbook-perfect blend of high-tech/high-touch. A recorded voice was first on the line. This is normally an irritant. Sony's master of ceremony made the announcement that calls may be monitored in an effort to insure prompt, professional service. The announcement was short and sweet and quickly gave way to soothing classical music, just the right choice for a company peddling high-tech, high-end consumer electronics.

Better yet was the pleasant, professional voice next on the line. This one was real, a real winner at that. She inquired how she could help, assured me that, even though I had called the wrong number, she could and would get me headed in the right direction with little or no further delay. She asked permission to dose me again with another shot of the classics and, in seconds, was back on the line with the correct number and a reminder that I would be welcome to call again if she could assist further.

Don't you just love it when all that attention to hiring and training actually pays off!

Next came the proof of the pudding.

Step into the Sony Gallery at the corner of Michigan Avenue and Erie and you may think at first that you have the wrong address and have stepped into a museum. The outside and the inside of the Sony flagship store have the solid, sophisticated look and feel of a first class exhibit. Gallery Manager, Elaine Reck, will tell you that this look is definitely no mistake.

Sony built the store as a showcase for its consumer products with the intent of educating the public. From the moment you step through the door, the educating process begins. The surprise? It is so painless—fun, in fact—as Sony puts on what must be the world's most low-key sales pitch.

Education is, in fact, the theme of this high-tech/high-touch shopping experience. Each "Sales Counselor" is a highly trained guide through the mystery of today's electronic gear. Product training takes place twice each week. Read that again, "twice each week." As if to underscore the point, the first smartly suited Sony employee I encountered on my visit was Rose, a corporate trainer who had been sent to the store especially for the purpose of conducting a session on the various models of the Walkman.

Formal training is also available to customers. Every two months, a public seminar is offered to introduce such electronic age information as "How to Create a Better Home Video," "How to Wire Your New House for Coming Electronic Products," and "Getting Comfortable with Dolby Pro-Logic."

Customers who purchase Sony products are offered delivery and setup service, plus personal training on how to get the most from their system.

Even Sony dealers have made the trip to study the revolutionary design of the store. Some have taken ideas to recreate, as is. Others observe and think of interesting adaptations that are more appropriate for their own particular situations. But some innovations have worked so well that Sony has made a commitment to make them available system-wide.

For example, so many customers have been startled to learn that they could actually make their television and stereo sets work as a system that Sony has decided to market a home-entertainment system already prepackaged including the cabinet, so that dealers can now offer more than individual products. Now they will be able to demonstrate the concept in one well-configured display.

Few of the ideas that make the Miracle Mile merchants stand out could be called by any stretch of the imagination...revolutionary. Evolutionary is a far more accurate description.

The store is a showcase for every Sony consumer electronic product, from a "video bar" that features seven cameras to an entire apartment with home office that shows how to integrate Sony products into any lifestyle.

Customers are quick to react with comments such as "I never thought about putting a TV under my kitchen cabinets," or "Who would have thought that you could hide a movie screen in the ceiling and turn your living room into a theater?"

At the video bar, customers can get hands-on experience with every model of Sony camera now on the market. A beautiful, well-lighted floral arrangement is situated neatly in a specially designed recess in the facing wall. Camera buffs can test each camera's faithfulness of reproduction as well as other features, such as zoom and titling. The scene changes frequently, sometimes including sculpture or other art.

The retail space really does resemble the interior of a museum, only this one features Sony electronics as art. In fact, the ambiance is so laid back that the overall feeling is like attending a gala opening of a fine art exhibit, rather than shopping for a replacement VCR.

The upstairs features a variety of Sony products in their "natural" environments. Walkman radios and disc players are shown on wire frame mannequins that are caught mid-stride as though frozen while jogging or wind surfing. Wireless headphones dangle from the ceiling enticing the curious to try them on for a test listen.

Everywhere there seems to be just enough product information to answer common questions, and there are plenty of non-aggressive salespersons available to handle the more esoteric questions of the true audio or videophile.

In the auto sound display area, customers can listen to incredible Sony products in the comfort and fantasy of a pair of Ferrari bucket seats. Mini televisions and videotape players demonstrate that there is room for yet another gadget in the true believer's car. And workhorse amplifiers prove that added watts can boost sound to the level of a low-flying jet.

The big risk, of course, comes from defying conventional retail wisdom in a hundred small ways. The floor is not packed with merchandise. There is only one of any item, but one of absolutely every item. Merchandise is delivered quickly from the stockroom, which is not far removed from the sales floor. Even the customer service function is handled in a startling manner.

Customer Service is located in a separate office and staffed, not with grease-monkey techies, but with well-trained service personnel, who greet the customer from behind a desk in a modern office setting, but wearing the same smart uniforms found on the sales floor. The staff has standing orders to do whatever it takes to be absolutely certain that no customer leaves unserved or unsatisfied.

Gallery Manager, Elaine Reck, came to the venture with plenty of credentials as a practitioner of industrial showmanship. In charge of introducing Sony Eight Millimeter video equipment to a skeptical public throughout her midwest territory, Reck visited the Detroit Grand Prix and dozens of other outdoor sports events to hand out demo cameras to spectators and invite them to put the cameras to a test.

She placed rental units in video stores and underwrote the conversion of the tapes to the then-standard VHS format. The results? Today, eight millimeter video equipment accounts for more than 50 percent of video equipment purchases. These same "put your hands on it, try it out," entreaties drive the Sony Gallery.

When asked what is the most important feature of the store, Reck is the epitome of sincerity as she answers. "Our people," is the gist of her response. She believes that educating the consumer is first and foremost, and that her well-selected, superbly trained, all-salaried staff make it possible to achieve that goal.

The reason for her evangelism stems from the fact that "most things in electronics are black...they aren't self evident." In other words, features, advantages, and benefits are not readily apparent in a high-tech electronic device. From the outside, a radio is a radio is a radio. It's the guts and what it does and how well it does it that justifies the difference in price. But if the customer sees only a box and thinks only "radio," then it will remain a challenge to sell quality product in a world of look-alike products.

So Reck and company have built a "consumer training store. They play with it, touch it, get familiar with it." And hopefully, they buy it. And that is the simple goal of Sony Gallery, whether the sale is made on Michigan Avenue or in a small town appliance store when Gallery visitors return home. Sony has made a sale by recognizing that an educated consumer is a Sony customer.

Nearly 50 percent of visitors to the gallery are tourists and the other 50 percent are likely to be locals who have made a special trip in from the suburbs just to look around. And look they do. The average Saturday count is a crushing 5,000 to 7,000 shoppers. And the gallery is definitely not a huge space. It comprises two rather small floors with the only advantage being that only one of each item is on display.

Just Do It

Nike Town sits right next door to the Sony Gallery. When Sony went for understatement, Nike went for the gold. Throw in a healthy serving of showmanship followed by a heavy dose of self-marketing. Nike Town marketing is so charming that, what elsewhere might be interpreted as braggadocio, at Nike Town is only part of the show.

The Visitors' Magazine that seems to own a share of every Chicago hotel room is a typical example of why the public should feel lucky that Nike products are as good as their marketing. Otherwise, no telling what Nike would have us wearing!

Under "Sporting Goods," the Nike Town listing stands out in typical Nike fashion. Just above their listing is an entry that reads, "America's largest sporting goods chain with over 260 stores nationwide." Ho-hummm.

Nike Town weighs in with this feel-good copy: "Nike out the yin-yang. No other store sports more cool stuff. You'll be motivated, educated, struck with awe, and inspirated (their word, not mine). You might want to plan two trips...one to see all the cool displays and another to do your shopping."

Get the point? Nike makes you salivate before you even lay eyes on the joint.

When you actually get to the source of all this hype, you are surprised to see that at first blush, ol' Nike Town doesn't seem to hold much promise from the street.

Nike Town makes a feeble stab at blending with the nose-in-the-air glitz of the neighborhood. But a closer look, and it's apparent that if Nike Town had a nose, it would have a thumb beside it.

On the facade of the building, Nike athletes cast in dull aluminum are freeze-frame monuments to those who insist on "just doing it." Caught in mid-shot, an aluminum basketball player takes aim on the goal, never knowing if the shot would be good or the clock has run out. A woman does her aluminum aerobics nearby, while a runner races from a cyclist who will never get up sufficient speed to break free of the stone facade.

Posted next to the doors, a store hours sign that, even for the terminally dense, is proof that Nike Town isn't going to be another trip to Wal-Mart. The store hours for Monday through Friday are listed as being from 10:08 a.m. until 8:09:07 p.m. Right.

Look a little closer, and you see that some space cadet has created a paddlewheel-like contraption with Nike shoes at the end of each spoke. The wheel makes endless tracks across a treadmill that, like the Energizer Bunny, keeps going and going and....

Inside is where the fun begins in earnest.

First-time visitors are surprised to see what could easily be interpreted as a Michael Jordan memorial, and the guy, at last report, isn't even dead yet! But there he stands, hangs actually, in life-size, non-living color. This Michael Jordan is the gray-white color of the plaster from which he has been cast. The only color about the scene belongs to the huge pair of, you guessed it, Nike shoes that support Jordan in mid-jam.

The walls on either side of the entry are covered with Sports Illustrated covers. If you have any hope of joining this gallery of sporting greats, you had better be good and you had better be wearing your Nikes.

Two automatic doors part with a swish and invite the visitor into the inner sanctum. There begins a history of Nike that includes a waffle iron, said to be like the one that served as the mold for the original Nike outer sole. What is most interesting is the quote from Nike founder, Phil Knight. It seems to have set the pace for what now can only be described as the Nike spirit.

Asked what he thought he could do to improve his time as a runner, founder Knight said, "Run faster."

The rest of the store is nothing less than 68,000 square feet of retail-awesome.

Rounding the corner, I was faced with a first look at what Nike calls the "Town Square." More accurately, it is a huge, open atrium that extends upward to encompass all three of the sales floors. Standing guard at the entrance is what Sam Walton would call a greeter. Nike has its own groupie in the person of one bright and chipper cashier-cum-hall monitor by the name of Darcy. Darcy was one of the 100 or so employees selected from nearly 3,500 applicants. She loves Nike. Always has.

What better person to greet the customers than a customer? And Darcy is nothing if not a super customer. She probably has a larger collection of Nike clothes and paraphernalia than the corporate honchos. A Nike customer from childhood, Darcy presents the ideal Nike image, dressed to sweat in her Nike Town work-out clothes. But even "Miss Nike Enthusiasm" can't keep you from gaping at the incredible sight of the atrium.

A trio of plaster cyclists race through the ether in a short file that launches from the third floor balcony and swoops toward the plaster casts of Scottie Pippen and David Robinson. These two are caught in a basketball game stuck in eternal overtime.

Allow yourself to be drawn closer into the action, and face the tough decision of which of the 18 mini-departments, representing 20 sports, to visit first. Most visitors cannot resist heading straight for what appears to be a hole in the floor, wood planking scraped away to reveal an ocean just beneath the surface of Chicago. It's like discovering the secret lair of Batman's nemesis, Penguin, or digging so deep that, just like your mother predicted, you would fall all the way to China.

What you are actually seeing...and hearing, is what Nike calls the "video pond," a wall of video monitors gone horizontal and covered by thick plexiglass. Everyone wants to walk on the scenes of aquatic life...a roaring surf, a tide pool, and close up photography of colorful fishes. Some folks are timid at first, wanting to test their luck in the water but not altogether certain that they can keep their feet dry.

To complete the scene, a huge, 22-foot aquarium serves as background to a collection of Nike Aqua Gear. Each fish has been carefully selected to match the color of the Nike products! Decadent attention to detail.

Runners are celebrated early on the ground floor, where the International Pavilion features a six-foot rotating globe and compass set into the floor. The displays, in addition to more Nike goodies than can easily be imagined, feature the accomplishments of such running greats as Mike Powell, Sergy Bubka, and Patti Sue Plummer.

Visitors don't begin to actually shop until they have first been dragged by their senses and churning imaginations from floor to floor, attraction to attraction. Even the escalators have a curious look. The simple act of replacing the familiar white lights along the side with glowing green tubes creates a subtle but somewhat haunting change.

The tennis department features the sound effects of a tennis match...in stereo. First the serve from the left, followed by a return from the right. Tennis balls appear to be embedded in the floor, and the try-on benches look as though they were fashioned from a real leatherette tennis court.

In another department, a tongue-in-cheek solar system rotates from the ceiling. Orbiting a basketball sun, there is a complete set including the ping-pong planet (Pluto), the golf-ball planet (Mercury) and, of course, planet Earth. (Well, you figure which ball Nike reserved to represent the earth. If you guessed "goofball," you are being logical but you are wrong!)

A favorite attraction is the poster department. Not only are the posters beautiful, they are mounted and displayed much as you would expect of a fine art gallery. Nike T-shirts get the same treatment. They, too, are mounted. A wall of flip frames holds the mounted shirts and allows shoppers to browse through the surprisingly beautiful shirt art, as though they were selecting a print to be framed rather than worn over baggy shorts.

A small, very black, acoustically balanced rotunda serves as a stand-up theater where Nike brazenly exhibits Nike commercials in a sight and sound experience unlike any you have witnessed while rummaging through the fridge at half time. The mix includes wonderful footage of Nike athletes and customers doing their thing, set to inspiring music and benefiting from creative photography.

At the other end of the building is a show-stopping sight, a near half-court basketball set-up, where shoppers are invited to take their new purchases for a test drive. I ran into six bubbly teenage girls who had decided to visit Nike Town in lieu of a spring break trip to Florida.

Not really.

Actually, they were on spring break and had taken the train into the city to see the sights. That's no surprise. At the Chicago Tourist Bureau, the number one request is for information about Nike Town. For two of the girls, this was a second trip and they were acting as tour guides for the rest of the group, showing off the store as if it were their own.

They had gathered beneath the basketball goal that hangs in front of a huge, probably 15 feet or so high (is that life-size?), photo of Michael Jordan. They wanted a photo. Actually three photos, one for each of the cameras they had brought. (It seems photos are the rule rather than the exception. I saw numerous visitors with video cameras and many more staging shots in front of displays that they found especially interesting.)

I had the girls pose in front of the net. Two stooped to lift two others to their shoulders. As the top two smiled and grabbed the net triumphantly, the remaining two laid across the scene, propped on elbows and feeling, oh-so glamorous. And that's just about an accurate description of how many Nike Town visitors feel, glamorous and part of the action.

Even if they only wear their tennis shoes while watching a match on TV, at least for the time that they are at Nike Town, they feel like they are "just doing it."

At Nike Town, everybody gets into the act. The biggest game is trying to see who will be the first to spot the next clever innovation. There are the shoe tubes which must be discovered, then deciphered. The huge plexiglass tubes with the strange lighting seem to pierce the building in a dozen places, from basement to roof, perhaps shooting sustenance to the God of Sweat who lives somewhere in the inner spaces of the building.

Stand and watch. You will see that the God must eat Nike shoes. The shoes are elevatored up and down the tube system as they shuttle from stock room to customer in a matter of seconds. A Nike employee finally explained, "They free up display space, give room to display more styles and, of course, allow us to spend more time with the customer."

Cash registers are all black and sit on curious black stands. Wrapping stations are also black and emit a curious blue glow. The stools have seat cushions that are air-filled, much like the now famous Nike Air shoe. Everywhere you look, interesting sights and sounds invite you to participate and draw you to buy. Never has sports merchandise looked so attractive or been so much fun. And fun is only one of the key points of Nike Town.

Values are the other. And we're not talking about anything related to the sticker price found on the heel of a pair of Nike shoes, a number that, although often considerable, is outweighed by the social values that Nike offers as part of what can only be interpreted as a corporate sermonette. What is surprising is that the customers seem to be buying Nike values right along with the cross trainers and tennis shorts.

Values. What an odd topic. Not many years ago a discussion of values would have been quite out of place in most business settings. Today, many companies are discovering that corporate values are, or at least should be, driving forces in the conduct of company business.

At Nike Town, corporate values hang on the walls and on the lips of the employees.

I visited with Anne Towers, the assistant manager, about Nike values. She said that there are several that shape their every move. Values are so important that the first crew of 55 sales and service staff was flown to Portland for two weeks of intensive training, which heavily emphasized corporate values in addition to the expected programs on product and procedure.

Think about it. Two weeks of out-of-town expense for more than half a hundred new hires? Somebody had to be awfully committed to just doing it...right.

In fact, the staff is not the typical retail clerk demographic. Most are college graduates, and all were selected for their dedication to what Nike calls their "Gold Standard Service."

"That means that we put our customers first," explained Towers. Then she added, "And we don't just talk about it...."

"I know," I interrupted, "You just do it."

I earned another smile. I was catching on!

Towers raced through her idea of Nike corporate values.

First came *Performance.* Towers pointed out that all Nike athletes are performers. Not playboy, high-profile endorsers, but serious athletes who are committed sports professionals. These spokespersons do more than simply attract the attention of the public. They are, in a larger sense, role models for the people of Nike. At least they are for Towers and, no doubt, Darcy down at the door.

Authenticity came next. It means that at Nike, it is not necessary to be a world-class performer. It's only necessary to deliver whatever is your personal best. This value seems right at home with the sign that customers see as they leave the store: "There is no finish line."

Plus there is the idea that Nike products should be true to purpose. There are shoes for running, shoes for walking, shoes for every sport, variation, and athlete. Nike wants you to have the shoe that is right for you. Not the shoe that has the highest price, but the shoe that works for you and your lifestyle.

Authenticity to Nike means a dedication to making a customer, not just a sale.

Nike trains its sales staff to offer solutions, not products. The product should solve a problem or remain in the store.

I offered that *Risk* must certainly be a Nike corporate value. Towers agreed, adding that *Innovation* was another word that belonged in the equation.

"It's easy to say what is wrong. It's a lot harder to come up with a solution. We ask our employees to contribute and they do."

Commitment had to be on the list, and it was. Simply stated, it is the Nike version of no bad hair days. The finest athletes take to the court or field 100 percent focused on performing to their personal best. They leave aches and pains, even heartaches and pains, on the bench. "They just don't let other things get in the way."

I was writing fast, and thought we were at the end of the list. "Have I got them all?"

"One more and it's a big one. We have to include *Teamwork.*"

The explanation that followed was that teamwork meant more than just working together. It meant working together to serve the customer. At Nike, department lines blur and everything stops if a customer has a need, no matter what department has official jurisdiction. If you can help, Nike wants to see you jump.

If there is such a thing as a boss at Nike Town, it comes in the form of Stuart Nishikawa. Nishikawa has all the energy that his track suit seemed to promise. He, like Darcy at the door and anyone who is involved in business success, is in love with his job. He came to work dressed to play, not a bad analogy for the rest of us. If you want to be successful, play a game you enjoy.

"Most customers don't focus on one thing. They just walk in the door and are overwhelmed by the totality of the visual effect. It's like, WOW! What is this place?"

Nishikawa explains that Nike is sensitive to its dealer network. At Nike Town there are no sales, no discounts—just every style and color of every product that Nike manufactures.

Nike Town relies on the ability to inform the customer about the product, and the incredible selection, to develop a sale. But in spite of a hard-working decor package, in the end, sales are highly dependent upon quality service. Surprised?

"Bottom line. No matter what happens, no matter how great we look, in the end our image is no better than our service. You see an exciting store and you *expect* exciting service."

It's a Small, Small World

If Stuart Nishikawa thinks that Nike Town is part Disney, he should take a short walk up Michigan Avenue to FAO Schwarz. FAO took a page or two from the Disney playbook, scrunched the result into a retail store instead of an amusement park, and came up with a product that puts your eyes on stalks!

Marketing to kids is no different than any other marketing. You have to learn to view the world through the eyes of your customer. It helps if you like your customer and it helps even more if you are like your customer. Then you have a commonality that helps you select on behalf of your customer.

I like kids and usually kids like me. When it comes to kids...I are one! And the same must be true for the genius behind FAO Schwarz.

(There's a kid here in the gate lounge waiting with his mother to board the same flight. He has a huge, sticky chocolate donut in one hand and a huge chocolate smile to match. I'd like to steal his donut but I'll settle for him not taking a sudden liking to me. I'm down to my last clean white shirt.)

From the street, FAO looks like a giant toybox. Although the numerous windows are each a show in themselves, the attention of all but the most jaded of passersby is captured by a huge Teddy bear, lording over Michigan Avenue from his window on the real world. Weighing in at a generous 5,000 pounds, Teddy is a masterpiece of ingenuity, his mechanical paw waving and his servo-mechanical eyes rolling as if he had just heard a mechanical joke.

Later I learn that Teddy has a bow tie that is five-feet-wide, a fact that is not all that obvious due to his enormous size, a whopping 20-feet-high by 12-feet-across. He looks soft and cuddly from my vantage point across the street, but a closer look might spoil the secret that he is really foam, plywood, and fiberglass-reinforced polyester.

Sharing Teddy's lofty perch are three brightly colored toy building blocks, appropriately sized at three-feet by three-feet. They announce that, indeed, this is the place, spelling F, A, O in letters on each face.

As inviting as the exterior may be, the inside of the store more than matches the promise. Stepping through the door is the rough equivalent of walking into a time-space warp, transporting the corporeal self instantly to FAO's version of a hands-on Small World from Disney, complete with a children's chorus that changes timbre but not rhythm as the appealing lyric draws you through the store.

"Welcome to our world, welcome to our world, welcome to our world of toys..." sing the unseen voices of what must certainly be a chorus of dolls brought magically to life just for the occasion.

Eyes and ears have difficulty staying in synch as they are attracted by what seems to be an endless source of color, sound, and invitations to play. The lower floor is dominated by stuffed everything. And we're not talking small. From the expected stuffed bears to the unexpected stuffed giraffe, gorilla, and tiger.

Riding the up-escalator is an adventure in sound, as mechanical creatures invite the visitor even further into the retail fantasy created by the genius of FAO Schwarz. Along the way, a giant version of what may be a Kachinko machine hurls bowling-ball sized globes along an enclosed metal frame from the top floor, looping and swirling to a climactic end near the front door at speeds nearing 200-miles-per-hour.

FAO is not the world's largest toy store. It does not carry the largest selection. It is, however, simply the best. The selection of toys includes only the best of its kind, not outrageously expensive and by no means selected for their snob appeal. Just great toys selected for their kid appeal.

But the magic lies not in the toys. FAO probably does not carry a single toy that you couldn't find at another fine toy shop. The magic lies in the inventive manner in which the toys are displayed. Like Nike Town and the Sony Gallery down the street, FAO Schwarz is a hands-on operation. And that is the magic. Participation.

FAO says, "Come in. Touch. Try it. Welcome to our world."

In the remote- and radio-control department, visitors are invited to try their hand at maneuvering the latest battery-operated cars and construction vehicles.

"We can put a battery in that one if you'd like to take it for a spin," offers one of the stores' professional kids.

Everywhere there are young-spirited folks who seem to have been hired not to sell toys, but to help customers get their hands on the goodies. There again is that awesome secret. Get the customer involved with a great product and there is no need to sell. The product, and the experience, do the selling.

A toy soldier turns out to be "the" Toy Soldier. Standing a handsome but not imposing six feet plus, this soldier moves and acts, talks and acts, as ringmaster in a multi-stage toy show that is playing out simultaneously throughout the store.

If you are just overwhelmed, too far from the freedom of youth to decide, an FAO personal shopper is available to help you make a perfect selection. By telephone or in person, on the sales floor or in the privacy of a cozy, living room-like office, the personal shopper is trained to ask just the right questions to pick a toy especially for the lucky kiddo.

Everywhere is the invitation to touch, to experience. The children's book area is reason enough to get any child excited over the joy of reading. A talking tree that is home to a crowd of stuffed and animated creatures invites little readers and readers-to-be to pick out, not a book, but an adventure.

FAO seems to understand that there is a bit of child-like wonder left in all but even the most jaded adult. They offer to clear the store and make way for bigger kids by making it available for private parties. Who could imagine a more whimsical location for an evening of fun and general tomfoolery?

FAO recognizes that we all need to play, and they have created what has to be one of the world's greatest playgrounds. The twist? In addition to just plain fun, the cash registers raise a chorus that would brighten the heart of Scrooge himself.

And all this to the tune of "Welcome to our world of toys."

More

Everywhere retailers are coming to the conclusion that consumers, at least sometimes, want more than product in a box. In a world where shopping time comes at a premium, consumers are asking for an opportunity to combine shopping and recreation. They are willing to pay for the pleasure. Our job is to come through when they ask themselves "is it worth it?"

In Minneapolis, developers have built a shopping experience so-big, so-grand that it has become a travel destination. Who would think that a shopping mall could ever become a vacation Mecca?

Well, the Mall of the Americas has become just that. Every day, tour operators deposit thousands of bus-riding tourists at the entrance. Hours later, they will drag back onto the bus, totally awed and absolutely exhausted.

Jammed with a representative of nearly every retailer in America plus scores of independents, the Mall of the Americas can't truly be appreciated in a single visit. But you could spend all day and never have to worry about things to see and do.

In the central court, you can ride a roller coaster. If you get dizzy you can visit a doctor. Feeling better? Then head for one of dozens of restaurants and eateries.

What many Americans have come to dread, a trip to the mall, has now become an eagerly anticipated event.

A Sanitized Los Angeles

"Sanitized Los Angeles," that's what the Wall Street Journal called the newest addition to MCA's Universal Studios attraction. Already there was an 18-screen theater attracting a whopping 15,000 movie buffs every Saturday night. Now they have a way to extend their visit without leaving the grounds.

Called CityWalk, the two block "shopping environment" is a faux Los Angeles, recreated as a microcosm of shops and restaurants. If you took most of Los Angeles's most familiar street scenes, cleaned them up, smooshed them together, and erased their attendant blemishes such as the homeless and litter, you would have a pretty good look at CityWalk. Add in the high-tech entertainment of Disney's Epcot Center, plus a crowd of tourists on foot, and you have a look at Los Angeles if it had been designed by Hollywood. Most of the excitement without most of the danger and inconvenience.

At CityWalk the bikini weightlifters, like those in Venice Beach, play in the sand as a 40-foot TV cranks out sports programs nearby. Street performers entertain as visitors wait their turn to experience a motion-simulated ride-film, or to someday soon visit the futuristic electronic pavilion to be designed by Spielberg himself.

Who can say if we are looking at the future of retailing or nothing more than a one-of-a-kind experiment? Though it doesn't seem likely that consumers will demand beer and circus at every turn, for certain these exciting new retail ventures are upping the ante as they raise expectations and put imagination next to the cash register.

Feel Me, Touch Me

The rock opera "Tommy" said it all. We all want to be touched. We all want to participate and be a part of the fun. That is the lesson of the retailers' delight playing daily at a "retail theater near you!"

Call Betty at (800) 635-7524, Monday–Friday between the hours of 9 AM– 4 PM (Central) for a free copy of our IdeaLetter.

CHAPTER NINE

Getting Started

- Ask your customers what they consider good, great, POS.
- Find out if they are willing to pay for it.
- Find out how much of an advantage such service could be.
- Provide basic information on demographic analysis and customer survey.
- Create an initial goal statement for the business. Remember to include who you are in the statement. Keep it short and simple; keep it in the face of everyone.
- Lead the way through an outstanding example.
- Determine what kind of showmanship you can deliver. Be careful not to make it overly standard.
- Create a profile for associates who can and will deliver the promise that you have established. Then hire to that profile.
- Be willing to pay a little more than standard.
- Create a leadership development program that establishes both a climate and a crew for creative customer care. Be the first to participate in the program.
- List the characteristics of an effective leadership training program.
- Create a training program that delivers the training and tools

that the crew will need to deliver.

- List the characteristics of excellent training.
- Create a customer/associate feedback system that rewards great performance and corrects less-than-standard performance. Be certain that the feedback is immediate to both customer and crew.
- Review and revise daily.

CHAPTER TEN

Service Magic

Watch!

The audience of customers and customers-to-be hangs onto every word and gesture. Undisturbed by the parade of people and noise that pass not more than a few feet away, there exists in this world, for this moment, nothing that is not under the tent.

The wordsmith slices and dices a careful cadence, more finely separated than the vegetables that are falling under the knife. No ordinary knife, a Ginsu knife. A tool with a million uses if you are willing to step a little closer and fall gently under the spell of the shaman.

He uses humor and reaches verbally into the audience with offers to play. Every move is rehearsed but it doesn't matter.

Some in the audience will buy, certain to have earned bragging rights over the treasure that lady luck plopped into their laps, manna from Heaven, or at least Taiwan.

Others will escape—those who had remained, through force of will or force of crowd, on the edge of the mini-revival that repeats every quarter hour. They may mumble disparaging words about the "suckers," the fools who had been parted from their money. But secretly they will wonder how their lives could have changed, had they the cash to acquire a household miracle not "available" in stores at any price, but worth all the more when the special bonus extras were considered.

When the hands on the sign hanging on the front of the tent have moved to the next quarter hour, nothing will have changed, save perhaps a fresh supply of product and a bushel of sacrificial vegetables. The pitchman may be different, but with eyes closed there would be no telling that a fresher horse had been substituted.

Patter Science

Showmanship is an art. Or is it?

To the curious, there are several principles at work. The old timers may have a difficult time finding just the right words to describe how a good pitch takes form. But even they will recognize the pattern of the patter.

Patter. It's the script that a good pitchman follows to capture his audience or mark. Patter is not the same as the routine offer of "Cheese?" or "Large?" that you hear at a quick-service restaurant. That is merely a statement not much different than a trolling line set for the unlikely event that a fish will happen along. Troll enough lines long enough, and eventually catch a fish. It's a numbers game. It is nothing more than simple suggestion.

You wanted cheese or the large size from the moment you walked in. All that happened to make the sale was that you were reminded of your need or desire. You wanted a milkshake but you are on a diet.

"If they mention a shake, I'll get one."

They mention. You buy.

Patter, good patter, draws you toward conclusions that you had not imagined. You get the message and want to take it home.

All great pitchmen and speakers use patter to make the sale whether the product is a Ginsu knife or an idea. What makes patter different from simple suggestion is that it is a calculated plan to change your mind, literally.

The Show Is in the Story

Storytelling is the secret weapon of the showman. Kick up the dust with compelling word pictures, and the mark is inevitably drawn into the spell of the moment. And "spell" is exactly what happens.

Some say that a good story creates a trance-like state that enables the audience's imagination to go to work. And everyone knows that imagination beats reality everytime.

Don't get hung up over the idea of creating trances. It's not voodoo but, in many respects, it is a bit of magic. A trance is an ordinary state of mind. We all achieve various levels of trance when we meditate, pray, daydream, jog, or simply fall under the spell of repetitive work or even a good book. (You're getting sleepy...your eyes are beginning to feel heavy.)

The beauty of a trance is that, when you are in the trance state, your attention is focused to the partial exclusion of external stimuli. Check out the intro to this chapter again for a clearer picture.

Recently, I spoke to a large audience known for continuing to conduct business during the speaker's presentation (or even walk out if the notion suited). An amazed and obviously delighted meeting planner gushed after the meeting that, "Even when you lowered your voice to a whisper, there wasn't a soul talking! How did you do that?"

Simple. Trance. That and the armed guards posted at every exit!

Actually, there are some secrets to drawing an audience close and creating a trance. These are the best-kept secrets of the showman's trade.

Grady Jim Robinson, a storyteller of considerable talent, reported in a recent article on the mechanics of how great stories create comforting trances. He says that getting a trance started may be as simple as offering a point of conversational fixation. Something that is the rough verbal equivalent of the hypnotist's swinging pocket watch or flickering candle.

What is surprising is that almost anything can serve as the catalyst to the process, as long as it helps to fix the listener's attention. And the single, most effective tool is a story.

Storytelling is the secret to showmanship. Every great example of showmanship involves the use of a story.

Sometimes the story is told by the showman. Sometimes it is served up as an opportunity to participate in self-created fantasy with the show-off supplying only the raw materials.

But always there is the story.

Is There a Mechanic in the House?

The mechanics of showmanship are simple. Create fixation through cadence, imagery, pitch and tone, and body language.

Recall please, the image-rich cadence of Dr. Martin Luther King. His "I have a dream" speech may be the best example of cadence. Even today when that famous speech—call it sermon, if you wish—is replayed, audiences are suspended in anticipation of the next use of the line.

The Reverend Jesse Jackson does a second-best imitation that still manages to capture attention wherever he speaks. The tradition of fundamentalist preachers is to use the magic of pitch and tone and the hypnotic effect of cadence to mesmerize the minds and hearts of their congregations. Sit through a fire-and-brimstone Southern Baptist sermon and catch yourself anticipating the next line.

Corporate marketing departments, televangelists, even the local grocer are learning to use the techniques of showmanship to communicate to their public. Visit a theme park and notice how color, sound, and costume have been employed, not to change reality, but to amplify it in an attempt to fixate attention and suspend disbelief.

Ride through Disney's Small, Small World exhibit at the southern California park, and tell me that color and cadence have no effect. Readers who have shared the experience are right now starting to hum that nauseating lyric "It's a small world after all, it's a small world, da, da, da, da, da...."

See what I mean?

Focus the attention and the audience will self-direct through the rest of the process. Once the attention is fixed, the imagination begins to take over. Helped along by images supplied by the pitchman, the imagination works in the foreground of thought, processing the images—real and imagined—until it can draw a new conclusion about the product or idea being offered from the stage, the screen, or across the counter.

What the master knows, perhaps only intuitively, is that the average bear needs help fixating attention and juicing up the imagination. Some folks will dream or fantasize without any prompting.

On the job, we think of that behavior as laziness when, in fact, it may be the prelude to a creative thought or solution.

But most folks need a little help. "Give me an example," is frequently heard in classrooms and seminars everywhere. Unwise teachers interpret that as a sign that the student is too lazy to think on his own. Not so.

"Give me an example" is usually a request that should be heard as "Give me a picture."

Too many presenters open with a joke, which is humor without the story, and fail to fixate attention. When they do manage to capture attention, they turn it away by failing to paint a clear enough picture for the listener's imagination to take over.

Showmanship, whether it is on the stage, under a tent, or "performed" tableside, requires that the Show-off provide a sufficient image for the imagination of the audience to kick in. Word pictures usually do fine. Sometimes a simple prop or the addition of a gesture may boost the story from so-so to engaging. All the elements of cadence, pitch and tone, imagery, and body language can work together.

The only way people learn is by doing. Period.

If that is so, a logical question might be: "Then why am I wasting time reading this book, if I can't learn by any means other than doing?"

Glad you asked.

If the word-picture is skillfully painted, the audience can be drawn so far into the story that they are actually experiencing the emotions and physical environment of the characters. The audience trades places with the characters and steps into your imagination, enjoying the new world that you have created through cadence, imagery, pitch and tone, and body language.

They learn by doing in an imaginary setting. But none of this can occur if you do not paint the new world fully enough for them to participate.

Think for a moment how poor language skills compound the problems of learning. Without the ability to translate a word into a mental picture, or in the presence of a teacher who "paints" poorly, the audience simply won't "Get it." And what they are not "getting" is the picture. This is why great showmen use more than words when they communicate. (See the story of Emmett Kelly and the Watusi warriors.)

During college, I had a program at Lenny's...I mean Denny's...to teach the hearing impaired to work as short-order cooks. It was a fun program that did good for others, and made my college days even more interesting. One lesson that I learned is that communication is far more than the written or spoken word.

One night, while goofing off after a particularly brutal dinner run, I decided to tell a "Knock, Knock" joke to my hearing-impaired partner.

By the way, this story also illustrates the effect of culture on communication. My partner, a hearing-impaired young man from Greece, had never experienced a "Knock, Knock" joke, which turned out to make my behavior even more puzzling by the time I reached the punch line.

We were restocking the cook line and I returned from the cooler with a bunch of fresh parsley that we used for garnish. Holding the parsley behind my back, I said to my slightly confused friend, "Knock, knock?"

He looked at me as though I had just arrived by spaceship. This was the late sixties, so I suppose that was possible.

I signed to him that he was supposed to answer, "Who's there?"

First of all, he didn't really care who was there. Secondly, he knew darned good and well that you don't have to knock at the door to eat at Denny's. But he went along and signed the appropriate response.

"John," I signed.

He didn't respond in formal sign language. All he needed to do was curl one side of his lip and I completely understood that there was an excellent chance that this joke was headed for the dumper.

"Sign back 'John who?' " I prodded. He did, still not getting that what was about to happen would be incredibly funny.

"John, the Baptist!" I signed, followed immediately by my free hand whipping the parsley, dripping with ice cold water in a motion that instantly baptized but in no way saved my partner.

We came within a hare's breath of bringing an all-new meaning to the phrase "punch line!"

One other student of my cook training program was a beautiful, young woman named Patsy. I was smitten by both her beauty and charm. She could sign something as simple as "It's raining," but with such grace that I could feel the drops.

One evening I made a sarcastic remark—you know, that harmless play that comes under the category of flirting. In response to something that she had signed, I replied, "Oh, women make me sick."

Well, it would have been funny even to her if I had remembered to tell my face that it was included in the conversation. But I didn't, and she was reading more than my clumsy sign language. She was reading the expressions that accompanied the hands. Not good. She clobbered me. Lesson learned.

Great showmen use their face and their body as part of the act. They use every possible resource to enhance the art of creating a picture for the the benefit of the audience's imagination.

Last Call

Creating a trance-like state for your audience may fail to realize its potential, if you fail to ask for the order. This is called...going for the close. Whatever conclusion that you want your audience to draw, help them to it. You've created a trance, given them support for their imagination, and led them to the point of concluding that they simply cannot live without whatever set of knives or ideas you have to offer.

But, for goodness sake, don't take them to the edge and forget to help them over!

At the end of every sermon comes the invitation to join. At the end of every pitch should come the invitation to buy. It doesn't have to be a product or service that you offer for sale. Like the sermon, it could be a powerful idea or simply an invitation to join the fun.

Ask for the order!

Call Betty at (800) 635-7524, Monday–Friday between the hours of 9 AM–4 PM (Central) for information on how you can be invited to our ranch-based Positively Outrageous Service seminars.

CHAPTER ELEVEN

Eaten by Tangibles!

Positively Outrageous Service or a small dose of showmanship may be just the thing to highlight your customer's perception of your service. And when it comes to customer service, perception is everything.

Years ago we attempted to move the then-state-of-the-art audio technology we used in drive-in (not drive-through) restaurants into the dining room. If you are old enough to remember, dining rooms came late in the evolution of fast-food restaurants.

In those days, customers would drive onto the lot, pull into a parking stall under a metal canopy, and use an individual speaker system to communicate their order to an operator inside. The brilliant idea was to use essentially that same speaker system to serve customers in the dining room.

Tests showed that in addition to cutting labor, a major expense in the restaurant industry, the system dramatically improved service times. That is, the tests said so. The customers had an entirely different opinion.

We should have known better.

Since dirt, it had been axiomatic that immediately after seating customers, the next thing was to get water and a menu to the table. Once that small service was provided, even if it was several minutes before a waitperson actually showed up to take the order, as far as the customer was concerned, service had begun.

Our gee-whiz table-to-kitchen electronic link provided a menu permanently affixed to the table. As soon as the customers were ready to order, they had only to pick up a telephone handset to be connected immediately to the operator near the kitchen. Even though the system was faster than a hog on ice, in the mind of the customer, service did not begin until the server actually arrived at the table.

Never mind that on the first trip to the table, the server was able to bring the complete meal. To the customer, sitting at a plastic table, talking on a plastic telephone while reading a plastic menu, service did not start when the order was taken. In their mind, service didn't start until the first face to face, human contact was made. And that was too darned long. In service, perception is everything.

A medical lab client of ours is careful to provide the fastest, most accurate service possible. They are proud to be able to pick up a sample, deliver it to their labs 45 minutes away, and return the completed test results in less than two hours. That's phenomenal performance by any standard...except the customer's!

To the customer, a service that takes two hours in this hurry-up world, simply takes too long.

In service, speed matters much less than perceived speed.

For years, the auto rental business has recognized the need to offer tangibility to service. Rent a car and, more often than not, you'll find a tag dangling from the mirror. The tag itself in no way makes the car run better or look cleaner. But like the toilet seat wrappers that said "Sanitized for your protection," they let the renter know that there is more to renting a car to you than simply handing over the keys.

Unseen Service Isn't

Service that is unseen is no service at all. Customers may enjoy your product. They may even remark how good it is but they cannot fully appreciate the value that you have added unless you tell them. Anyone who provides a product or service should make tangible the value-added ingredients, materials, and services.

Restaurants:

"We use only the freshest ingredients. Our chicken arrives fresh. We hand-cut each piece to our specifications and marinate for 22 hours under exacting conditions. There are no canned products used in the preparation of your meal. From time to time, certain menu items may not be offered if the ingredients currently available do not meet our high standards."

Auto Repair:

"The mechanic responsible for the repair of your vehicle has successfully completed an intensive, factory certification program, and receives frequent continuing education. We use only parts provided by the original equipment manufacturer. All this, including a test drive of each vehicle prior to delivery, will make sure that you leave with a vehicle that allows us to earn your continued confidence."

Electronic Equipment:

"Each and every product that we manufacture undergoes an intensive test routine to make absolutely certain that it performs under the conditions likely to be encountered once it is put into service. It costs a little more, but we think you will agree that products you can depend on are worth our extra effort."

Hotel:

"Your room is cared for by a housekeeper who has been trained to pay attention to the details. We think that when it comes to cleanliness and comfort, it's important to be picky. You can relax knowing that your room has been serviced by a professional."

Airline:

"Airplanes make lots of noises. You'll hear the sound of the control surfaces moving into position and the landing gear retracting into its bay. Whatever the sound you hear, you can relax knowing that our flight crews are the best qualified in the industry. They are highly trained to put your safety first and to provide for your comfort. So welcome aboard!"

Public School:

"Your child is under the care of teaching professionals. Each of our teachers are carefully selected for both their technical knowledge and their ability to inspire young people. Our classrooms are frequently monitored by a staff of experienced administrators who insure that your child gets the finest possible educational experience. We have made full use of the latest technology, so that your child's education will be relevant to the real world. We invite you to attend parent-teacher events so you can experience our program firsthand."

Police Department:

"Each of our officers has been carefully selected and rigorously trained to serve our citizens. In addition to police procedures and legal issues, our officers are trained to assist with minor medical emergencies. And, many of our officers perform volunteer community service in their off hours. When you need help or protection, we're here to serve!"

** ** **

"Ladies and gentlemen, the captain has illuminated the seat-belt sign to indicate our preparation for landing. Please stow all carry-on articles, and return your seatbacks and tray tables to their original, upright and locked position...."

I had to stow the old laptop just about here and decided to spend the rest of the flight with the United Airlines in-flight magazine. The pages fell open to an ad for Coleman water jugs. What made the ad special? It used storytelling, a form of showmanship, to make tangible the craftsmanship of Coleman products. Very clever!

The story is of a husband-wife couple who were flying by private aircraft over a remote part of Baja, California, when they spotted a downed plane. In the sand near the plane, they could see a message scrawled by the plane's uninjured but thirsty occupants. "WATER" was the single, all-telling word in the sand.

The would-be rescuers dropped juice boxes only to watch them burst on impact. Unable to land in the rough terrain, but recognizing the desperate straits of the two below, they gambled on the strength of their Coleman water jug. From a hundred feet, they watched their Coleman drop to the desert floor. Not a single drop of water spilled!

According to the ad copy, the couple refused hero status, saying that they were only a couple who dropped in for a drink!

Now that is making an intangible quality highly visible and memorable!

Taking off from another airport and fortunate to be flying first class, I got another opportunity to see tangibility in practice. American Airlies has made great progress with the quality and selection of their in-flight meal service.

Some genius must have had the idea that airlines could serve good food if they would just admit to the limitations imposed by the circumstances of flying. Now they are attempting to serve simpler meals, often served cold but prepared with more than a little flair and imagination.

Tonight's dinner, get this...

...An assortment of warm mixed nuts to accompany your preferred cocktail or beverage. Followed by chilled shrimp. Then, as you would expect...salad of the season offered with grated Parmesan cheese and herb vinaigrette of Caesar dressing. Sounds like the perfect precursor to...herbed salmon enhanced by fresh herbs and a lemon vinaigrette, served with barley pilaf and a vegetable medley of sliced squash and carrots.

I would tell you about the dessert, but it was soooo good that it would only distract from the point that the menu enhanced the perceived quality and value of the meal. (I even ate the vegetables because they weren't just green stuff. They were a "medley," for goodness sake!)

The Invisible Cleaner

You can even make a human being "tangible." The best example ever arrived by mail. It was a letter from Chris Ballard of Richmond Hill, Canada, a suburb of Toronto. He says it best, so here's Chris....

"I've got a story to share about POS—how I stumbled across it and what I believe is at the root of it.

"Years ago, I took a year off following graduation from high school. I spent the best part of it working straight nights as a cleaner at Kodak's Toronto plant.

"What a hellish job for someone who's a morning person and who thrives on working with people, not in isolation.

"Anyway, I never saw the office workers whose premises I cleaned, and they never saw me. I was the 'Invisible Cleaner' who magically removed their grime and trash in the night. If a coffee was spilled on the floor, chances are they'd leave most of it knowing the cleaner will get it. Most would leave their desks a mess, making it harder for me to dust and tidy. And the washrooms...well enough said.

"About three long months into this routine, discouraged, exhausted, upset with myself for getting into the situation (but needing a good paying job to afford college), angry with the people I cleaned for, I decided that either things would change or I would quit.

"The problem, I knew, was that I was the 'Invisible Cleaner'—anonymous, invisible. I figured if they didn't know who I was, they wouldn't care about me or what I did.

"So I invited them to play. At first it was fun stuff, like refilling their office candy jar and leaving a note from the 'Night Cleaner Candy Fairy.' Then, despite the unwritten rule that said cleaners had to vanish before office workers arrived, I began to hang around a little longer to dust— and introduce myself.

"At Christmas I decorated the door of the cleaners' closet. It's in a well-traveled hallway and really got attention with its flashing colored lights, cardboard Santa, and best wishes to all my workers.

"Once while dusting a desk, I found a $20 bill hidden beneath a desk mat. I put it back with a note: Thanks for the tip, but $20 is really far too much for tidying your desk—$5 would be plenty. I heard about that one for months.

"People began to notice me, say 'hi' in the hallways, leave funny notes, thank me for the candy and the extra-special jobs I did cleaning up after them.

"And another interesting thing began to happen. They began to clean up after themselves. Coffee was mopped up, overflowing wastebaskets emptied, desks tidied, apologetic notes left for big messes, cleaner washrooms...a miracle!

"After years of thought, I've come to understand that I had unconsciously humanized the job of cleaner. I'd given it a face and name. If coffee was spilled, then the owner would wipe it up so that Chris wouldn't have to do it.

"I'd inadvertently discovered what happens when you give POS, invite people to play, and generally humanize the situation.

"And that, I think is a key to POS—treating people like people. Putting a name to a face. We all know we're special and it's wonderful when someone else acknowledges it. Our society is too anonymous, and POS allows us to show our customers that we know they are real, live, unique people—different from anyone else in the world.

"The outcome of my experiment at Kodak was that my job became easier and more enjoyable. I still had to work nights, I still had to work by myself. But there was always something unexpected that happened—whether it be a nice gesture to me in the form a note, of candy, or an opportunity for me to give some POS or invite someone to play with me."

Tackling Tangibility

Think about adding value to your product or service by revealing its "personality."

People often mention that the better they got to know someone, the better they came to like them. As you become more familiar with someone or something, a sense of ownership develops. Regular customers can and often do help themselves. They feel like they "own the joint."

By making the personality of a product or service more tangible, you create a sense of familiarity, a sense of ownership and comfort that adds value and builds loyalty.

We have heard nothing but raves about Ben and Jerry's Ice Cream, a product that exudes personality. One night we were invited to a friend's home for dinner and, unable to resist the opportunity to conduct a little basic research, he lined up identical bowls along the kitchen counter and filled them with samples of ice cream from Ben and Jerry and from a Texas-based creamery, Blue Bell.

In a blind taste-test, all five of our tasters chose the local, much less expensive product. Before revealing their choice, he told them the brands that they had been tasting and asked which they expected would be their favorite. Without hesitation, the group said that Ben and Jerry's would be the best.

They cited rain forest projects and all-natural ingredients. They knew all about the political stand that the two maverick men of mocha had taken on a number of social and environmental issues. What they couldn't tell him was which ice cream belonged to the myth and which had simply been trucked in from a small town in Texas.

Ben and Jerry's make very good ice cream. But they are even better at creating a personality for peach and pecan.

1. *Share Insider's Details.* Think about the little details that you believe make your product special. How could you share that information in a way that won't put customers to sleep? Use imagination. Tell the story as you would tell it to your kids.

2. *Tell About the Obvious.* So called "obvious" details are often worthy of note. Simply calling attention to the obvious adds value, especially if you tell it in an interesting way.

3. *Create a Myth.* People love to read or hear a good story, so tell one. The more outlandish, the better. Tell the world that your product was inspired by elves or was mined at the very center of the Earth.

4. *Add a Label.* Sometimes simply stamping a product with a single word like "Inspected" changes its personality enough to add value. If you put your mind to it, you can probably think of a half-dozen short modifiers that will add personality to your line of business. One great word is "Certified." Just make sure that you are completely truthful.

5. *Tell About the Exception.* Nobody expects that they should be able to drop a Coleman water jug from 100 feet without busting it into a million pieces. But there is an aura of toughness about a Coleman after you've read that story.

6. *Name It.* Consider a name for your product or service that serves as a description of its unique properties, drawing attention to qualities that may not be obvious. Rain Forest Crunch is a great example of a product name that also creates a visual/real mystique.

Making product or service characteristics more tangible is just good marketing. It's also a bit of built-in showmanship. Creating or featuring product personality appeals to the customer's need for an experience and gives them a sense of ownership that builds loyalty.

Call Betty at (800) 635-7524, Monday–Firday between the hours of 9 AM– 4 PM (Central) to order a videotape of Scott's keynote, Positively Outrageous Service.

CHAPTER TWELVE

Micro-Insults

Looking for an opportunity to try out a little industrial-strength show-manship? Then why not work a little magic on some of the dozens of micro-insults that customers face every day?

Micro-insults are the little things that we do to inconvenience customers in subtle yet irritating ways, usually in the name of "policy."

Little things like not being willing to make appointments for auto repair. Somehow we are convinced that the car needs to sit for a day or two on the lot before we can look at it. In the meantime, the customer is hitch-hiking to work.

The phone company is famous for a variation on the no appointment game. They try to make appointments, all right, for Thursday. No particular time, just Thursday. And you feel grateful that they didn't agree to come on "a Thursday"!

Then there are the serpentine lines that rental car agencies construct to eliminate weaker travelers. "Too tired to walk through three miles of rope and posts even though there isn't a single customer ahead of you? Then you aren't fit enough to rent from us!"

Or here's one. You stand in line waiting your turn. When you get to the head of the line and have dropped your bags in relief, you discover that the clerk wants to help you "over here!"

How about voice mail? Now there's the biggest insult of the century! People ask you to call them, but their voice mail answers instead.

"I'm in the office today but I'm not able to take calls (from you, Dirtbag!). Please leave a message and I'll return your call as soon as possible" (or when I feel like talking to you, which may be never).

Or better (worse) yet. How about the voice mail systems that give you a list of several dozen names and extensions, repeating each name and number in case you are terminally dense. Ten minutes later, you finally hear the name and extension of the person you want. Then when you dial the extension you get...I think you know which message.

As long as you are going to put merchandise exchange at the end of the same line you put gift wrap, credit, and customer restrooms, why not add a miniature campground and cafeteria to make a few bucks on us while we are waiting?

Lines can only form if customers are arriving faster than they are being served. That's why it makes so much sense to wait until the line is really, really long before you open another.

Did you know that once a line is formed it will persist as long as customers continue to arrive at the same rate they are being served? Every minute of delay in opening a new line is a minute wait for *every* customer that follows.

Here's a favorite. Ask for a large drink of water at a fast-food restaurant.

"I'm sorry (right). I'll have to charge you full price for the cup...or you can have a bunch of these (no) 'courtesy' cups."

Feel like taking communion? That's the size of the cup they offer. Now that's hospitality!

One cute, little insult is simply the lack of attention to detail. Like the airline breakfast of cereal and bananas that had to be eaten with a plastic spoon no bigger than the one you would use to feed a toddler. Chopsticks would be easier.

The American Airlines flight attendant just interrupted to announce that they "...will be serving dinner shortly. Tonight we have the all-time favorite cheese ravioli, topped with a delicious marinara sauce and dusted lightly with a parsley garnish. And if that doesn't hit you, may we suggest the chicken...."

Speaking of airlines, the structure of their fees is so complicated that the ordinary traveler cannot begin to understand them. Does that seem like great customer service?

Let's not forget the rocket science engineers who designed the plug for airline headsets. Why do you think they put the plug below the top of your leg? So that the little tubes would bend closed when you breath. That's why! These are the same geniuses who put hotel shower heads at belly button level. I hope a different team designs the engines.

Speaking of hotels, how come they have one guy to carry your bag the 30 feet from the cab to the front desk and then another to carry them to your room? Why? So you have to tip two people instead of one!

Or grocery stores that pre-wrap the produce so that you have to be satisfied with their idea of the correct selection and package size. What about in-store bakeries that package muffins four to a pack and then whine when you ask if you can purchase only two?

There is the gas station that makes you pre-pay for a fill-up causing an additional trip into the store to get your change. The department store that hems men's trousers for free but charges for the same service for women. The automobile dealer that tries to sell you based on the size of the monthly payment you are willing to bear. And anybody that says, "I'll have to talk to my sales manager," at any time for any reason.

Think about it. There are zillions of times when dumb or simply devious policy puts customers on edge, insults integrity and intelligence, and sends them straight into the arms of a competitor. How could you use a little Positively Outrageous Service, a little showmanship, to turn these and other situations so far around that they become a source of joy rather than irritation?

It can be done. The truly great service providers are doing it!

CHAPTER THIRTEEN

Survey Says!

Didn't you just hate it when that slimy character on Family Feud started planting mushy kisses on everyone and everything in sight? That guy would kiss a pig on television...in fact, I think he actually did kiss a few.

But we stray!

What makes "Family Feud" interesting? The opportunity to out-guess the surveys conducted of earlier audiences.

But why that would be so unusual is amazing, since trying to guess the opinions of our customers is an everyday occurrence in the world of business. While there is plenty of guessing about what customers want and how they want it, there is not much that could pass for genuine research, formal or otherwise.

The big companies do it. In fact, they have made a science of consumer research. The little guys can't really afford to do sophisticated consumer research but then, it is probably the lack of such research that explains why little guys tend to stay little guys...if they aren't beaten out of existence by the big guys.

The heck-of-it-all is that customer research need not be all that expensive. In fact, and this is so for good managers regardless of the size of their companies, taking the pulse of customers can be done quite effectively with little more investment than a few, well-thought-out questions asked on a more or less regular basis.

Business is nothing more than filling customer needs. Find an unsatisfied need and then fill it in a way that will attract customers. Sounds simple and, in some respects, it is. But the problem remains that most, emphasis on the word *most*, most businesses fail to do any but the most rudimentary market research if any at all.

And that's goofy. Or suicidal.

Because, as customers and technology changes, so must the business if there is to be any hope of survival much less prosperity.

Take My Dockers...Please

Pardons to Henny Youngman for the pun.

Dockers, the pants made by Levi Strauss, are a premier example of a product born of recognized change. You've seen the commercials of the Boomer-aged men reminiscing about their high school and college days. The pants they are wearing are an admission that the market for Levi products is getting older. Tubbier, too! Levis are made for the man who needs "a scoche more room in the seat and thigh."

What is remarkable about both the ad campaign and the product is that this highly successful product would not have made it to market had it not been for heads-up research and the guts required to follow up. Simply continuing to produce the world-famous Levis jeans and related products would have been the easy way out. By not listening and acting, Levis would have missed both a trend and an opportunity.

Listening is the foundation of good business.

Listen to discover unsatisfied needs.

Listen to learn about new ways to solve old problems.

When smart executives think about listening to customers, they realize that perhaps their most important constituency is their internal customer.

Particularly in service- and knowledge-based industries, but even in sophisticated manufacturing operations, the assets of the company do not consist mainly of inventory and equipment. It is the skill, loyalty, and creativity that account for the bulk of corporate value. That being so, smart executives consider it a primary function to keep an ear to the ground, listening to the troops.

Employees often have the solutions to major corporate problems locked tightly in their brains where they lie waiting for someone to simply ask. Asking employees for their thoughts and opinions is nothing more than internal market research.

Camille Keith, vice president of special marketing for Southwest Airlines, said it best, "Most of what I've ever found out that had value, was something that I didn't set out to know."

The message is simple: Make listening a habit and stand by to be surprised at your discoveries.

And if asking your own employees for input doesn't excite you, consider Keith's technique, "Sometimes I sit in the gate area of our competition and listen to their employees. The things that they talk about and complain about tells me what our future problems might be."

Southwest has turned listening to employees, apparently any employees, into a science. Has it worked? Well, consider the article that appeared in this morning's local newspaper that reported that Southwest "has been overrun by job seekers so eager to work for Southwest that they'll take pay cuts and accept less glamorous perks."

Having trouble finding winning employees? Maybe the solution isn't much more than a matter of listening to the ones you already have.

Management by...

Tom Peters made it famous. Thousands of managers have tried it out. It's the old "MBWA" (management by walking around). The good news is that it is a simple management technique that really works. But some folks try MBWA and find out that it doesn't yield much more than sore feet and valuable time spent away from the desk and phone.

Two reasons. First, many managers are simply more comfortable in the office than on the floor. Second, a few simple techniques make MBWA pay off. MBWA is not a matter of simply walking around; you have to know how.

As all good managers know, the action occurs on the floor. But over the years, we forget the skills that brought us to the party and gradually we begin to practice skills more appropriate for survival in the executive suite. (Like kissing up. And political maneuvering.)

Managers who understand MBWA may not necessarily be the fastest bumper installer or the best pants presser or the most proficient draftsperson. But they are in touch. Rusty, maybe, but thoroughly in-touch with the reality of life in the trenches.

Dad always said, "You should never have to deal from a position of power."

In other words, you should try not to rule by fear. He also said that good managers *can* operate from a position of power if they are forced to do so, because power managers remain in touch with the job at hand. While they may never have to deliver an order personally, they could if they had to.

It starts out as a fad by which top executives are soon excused, until layer-by-layer, lower-and-lower into the organization it sinks, and eventually everyone forgets. We're talking about the idea that everyone at the Puzzle Palace should work at least one day every quarter or so directly serving customers.

When I had a real job, we had a rule that said no matter what your position at corporate, you would first have to qualify yourself at store level. The company was Church's Chicken. Eons ago, we had a program called the National Executive Candidate program designed to recruit executives with proven talents in non-food related fields and transfer their experience to what was then, one of America's fastest growing restaurant chains.

No one, absolutely no one, was allowed to drive a desk until he or she could cook and serve Church's Chicken. And you wouldn't believe what a sense of reality that put on decisions made at corporate!

When the company got bigger, somehow the things that had brought us to the party in the first place got pushed aside. Suddenly, we were no longer chicken cookers and servers, we were financial wizards much too smart to walk around in puddles of shortening and clouds of flour. But, while it had been a hardy band of men and women cutting, cooking, and serving mounds of the world's best and freshest fried chicken that had built the company, it took only a few MBA types who "knew better" than those yokels in Texas to tear the company apart.

If listening to the customer, both internal and external, is the key to success, so is the refusal to listen to an invitation to certain failure.

Do the MBWA...

The best way to do MBWA is to supplement it with an all new step that we'll call MBDI, Management By Dropping In.

Time-management courses teach that managers, who value their time, should schedule meetings to be held somewhere other than their own office. Good idea, because it allows you to leave when the meeting is over or when discussion has slipped into idle conversation.

But MBDI is not about encouraging idle chit-chat. It is simply about creating an atmosphere where employees, any employee, feel safe telling the boss what is so. MBDI just isn't going to happen where employees have a good chance of opening their mouths only to swallow a large sacred cow.

If the boss keeps pets, unexpected guests will be few and far between, except from animal lovers, and you know what kind of animals they will profess to love. Big, ugly, sacred ones. The kind that are too expensive to keep and too beloved to eat.

MBDI begins by putting titles and politics to rest. Really great managers do not have to hide behind formality and titles. Really incompetent managers need the added protection of legislated respect.

Another way to encourage MBDI is to join the crew in play. Some managers think that playing with the troops means drinking until the wee hours. These aren't great leaders, although they may be great drinkers. Alcohol and business do not mix. And playing with the troops does not require that managers become party animals.

One manager that I have long admired is a fellow by the name of Ernie Renaud, the leader of the Long John Silver chain through their years of rapid expansion. He later took over the reins at Church's Chicken, where he had engineered the beginning of a turn around before the company was swallowed in an ego-driven take-over.

Ernie is the kind of guy that you want to call "Mister Renaud," not because it was required, but precisely because pomp and circumstance had no place in his presence, a fact that earned respect from all. His idea of playing with the troops was clearly presented when, at the end of the first day of a company convention, Ernie and his wife invited all comers to join them in the hospitality suite for an old-fashioned sing along.

Song sheets were handed around and, in an evening that ended all too soon, employees and franchisees became family.

Play with the troops so that you feel comfortable. The objective is to rub shoulders, not break bones. So make it gentle and not overly competitive. And, oh yes! The best bosses are those who can and do lose graciously.

Bill-Paying Customers

MBWA works best with bill-paying customers when you do more than offer pleasant conversation. And asking the time-worn, "Was everything all right?" is hardly worth your breath. You won't hear the things you really need to know.

Camille Keith, mentioned earlier, is a master of listening. She often responds to customer complaints by calling the customer and asking how they think problems should be resolved.

A California senior citizen wrote to Keith complaining that the ad announcing the Southwest policy on Senior Discounts was misleading. Keith simply called and said, "I'm the person who writes the copy, how would you change it?"

An elderly customer wrote to complain about a policy requiring gate agents to write the age of customers who need to be escorted on the ticket envelope. The customer said that such a policy was embarrassing. Keith listened.

After consulting with the staff, Keith wrote the 78-year- old customer that indeed the policy was poorly conceived, that it was only necessary to write on the jacket that the customer's age had been verified.

"I think you are right," wrote Keith. "The reason that it has taken a while for me to respond is that I wanted you to see that we listen. Here's a copy of our new policy."

How to MBWA

Ask questions that require a thoughtful response. "Was everything all right?" asked when you have your nose buried in the cash drawer, isn't likely to get more than a grunted, non-revealing response.

Instead ask:

"What did you think of our service today?"

"What could we do to make your visit more enjoyable?"

"Where else do you shop for...?"

"Who do you think is our biggest competitor? Why?"

"What could we do to get you to come in more often?"

"What other stops are on your list today?"

"Do you know anyone who is unhappy with us? Why?"

"How did you hear about us?"

"How often do you do business with us?"

"Why did you decide to shop with us today?"

"Tell me how we're doing!" (Thank you, former Mayor Ed Koch!)

The technique for MBWA for internal customers is not all that different. Try these on just to get you started:

"What could we do better?"

"Why did you decide to apply here?"

"What are we doing that is really stupid?"

"Tell me what may be getting in your way."

"What do you hear from our customers?"

"What are we doing that really bothers you?"

"How could we improve our product or service?"

"Do you have the tools and training that you need?"

There is one final question that you should ask often. When interviewing, I like to end with this question, "What one question did I fail to ask that you thought for sure I would ask?"

Or sometimes I try a variation on the theme, "What one question did you hope I wouldn't ask?" Or even, "What question, that I have not thought to ask, do you think is important to my understanding?"

Get the idea? No matter how clever you may be, at least occasionally ask your customer, "Is there anything that you think I should know but forgot to ask about?"

Sometimes the words that customers use are the most important part of the message. For example, if you ask a customer about your service and get an answer, "Well, today it was pretty good." Did you hear the not so hidden message? The customer said that the service today was acceptable, but hinted strongly that there had been previous offenses that needed to be addressed.

Listen. Listen to what is said and listen to what is not said. Listen to how things are said.

With employees, there is a certain sign that more listening is in order. When you hear employees talking about the company in terms of "They." "They have a policy," or "They do it this way," are sure signs that more than a little listening is in order.

Survey Says!

The four biggest problems with satisfaction surveys are:

We don't do them.

We don't ask the right questions.

We don't ask questions right.

We don't pay any attention to the responses.

Other than those few problems, surveys seem to be working just fine, thank you!

Let's focus on a simple technique for getting useable responses.

What if you did a survey and more than 90 percent of respondents checked a box that said that price was important to them. Would you immediately lower prices? If you do, you could be making the mistake of a lifetime.

Poorly constructed surveys are the source of many marketing missteps. Think about our example.

What human being would not check a box saying that price is important? As a business person, you don't care that price is important. Heck, that should be a given!

What you care about is not that price may be important, you want to know how is price important and how important price really is!

Every survey, whether written or verbal, should come equipped with its own qualifier. In column "A" ask the base question, and in column

"B" ask the all-important qualifier, "How important is this in your decision to do business with us?"

You will discover that price, just to continue the example, is always a consideration. But to your customers, it is the least important factor in the buying decision.

For example, if you are a foodservice operator in an airport, then customers expect high prices. So price may fall far lower in importance than say speed of service and the ability to purchase a healthy snack that is not messy and can be held in one hand to be eaten.

By rating survey responses, customer feedback can be quickly put into perspective. A men's clothing store might discover that prices that are too low reflect badly on the quality of the merchandise, or perhaps remove the aura of exclusivity that is an important draw to this particular clientele.

The key point remains: Survey, but survey intelligently. Ask your respondents to quantify their answers, and be certain that you ask the important questions by asking the audience first what is important to them.

My appendix burst one Friday night. By Monday, I had no energy to fight off Melanie's wise insistence that I visit our local medicine man. A few days later I was pacing the floor hoping that the doctor would see it in his heart (or invoice) to let me go home, when a knock at the door broke my concentraton.

"Mr. Gross?"

"Yes, Ma'am."

"May I come in? I'm doing a survey for the hospital foodservice department."

"Pull up a chair. I have plenty of time."

"Was your food hot when it should have been hot, and cold when it should have been cold?"

"You bet."

"Were you happy with the size of the selection?"

"It was more than ample."

"How about portion sizes?"

"More than I would eat."

"Were the choices the kinds of food that you might eat at home?"

"In concept, we're in agreement."

"Thank you. I appreciate your time!" With a smile, my inquisitor rose to leave.

"Hold on! Don't you want to ask me how the food tastes?"

She looked over her survey form before smiling, "I'm sorry, Mr. Gross, that isn't one of my questions."

"Well, it is now! Write on there that if the food here didn't come in distinctive, Day-Glo colors, I couldn't tell one item from the next. Most of it is mushy and tastes like everything else on the tray. Some of it is crunchy, but I think that is supposed to be soup."

"Now, please go and tell your boss that the food is served on time and at the right temperature, there is plenty of it and the selection is just fine, but that none of those fine attributes is worth a tinker's damn if I can't eat it!"

There. Ask the right questions, ask everyone in sight and a few who aren't. Qualify every answer and whatever you do, don't eat hospital food!

CHAPTER
FOURTEEN

Seeker Targeted

"How do you build a church that doesn't look like a church?"
— *Randy Mayeux,*
Pastor, Christ Church North

"Can a guy who likes professional wrestling be worth your time on Sunday morning?"

That is the message that jumps from the page of the slick direct-mail piece that greeted Dallas residents, challenging them, almost double-dog daring them, to spend at least a few more seconds to investigate this one-of-a-kind invitation to visit Christ Church North.

Holding a box of popcorn and watching a sweating duo wrestle at ringside, Randy Mayeux strikes the pose of an excited fan and a most unconventional man of God.

We've always suspected that modern religion, particularly the tele-vised versions, must be nothing more than shrewd marketing. But Mayeux has no problem confessing his child-like interest in wrestling and doesn't even blink at discussing marketing and church-building in the same sentence. In fact, it is Mayeux's marketing decisions that have made Christ Church North something...different.

Mayeux wouldn't mind being thought of as different. Different was his objective. And different is the result.

Mayeux, a refugee from mainstream fundamentalism, had tired of preaching to the saved. Growth at the churches that he had pastored had been spectacular, but most of it had been at the expense of other churches. Men and women who have dedicated their lives to winning souls find a hollow victory in simply moving them.

Mayeux knew there had to be a better way, a way to attract persons who were non-churchgoers but seeking. According to the press, the Baby Boomers had been coming back to the church in droves. The unreported story was, they were leaving as soon as they discovered that the things that had turned them off in the first place hadn't changed in the intervening years that they had spent acquiring children, houses, and ego-stroking sports cars.

Mayeux's experience is in growing churches from coast-to-coast, landing finally in tony Highland Park, the Beverly Hills of Texas. There he continued his record of growing churches, enjoying a terrific salary and hating the idea of church-turned-fashion-statement.

Mayeux's mailer promises a church experience that is "surprisingly different," a message that is carefully constructed to target the spiritually hungry but commitment-shy boomers. Mayeux thought that "seeker-targeted" marketing and program-design might give him the chance he wanted so desperately to introduce his Savior to the experience-starved Boomer generation.

Read the mailer. It is nothing like the staid messages served by traditional churches. And that's the point. The traditional message wasn't working and Mayeux was willing to risk his career and security by taking the path less traveled.

Showmanship was the answer. Mayeux had to read the definition of showmanship in Positively Outrageous Service before he could finally feel comfortable associating with a word that he thought had more application to the circus, and things slick and perhaps a bit questionable. But the "fact is, we're heavily involved."

No kidding.

We'll let the copy from the mailer, first of a series, speak.

"When he's not ringside, Randy Mayeux is our pastor. We're Christ

Church North, a brand new church in North Dallas. And while we don't whole-heartedly support Randy's affection for wrestling, we overlook it. Because he's a great pastor.

"Mayeux understands how much we all need the touch of God in our lives. And his sermons aren't about guilt, or raising money for a new building. He wrestles with hard issues—like discovering God's love and making ourselves the best we can be.

"You'll find that Christ Church North is a different kind of church. We have an upbeat band, and we regularly use drama sketches and movie clips. What's more, we think Sunday mornings should be the happiest part of your week. So come visit. Whether you're single, married, or divorced, you'll feel welcome. (And we won't hound you for money.)

"Come see. Dress casual. Maybe with your help, we can talk to Mayeux about this wrestling thing."

See what we mean? Mayeux is a man on a mission. He has created an environment where the non-churchgoers can get reconnected and feel good about it.

Sunday services, or should that be "performances," are definitely not going to intimidate anyone. The congregation or audience (heck, you could even call them customers) is invited to participate emotionally, but not required to sing, sign, or give. And the prospect of singing, signing, and contributing to someone's building fund may be precisely why so many Boomers check out church and then check out for good. When the plate is passed, it is with the reminder that the "service is our gift to you," and that when the offering is taken "it is only a chance for the rest of us to participate."

Pretty daring for a church founded on a shoestring where the church secretary and janitor are also the pastor.

"Americans," says Mayeux, "are hungry for spiritual life, but they've about had it with religion."

Maybe the same could be said of Mayeux, who turned his back on an approach to religion that he saw as failing to deliver. Still, talk about risk and Mayeux thinks you are calling his name.

Christ Church North is independent, founded on the family savings account and faith. What a concept.

"The risk was enormous. There are times when I think I'm an idiot, especially now when things are so tight (financially). But most of the time, I just wonder what took me so long."

Mayeux doesn't have an orchestra. He couldn't afford one. But he does sport Dallas' top jazz fusion guitarist as his music director. The latest marketing piece features a photo of Christ Church North's sparkle of a program director, Brittany Haddock, teasing him into the photo by pulling on his tie. Mayeux, the less subtle of the two, is pulling on his ponytail.

The copy reads, "He's a little shy but he's a great guitarist." Then follows an invite to Christ Church North for a first-hand demonstration of modern day spirituality.

Sounds pretty traditional...until you discover that the ad will run in the "Dallas Observer," an alternative paper that includes ads for men seeking women, women seeking men, and men and women seeking, well, you know.

But Mom always said that church was supposed to be a hospital for the sinners, not a rest home for the saved. Mayeux is only fishing where there are fish.

Mayeux's not shy about using clips from "Field of Dreams," "Return of the Jedi," or "City Slickers" to make a theological point or two. Find yourself humming a Beatle's tune, and you may be about to experience an object lesson that Mayeux has cooked up just for you.

The intention is simple if the delivery is not. "Create a church service that will get your attention...and keep it."

Asked if he had ever lost any "customers" because of this non-traditional heresy, Mayeux doesn't hesitate for a moment.

"You always have people who come, try out, and go. People who want the traditional church just don't stay. They need the organ. They need the choir. They need the formality for church to feel like a church. And that's okay, because they're not our customers."

Mayeux has been deviled (sorry!) by the admonishment of an acquaintance to "figure out why people don't go to church, and then make sure that you don't do that."

Here lies a lesson for us all. Mayeux says that we all need a regular way to listen to our customers. His favorite question is, "Why don't you go to church?"

What makes Mayeux different is that he is not making a suggestion of guilt. He really wants to know.

Hanging on the wall in Mayeux's office is a framed challenge from Peter Drucker: What is our business? Who is our customer? What does the customer consider a value?

But value can come to the server as well as the served. "I don't think it's worth your time in life if what you do has as its only purpose to make money."

It has been suggested that Mayeux and friends name their church "The New Age Happy Place." But they miss the point.

Mayeux is insistent that credit for the miracle in the making that is Christ Church North does not accrue to him alone. He wants to share both the kudos and the message. But, whoever should be listed in the credits on this bold venture, Mayeux is the leader who did more than dream. He did.

"I really believe that when Christ is viewed honestly, he is not a turnoff. It's religion that's a turnoff."

CHAPTER FIFTEEN

Eskimo Joe!

"The best perceived value is a good time."

— Stan Clark

Eskimo Joe's is just another dive in Oklahoma...nah!

Actually the preferred term seems to be "juke joint," and if that doesn't get your respect, then standby to learn from a true master of showmanship.

Eskimo Joe's and two other restaurants make up the not-so-small constellation that dominates the college town of Stillwater, Oklahoma. Who would have imagined that two college students, talking more out of boredom and bravado, would open what has to be one of the most successful restaurant companies in America, or most certainly, in Stillwater?

Announced by a smilin' Eskimo and his wonderdog, Buffy, Eskimo Joe's is just one of those oddball places that people love to visit. When Stan Clark and a college buddy decided to open a bar, about the only remarkable thing about the plan was their parents' reaction. Actually, even that was not all that unexpected. Something like, "Oh, great! All this money on an education...."

You've got the picture.

But today, little Stan Clark has earned the right to a sincere apology from any relative who had doubted the wisdom of the deal. In fact, it had been motivated by not much more than the curious fascination that you could pull a handle and beer would come out of the wall.

Working a modest investment of $15,000 into what today is a multi-million dollar food-and-beverage operation, the history of Eskimo Joe's—and the concepts to follow—is a story of shrewd marketing, a dash of luck, and an absolute dedication to showing the guest a good time.

Luck, they say, is when preparation meets opportunity. If there ever was a perfect example, Stan Clark has got to be it. He has elevated showmanship, not to an art, but to an obsession. It's not that he does anything that you wouldn't see other places. Clark's mark of distinction is that he seems to do every great marketing idea at once.

First the luck part.

In the early eighties, Oklahoma raised the drinking age from 18 to 21, and ruled that the newly created class of minors could not patronize bars unless accompanied by a parent or guardian. Tough news for a beer bar in a college town.

Clark knew that his only salvation was to become a restaurant, a definition requiring that less than half of his sales come from alcohol.

Almost overnight, Eskimo Joe's added food service, while sticking to the basic principle of "show 'em a good time" that had paid the bills since day one. Only now, instead of the single quality admonition of "keep the beer cold," there were a few more standards to uphold. In the end, food sales accounted for 50.4 percent of sales by the time the new law went into effect. Whew!

Today there is more to Eskimo Joe's than cold beer and fat, juicy burgers. There are the T-shirts, the golf balls, the hats, night-shirts, and of course the baby bibs. It seems that when you show people a good time, they naturally want a memento of the occasion. These small novelties begin to add up.

In fact, the economic impact of Eskimo Joe's, Joe's Clothes, and two restaurants that have been added to the fold is difficult to measure. The head count of employees runs to nearly 400.

Of course, there is the annual Eskimo Joe's anniversary and reunion weekend that is Stillwater's biggest event. Drawing over 60,000 revelers, the event pumps nearly 8.5 million dollars into local coffers, a bunch of it you can assume at Clark's place!

The remarkable bit of self-promotion and marketing that started the annual celebration began when he wrote and recorded a couple of songs about—what else, but—Eskimo Joe's. Clark managed to get air time throughout the state and before you could yell "another cold one!" the streets in front of Eskimo Joe's were full of party animals all paying homage to their favorite college hangout.

The rest, they say, is history.

Clark has tried about every fun marketing tactic known to man, and invented a few oddball gimmicks all on his own. To the Joe's Clothes catalogue, which by the way is now in glorious full color, Clark added a Joe's boat. No kidding, a powerboat decorated to look a lot like it had been part of the decor at Eskimo Joe's.

There is the costumed Buffy the wonder dog, who attends functions of all sorts; the Juke Joint Jog, an annual run to benefit United Way; and don't forget, Toys for Tots. In fact, if it's good and it happens in Stillwater, you can pretty well imagine that Stan Clark and company will have a strong hand in the event.

That's nothing more than the Law of Harvest that says what goes around comes around. But to give, you've got to get, and it is showmanship, pure and simple, that have made it possible for Stan Clark to play with the big boys.

Would giving up the showmanship impact sales?

"It could cut it in half," says Clark. "Fun drives the shirt business."

Clark counsels new employees to read the customer.

"If it's a serious business lunch, talking 90-miles-to-nothin', that's not who you go play with."

There are no canned routines like you see at many establishments that trade in fun. At the Three Amigos, as the restaurants are called, employees are given the freedom to play, to bring their personality to work with them.

"The number one perceived value is a good time. So show 'em a good time!" Here Clark nearly shouts with enthusiasm, adding that customers just want to know one thing: "How are you gonna make me feel?"

"I'm just so excited to see a guest, that it shows...if it weren't from the heart, it wouldn't work."

Call Betty at (800) 635-7524, Monday–Friday between the hours of 9 AM–4 PM (Central) to order an audio tape of Scott's Positively Outrageous Service and Showmanship.

CHAPTER SIXTEEN

King of Show

There can only be one king and Philip Romano is it. Not the king of a country, although he owns the better part of a small town, Romano is the undisputed king of showmanship.

Philip Romano is the founder-creator of Macaroni Grill and a host of innovative restaurant concepts. Wherever there is Philip Romano, a good time can't be far behind. Funny thing, Romano usually seems to be lost in thought. If this guy's a prankster, he certainly doesn't fit the mold.

Then again, fitting the mold is definitely not what brought Romano to the party.

First, a little history. Then we'll hear from the man himself.

When the world first caught up with Romano, he was working his newest incarnation, Fuddruckers, a single unit, poorly located, dimestore decorated burger joint in San Antonio.

This wasn't his first venture into food service, only his latest. But it was at Fuddruckers that Romano and showmanship became synonymous. In earlier operations, Romano had used all sorts of gimmicks, many that worked counter to conventional wisdom. But at Fuddruckers, he seemed to use them all at once.

One neat thing about Romano is that he's not afraid to borrow ideas.

Not that he isn't the most creative guy on the planet, only that if Romano sees something that works, he's not afraid to hijack the idea, tie it into an all new knot, and put it to work in a whole new way. And he's not afraid to reincarnate his own good work.

In a Florida operation that was under heavy pressure from the competition, Romano fought back by *restricting* entry! This guy's crazy! The rest of the world would have dragged out the coupons and discounted themselves silly. But noooo! Romano locks the door, makes entry available to keyholders only, and laughs all the way to the bank.

At Fuddruckers, Romano wanted a little press, so suddenly there are announcements that some international association of burger lovers has declared the Fuddruckers product the best of the best. Right. If the smell of grilling onions hadn't been so strong, someone would have noticed that the so-called association was a product of Romano's imagination!

Makes sense to me. If you need to be recognized by a prestigious association, well, just create one! I love this guy!

At Romano's newest, Spageddies, showmanship is everywhere. Ideas that were a hit at his Mexican concept, Nachomama's, appear in Italian dress. But the new twist, which seems so obvious that we all should have thought of it, is the idea to tag first-time guests.

A Texas-size, yellow tag identifies first-time guests, singles them out for extra special treatment. The manager is certain to visit with a personal welcome. Waitstaff will take extra time to help with the menu, maybe invite the new kid over for a game of bocci at a court just off the dining area. You do need instructions to eat at a Romano concept. There's just too much to see.

Great showmen and showwomen are students of showmanship. They admire smooth marketing when they see it. Just as magicians and comedians will fall under the spell of another performer whose artistry they admire, Romano is no different. He knows and appreciates a good show when he sees one.

In our last conversation, he didn't resist telling me about a micro-brewer who had put showmanship to work. He didn't remember the name, but he did remember that the delivery drivers were dressed in tuxedos, and that the trucks had been painted bright red and decked out with gold wheels.

"They made the beer into a class product by presenting it with class."

You could almost hear the mental file drawer shut with an idea involving tuxedos and flashy vehicles neatly tucked into a folder. Perhaps it would be labeled "in case of a brainstorm, open here!"

The fundamentals according to Romano are simple. But execution is not. Romano is more than an idea man. He can, and does, put his ideas to work.

When you visit a Romano operation, you'll see employees who are actually having fun. There will be hugging. Sometimes lots of it. But the food will be delicious and the surroundings will be neat. Because the fundamentals demand accommodating the customer, Romano's twist is that the customer should be accommodated in a way that has never been done before.

"Probably the reason that it has never been done before is because there is risk involved." When Romano dreams another dream, he never knows for certain that it will be a hit. There is that element of risk, which to the average person doing average things in search of average rewards, is too big of an obstacle.

"Is it going to work? I don't know."

And inevitably, with risk comes failure. Not necessarily the kind of failure that closes the doors, but the kind of failure that may cost a customer or two from time to time. To a guy like Romano, who lives for the applause, losing a customer is a big deal. A very big deal.

But you have to lose a few to win the many. The secret is in how and why you lose the few.

When the door closes on the men's room at Macaroni, crisp white lettering on the backside of the door spell out w-o-m-e-n. Not the kind of thing you want to notice once you are, how would you say, committed? Some people just can't take a joke. So Romano is likely to lose the terminally stuffy in favor of the happily stuffed.

"You can't make everybody happy. We try to make most of the people happy some of the time. You give people something they can go out and tell a story about."

Like the time you went into the men's room and....

"You've got to accept the fact that you *are* going to have accidents. If you make 90 percent of the people happy, you still have ten percent who may not come back."

And ten percent of a thousand covers a hundred unhappy folks. Not acceptable by any measure.

"It's how you handle the accidents that matter." Romano spends nearly as much time training how to handle accidents as he does on accident prevention. Naturally, he doesn't want accidents at all. But he does realize that a well-handled accident and great recovery, has a value of its own. Customers who have had a well-handled problem turn out to be even more loyal than those who never had a reason to complain.

Have an accident at Romano's place and you can expect to be dazzled.

"Take care of that ten percent," Romano is certainly overestimating, "and that's how you make them tell stories about how you turned the negative around."

Romano likes to recall that when Will Rogers died, they found an unexpected cache of lists. The lists were of things that he could do or say in the event that things went wrong. "See? A good showman always has something to fall back on."

But the best list of all is the one that you follow to keep the customer happy from the start. When Romano opened Macaroni Grill, he called in the University of North Texas to teach the waitstaff, standby...acting techniques!

"It's the same as the theater. If they like the performance, they come back. So I got the drama department to teach our employees how to act like the world's greatest waiters and waitresses."

And they do!

It would be easy to miss the secret of Macaroni in all the excitement. To really find out how and what Romano is doing, it makes no sense to take notes over dinner and perhaps steal a menu. What makes Macaroni so very special is that Romano is even better at attracting winners than he is at training them.

Ask Vic Paesano, Romano's long-time friend who takes up a post near the door on busy nights, making certain that anyone in need of a hug gets one. He is one squeezed fellow by the end of the evening!

"In my house, especially on a Sunday morning, all the people would come over. The women would be in the kitchen cooking. My uncle would make the wine. We'd go get the wine out of the basement and we'd set it on the table.

"This is an Italian tradition. Wine on the table. A jug of wine on the table...and everybody helps themselves."

Romano once said that part of the mystique of Macaroni is that you see something plain and then something elegant. The customer is taken up and then gently let down. Beautiful flowers, concrete floors. Fabulous food, wine in a jug. Up and down. Always a surprise.

Paesano continues, "This is like your home. My mother couldn't wash the glasses fast enough, so instead of putting them back in the cupboard, she put them on a small table in the kitchen. Always available.

"And always there would be flowers. If you didn't have a nickel for anything else, there would be flowers on the table on a Sunday morning."

And that's the decor at Macaroni.

"It becomes more of a home atmosphere. *Questa casa e la sua casa!*"

Mama mia!

What is showmanship?

"It's a marketing concept," says Romano without a moment's hesitation. "You gotta do something that is different and you've gotta do it better than anybody else in the industry. People don't notice anything that's being done the same way all the time...so do it different.

"Understand how things are done, then do it better. It's breaking standards. It's knocking down sacred cows.

"If I didn't do the things that people told me not to do, I wouldn't be where I am today."

CHAPTER SEVENTEEN

"That's a Pearl, Son"

"What's that buzz? Tell me what's a happening! (louder) What's that buzz? Tell me what's a happening? (chanted, now) What's that buzz? Tell me what's a happening?"
—*from Andrew Lloyd Wright's "Jesus Christ, Superstar"*

If a Sequoia tree could turn shaman, it would be named Paul Meunier. He moves around the audience, sucking them in with his pure, focused intention. They listen. Puzzled at first. This behavior doesn't match a man in a tailored suit.

He continues to march and chant. The audience is his, unable to resist joining the almost mystical lyric that this, their leader, is spreading over the room.

He continues until the group has the rhythm, "What's that buzz? Tell me what's a happening?" Now that he has them, he begins to drop in spoken footnotes..."You can feel it!" "What's that buzz? Tell me what's a happening! We're changing the industry! What's that buzz?

Tell me what's a happening."

The chant stops. There is not a single unsaved soul in the room. Meunier owns their attention and commitment to whatever he intends to build. They think he is talking about a business. He is. And he is not.

Paul Meunier is the president and CEO of Signature Flight Support, an Orlando-based company. But Meunier could just as well be pushing groceries or lumber, it's his people-moving message that makes him special.

He turns quickly, rattling off a list of things that have happened to put the company, Signature Flight Support, on-a-roll. Signature provides airport services. From the sometimes glamorous business of running FBOs (fixed-base operations) for private and business aircraft to the rarely more than tolerable run-of-the-mill airport services, such as contract baggage handling and fueling services, Signature is on the move. Meunier continues with his list.

"Sharper Image gifts, Godiva Chocolates, and Sparking sessions (brainstorming sessions)," his list of premium gifts and concepts continues. It is a mistake to think that Meunier is talking about business. He is, yet he is not. He believes and wants you to believe that he is building a team, a team that could run any business. The fact that they put dollars into the corporate coffers by serving a slice of the travel industry is only incidental. The product is outweighed by the process.

"I have come not to praise our past," he prepares the bomb for release, "but to bury it. Respectfully but terminally."

Meunier continues, brighter, building to an enthusiastic look into the future as it has been revealed to him. He has a dream to offer, and you are invited to join in for the adventure. Meunier wants those who choose to follow, to follow wholeheartedly.

"Commit to yourself...do this one thing for me...to live up to your full potential. And I commit to you to create an environment where everyone *can* live up to their potential."

"No longer will you be asked to check your brain at the door. But! If you don't want to step out of the box, take risks, if you are too embarrassed to stand out...I've got something to show you."

With the flourish of a magician or accomplished snake oil artist, this giant man pulls a cloth up and away to reveal a miniature prop, and announces dramatically, "the door."

"I want to see a new way of thinking about customer service. I want to hear new words when we deal with our customer...let me see what I can do...let me talk to the manager for you...welcome home, Mr. Customer.

"We're getting out of the FBO business. We're getting in to the FSO business. FSO, flight support operation.

"What's that buzz? Tell me what's a happening!

"We're taking the industry by storm. And the reason is that we're putting people first! Everyone on the payroll is in customer service. Everyone! Aircraft fuelers will come and go, but customer service people will stay forever!"

The sequoia turns to a flip chart and begins to list what is "in" and what is "out."

Nike's in. Reebok's out.

Leadership — in. Management — out.

Teams — in. Organizational charts — out.

Stories — in. Policies — out.

Training — in. Winging it — out.

Sharing — in. Hoarding — out.

Respect — in. Egos — out.

Communication — in. Indispensability — out.

Quality — in. Getting by — out.

Relationships — in. Overreaching — out.

Innovation — in. Habit — out.

Listening — in. Commanding — out.

Dreaming — in. Dozing — out.

Pro-act is in. React is out.

Profit — in. Perks — out.

Preparation — in. Gut reaction — out.

Caring — in. Taking for granted — out.

Professionalism — in. Profanity — out.

Future — in. Past — out.

And Meunier is the first to recognize that if the cultural leap can be made, Signature Flight Support will be in. The competition...they're out!

"The old days when someone from corporate would fly in, have lunch with the manager, walk through the hanger, and leave thinking he knew what was going on...are over."

Meunier continues by saying that management will learn to serve those who serve the customer. He introduces the idea of service to internal customers offering to turn the company upside-down and put the power of decision-making close to the customer, who is not interested in policy, only results. "Corporate," reports the ex-boss, "will be known as Mission Support."

"Our motto: Consider it done."

And then an explanation of the new name, why Page Avjet no longer fits and why Signature is the only logical moniker for a company that promises to take an industry by storm.

"What's that buzz? Tell me what's a happening! We put our name on the line everyday. That's why we'll be called Signature."

A visit with Paul Meunier is a visit to your personal sense of value. He is approachable. While many would blush to talk about business as an affair of the heart, Meunier is the first to make the point. Yet he understands the difference between the show and the showman.

Asked what value he thinks today's customers place on showmanship, Meunier is quick to respond.

"We think that the relative value is very high...the entire industry is a show, I mean, an experience. Unless you place a high value on experience, you wouldn't be a customer.

"As a chain, the difficulty is to create the customization that a single owner can create. Showmanship has allowed us to transcend the 'chain' product."

Notice, please, that showmanship is credited with the ability of narrowing the gap between the personalized customer service that is most often associated with an owner-operated business. Perhaps the reason is that showmanship requires flexibility on the part of management. Only an empowered employee can and will make the kinds of service decisions necessary to create a custom service experience.

"Custom" is a key operating word. If today's consumer wants to be touched, to share an experience in an increasingly impersonal world, then we must recognize that customer service is a relationship unsuitable for "design by policy."

"We believe," Meunier continues, "that we are a subcontractor for the corporate aviation department. We continue the experience of the plane. If we fail, that devalues the entire experience. This is the message that we try to convey to the corporate pilot. The chauffeur doesn't take his passengers to the gas station...not true for our business! We're part of the show. And our pilots don't want to be like an airline.

If "custom" is one key word, then "experience" must surely be the other.

"Over and over again, our customers are telling us that they both want and will pay for a quality experience. The smart operators understand that they offer more than a product definable in terms of units or pounds. The relationship between buyer and seller increasingly is regarded in terms of the experience that surrounds the sale."

For Signature, the cost of corporate showmanship has yet to be fully analyzed.

"We've never budgeted it or tracked it. Some of our events cost nothing, absolutely zero. On the other hand, our national events could run as high as $50,000.

"We threw a big party during the Clinton inauguration. We brought in a comedy team, catered food, the works for the corporate pilots that sat out the event at Signature. We've done the same thing for the Kentucky Derby and the Super Bowl. But most of the showmanship, our Positively Outrageous Service, has been a spur-of-the-moment kind of thing.

"We had a chief executive officer call one of our operations to tell us that he was supposed to meet his wife who was flying commercial."

It was their anniversary, so Signature did more than simply meet the plane. Remember, the definition includes "unexpected, out-of-proportion to the circumstances, and the customer is invited to play or otherwise be highly involved." They met the woman with a bouquet of roses and capped the moment with a serenade sung by a guitar-playing Signature employee.

She cried!

Then there were the military pilots who were on their last flight together. They were a male-female duo that had met and fallen in love while flying military brass. Regulations meant that their days sharing the cockpit would end as soon as the the ink dried on the marriage license.

Imagine their surprise when they returned to find the plane decorated with streamers, cans on strings, and "Just About Married" painted on the windscreen. Naturally, "wedding" photos were taken of the happy couple. These are the things of which service legends are made.

"Marshall" is the term used to describe leading an aircraft to its space on the apron. Most of the time, it is the responsibility of a ramp agent, driving a small vehicle signed "follow me."

What you wouldn't expect is for the driver to be a cow. You wouldn't expect that...unless perhaps the company you worked for was Borden and the flight support service was Signature. That's exactly what has happened on a number of occasions when the Borden pilots have stopped on one of their "milk runs!"

What makes for a better celebration than a birthday? An un-birthday, of course! Slow days at a Signature operation may signal that the time is ripe for an un-birthday. Customers are feted to a birthday celebration as Signature employees heighten the experience by pretending to believe that they really think they have selected the right day. The Signature idea of the "right day" is "any day!"

Dignity

Not everyone has the psychological presence to adjust to the odd juxtaposition of cows, un-birthdays, and other tomfoolery with the idea of cautious, dignified corporate management. And, not surprisingly, Signature has lost a few to the abrupt, harsh-for-some, shift in corporate culture.

One casualty told Meunier, "I understand what you are trying to do. I agree intellectually. I just can't get on board."

Explains Meunier, "Some people are not able to adjust to this atmosphere. You have to be able to be a little bit corny. Some people who have a rigid sense of what is and isn't 'management,' don't accommodate this well.

"They don't seem to grasp that the world is lining up into two camps...the devalued commodity and the valued experience.

"I'm a lawyer...we have everything non-analytical run out of us in law school. POS has opened me up as a person. (I've learned that) there is something in every person that wants to play.

"If POS counted for nothing in the customer's mind, we would still find it highly valuable for the changes it has brought to our partners (employees)."

Showmanship has its risks. In some industries, there seems to be an awkward fit at best. Signature is playing in a business that requires exact attention to detail. After all, we're talking aircraft, a breed of machinery not known for coasting to a stop in the event of a malfunction.

The risks are there for others, who for some strange reason have gravitated to the idea of bringing fun into the workplace. This is especially true of the scores of folks in the medical profession who have been delighted to receive our permission to lighten up. The same can be said of the credit unions and banks where the cat named POS has been let out of the bag.

Who knows why or how fun can find a home in such serious circumstances? Perhaps we all just need a little comic relief when the going gets tough. The lesson to be learned is that the mere possession of a sense of humor is not equivalent to being irresponsible. In fact, it may be the healthiest sign of all. Only individuals who can handle the dichotomy of serious fun can maintain the sense of balance necessary when things go awry.

Says Meunier, "In a way, we have a schizophrenia about us. We strive for a classy, subdued, consistent look." Signature partners sport a new uniform that is as sharp as the new image gracing Signature facilities.

"But at the same time, we want to play and have fun. Our culture is to do the job well but have fun doing it. Doing the job well is the price of entry."

And having fun on the job is the edge that keeps customers and partners in a state of pleasant anticipation.

That playful posture that we call showmanship, Meunier defines as a way to transcend the barriers that separate the server from the served, "role playing with your heart in it."

Corporate Heart

"Changing coaches can matter. A collection of players can be a failure, but under other leadership you can get a success. Good leadership is like adding an ingredient that causes a mixture to gel...when it happens, everybody knows."

It comes up in conversations with any natural leader that leadership and followership are a partnership of responsibilities made odd by the fact that, in many ways, the leader must follow and the followers may, in many instances, need to take the lead. We're not far from the analogy of flocking geese, who take turns leading the group, taking on the burden of creating a draft, a sort of vacuum in which the rest of the flock will find it easier to fly. The phenomenon is complete when the leader moves from the point to allow another member of the flock to lead, thus saving energy of the whole without exhausting any single member.

"When people feel the presence of leadership, they are able to dedicate themselves to a task greater than themselves. Every person has an innate desire to be a part of something greater than themselves. Maybe that's the way we gain immortality."

Pretty heady discussion for something that on the surface seems both simple and, in some ways, trivial. We are talking about having fun on the job, about playing with the customer, about showmanship, which is but a step away from the carnival midway.

"Leadership that creates belonging and dedication to a larger if not higher cause is," muses Menuier, "a fair explanation of the growing influences of street gangs." Perhaps we have left the responsibility of leadership to the "other guy" for too long. Besides, leadership is also about developing the strengths of the followers so that they, like the geese, may in turn take the lead.

"You have to have a vision of something that is to be. That is essential. A leader has to have a sense of environment for allowing people to grow. A leader is a lot like a gardener who creates an environment where things can grow."

For a moment, I thought that Meunier had fallen into an analogy that had been overused and underutilized. Then he added a perspective that made it all right.

"A leader is not like a composer who writes every note. Besides, the vision is never going to come out exactly as you originally envisioned it."

Of course not. If leadership is about empowerment, and others are given control of the day-to-day decision processes, the vision itself swells to the might of a symphony playing together, each individual adding a touch of creativity that cannot help but shape and improve the final result.

And sometimes, you've gotta break the rules. One example is the takeover of the FBO operation at LaGuardia. The rules said that you need a tough male manager to handle the rough environment of a big city airport.

Signature broke the rules and brought in a female. The rules said that to clean house and start fresh with new, inexperienced employees would be suicide. Bad habits or not, the old crew knew the ropes and could get the aircraft off the gate. Maybe not with a smile but at least off the gate. Signature broke that rule, too, spending a small fortune to train an all new crew in the Signature way of loving on the customer.

"We spent a lot of time and money, but the turn around was dramatic. People asked, 'What did you do with LaGuardia?' Fuel volumes increased by 50 percent per month, month-after-month. And all we changed was the way we treated the customer."

That was a matter of sharing the vision and then getting the heck out of the way.

"Leaders have to think big but, in many cases, the results will be even bigger. Did Edison have any idea what would become of his inventions? I don't think so."

The dearth of leadership in America may be that since the point of our formation we have had—not leaders, but—managers who thought it was their duty to hang on rather than lead on.

Meunier believes that leadership is about preparing others to assume the responsibility of guiding the flock. It is more about the development of the follower than development of the product. The product is only the excuse for connecting.

"Did you see 'Scent of a Woman?' "

"Not yet."

"Well, in the movie, whenever the kid said something profound, the old man would say, 'That's a pearl son, that's a pearl.' "

"So you agree that the product is not all that relevant, that it is only the excuse for connecting?"

"That's a pearl, son. That's a pearl."

Call Betty at (800) 635-7524, Monday–Friday between the hours of 9 AM– 4 PM (Central) for a free copy of our IdeaLetter.

CHAPTER EIGHTEEN

The Lion Laughs

"So, tell me. Just exactly what is it that you care about and what is it that you can do?"

That was the question tossed at the waitress who had breezed by the table dropping breakfast and a smile. She wore a badge that said, "I care, I can."

Yeah, right. Another marketing coup, no doubt belonging to some marketing know-it-all, while stretching his suspenders and sitting at the Puzzle Palace dreaming up yet another "brilliant" idea. If the grunts in the field don't screw it up, it'll put another billion on the bottom line.

We had seen this kind of motivationless marketing before. This time, things were different.

The folks at Red Lion Hotels and Inns are not about to engage in empty sloganeering.

"I care about you...and I can do anything it takes to make your stay with us perfect."

In the words of a famous author on customer service, I said, "WOW!"

The Red Lion "I care, I can" customer service program is more than empty empowerment. It's a lot more than simply giving the inmates keys to the asylum.

When Red Lion set about to discover its own strengths and weaknesses, it discovered pure gold. The funny thing was that they already had it!

Roger Long, director of advertising, said that focus groups revealed that the friendly employees, already a Red Lion staple, meant more to the frequent traveler than all the fancy soaps and doo-dad amenities in the world. Travelers mentioned other, higher profile hotels as being efficient and prompt but having no personality.

"We want someone to make us feel welcome. We get lonesome and bored."

Says Long, "We realized that customer service was important, we just didn't know how important."

It turned out that the crispy apple waiting at the desk for the late night arrival and the folksy, welcome-home attitude of the desk clerks were what made Red Lion a hit with road warriors of all stripes.

I witnessed that myself one morning in Oregon when a crusty, old-bat-of-a-clerk held court with truckers and executives alike, charming each in turn and sending them into the day feeling like Mom had just buttoned their collar.

After breakfast, I couldn't wait to put this "I care, I can" stuff to a test. Upstairs, the first button I spotted belonged to a short, round-faced woman who had a smile so big I thought it was a tattoo.

"So, what do you care about?" I tested.

"I care about whatever you care about," was the cheerful answer.

"Oh, yeah? Well, what can you do that is so darn special that you get a badge to tell about it?"

"I can do whatever it takes to make your meeting a success."

"Well then, I think one of those jazzy badges would make my meeting perfect." That was just a challenge to see how serious this walking cherub would take her mission.

"I'll be right back."

She disappeared. This part of customer service I had seen before. The surprise came when she returned a few minutes later, badge in hand.

"Ta da!" she announced as if her magician's license had just been approved. Then a pudgy hand opened to reveal an "I care, I can" badge just for me.

"Got this one right off my manager's coat!"

You Won't Believe...

What had drawn my attention to Red Lion was the showmanship of their ad campaign. A low-key campaign had placed magazine ads, each beginning with a hook such as, "We hate to tell you..." or "We probably shouldn't admit...." Then the ad continues to give only the slightest clue as to some service deed of a Red Lion employee. Each includes a somewhat misleading picture that could easily be misinterpreted and the invitation to dial 1-800-RED-LION to find out what happened.

Notice, please, the use of a story and the injection of personality. Now that's showmanship. Plus, to get the rest of the story, the customer must get involved long enough to call the 800 number.

What callers hear is the voice of the employee involved in the customer service incident. What is truly amazing is that nearly 40 percent of those who call remain on the line to make reservations!

My favorite begins with the headline, "We hate to reveal what our Salt Lake City concierge did to teach a guest a thing or two." The picture that accompanies the ad is a menacing meat mallet.

Stay on the line and you hear the concierge describe how a guest wanted to arrange cooking lessons for his wife when she accompanied him to Salt Lake City on business. The quick-thinking concierge realized that the hotel was chock-full of great chefs, so he arranged for the guest's wife to "apprentice" in the kitchen.

More! More!

Not all Red Lion service stories are appropriate for the ad campaign, no point in raising expectations unnecessarily.

But there is the story about the employee at the Vancouver, Washington property, a former military corpsman who answered the phone only to discover that the caller was looking for her husband to tell him that their baby was on the way. In fact, it was darned near on the line! Fortunately, the operator was able to talk her through the delivery!

Then there was the incident in San Jose when a customer left in such a hurry to attend a meeting in Los Angeles that he forgot both of his bags. A Red Lion employee who had recently acquired his pilot's license, gassed up and flew to the rescue!

In Durango, a guest with car problems left a credit card and his car with one of the clerks asking him to have the car fixed. The employee discovered that the problem was the fuel pump. Rather than have the guest pay for expensive towing and garage fees, he purchased a replacement pump and installed it on his own time. The bill? A grand total of a mere $27!

Today, the ad campaign continues, powered solely by letters from satisfied customers.

Stepping Out

Red Lion has its service program down to a science, which extends well beyond the four steps to great customer service that are preached to employees from day one. In fact, they are the subject of a video-based training program that follows the Red Lion experience from airport to hotel, showing some of the many ways that Red Lion employees are empowered to solve guest travel problems even before they enter the lobby.

The four steps are simple to the point of earning a yawn. Perhaps that's the point. Great customer service isn't a matter of rocket science. It is a matter of people science, a discipline that is astonishingly complex in its simplicity.

Smile and greet.

Show you care.

Show you can.

Thank them for their business.

So maybe you think that you now have the secret of Red Lion customer service. Don't bother to take out your highlighter. Those four steps taken alone don't mean beans.

Inquiring Minds

Me? I have to know how things work.

So I called Red Lion and talked with Kim Hansink. Now, Hansink is without doubt a competent executive. She answered my questions, steered me to the salient points when I got off track, and, in general, represented Red Lion very, very professionally.

But she giggles.

We're talking about those delightful little notes that people sound when they are talking to someone to whom they have given their complete attention in a conversation, about a subject that makes them smile.

That's it! WYSIWYG! Just like on your computer. What you see is what you get!

The people at Red Lion didn't create an ad campaign, they created themselves...nice people being nice to people. The ad campaign only serves to spread the news, not create it. And Hansink was the reflection of that simple fact.

When Red Lion discovered that friendly service was far more important than they had previously thought, they dreamed up not just a nifty ad campaign to promote service to the public; they created the "I care, I can" program to make certain that they actually delivered on the promise.

Don't miss that key point. Too often the marketing group spends about a gazillion bucks making promises, and then heads for a three-martini lunch, leaving the operations guys holding the bag. Well, making promises is a lot easier than keeping them. Red Lion gets high marks for:

1. building on an existing strengths;
2. making and keeping a promise that their customers are important;
3. creating an environment that works, to make certain that the promise could and would be kept.

All of this is dependent upon having people who really do care.

Red Lion spends an inordinate amount of energy in the employee selection process. Get it? That's "selection," not "hiring" or, worse, "body snatching."

Red Lion wants to hire the right people in the first place. To help in the decision process, they give finalists a personality inventory to assist in determining if the person really is naturally friendly and service-minded.

But hiring the right people doesn't count for much if they are not managed so they can use some of that service-minded ability. Hansink says that, to her way of thinking, showmanship is not much different than good management, "Creating an environment that allows individuals to serve other individuals."

Okay, so she was struggling to get the definition just right, but it's tough to define a word like showmanship.

She wound up and tried again, saying that at Red Lion, "Policy and tradition doesn't limit what we can do for a guest. The first level of great service is letting the customer tell me how we can serve. The next level is to anticipate customer needs."

"Are you worried about all the public attention on customer service creating artificially high expectations, or maybe even reaching a sort of critical mass when employees simply can't top one another?"

(sigh) "No! People stay because it's fun. This is a demanding business and the 'I care, I can' program affects how we relate to one another as well."

And apparently, it works.

(giggle!)

Proof in the Pudding

If showmanship had a name, it might very well be Pat Birmingham, the senior sales manager at the Modesto Red Lion. Birmingham discovered a potential sale to McDonald's Corporation and, not content to send the standard bid proposal, he created a video of himself wolfing down an Egg McMuffin...cut to the general managers's office where the GM is doing the same...cut to the coffee shop where employees are also eating Egg McMuffins.

Next came a video tour of the property, followed by a grand finale of Red Lion employees gathered in the lobby singing the McDonald's theme song.

Got any ideas which hotel got the job?

Then there was the $70,000 banquet that was threatened by the loss of air conditioning on a 101 degree day. Not to worry—Wayne Pipes, corporate director of engineering, and Curt Sauers, property director of engineering, climbed to the roof where the temperature was a crispy 134 degrees.

The dynamic duo managed to make a temporary repair that soon had the room cool and comfortable, but required constant monitoring throughout the event. And to think we call these guys "techies!"

At the Lloyd Center property, Lisa Tenney raced across the street to purchase a disposable camera, with her own money, when she discovered that her meeting-planner clients had forgotten theirs! That proved that she cared...and that she could!

But my favorite story belongs to the Salt Lake City property, where Lindsay Gray arranged for Santa Claus to visit a sick boy who stays in the hotel when he and his mom come to town for his medical treatments. Now that's Positively Outrageous Service. That's Red Lion.

CHAPTER NINETEEN

Poof!

Spellbound. That's the only way to describe the audience held captive by magician extraordinaire, Wayne Alan. First, the feint of friendly banter misdirects attention and expectation. Then comes the sudden start of amazement of an audience delighted, and bemused after-smiles of adults not used to falling so easily.

Alan works magic. Though he really does use smoke and mirrors, the magic he spins at trade shows and sales meetings is but a variation of the everyday magic worked by friendly sales clerks, amusing barkeeps, and concerned nurses. With these legendary servers, Alan shares the secret knowledge that causes the burdens of the world to evaporate.

If only for a moment, Alan can coax a laugh from the most jaded corporate executive, the most wary corporate purchasing agent. And though Alan himself seems to enjoy the magic of the moment, his corporate sponsors are distracted by the ringing that he creates for their cash registers. Most of his clients are Fortune 500 mega-hitters who have discovered that entertainment is good for more than a few laughs. It sells product.

"Most entertainers are driven by art," says Alan, who sounds for all the world like my Uncle Jack. (If you live in Ohio, the analogy may be helpful, otherwise take my word for it.)

Alan doesn't criticize the motives of those who are driven solely by the lure of applause, but with a degree in marketing and a minor in theatrical arts, Alan just figured that there was no point in being a "starving" artist. From the beginning, Alan has always had a corporate sponsor—testimony that business recognizes the value of an entertaining pitch and that Alan's folks didn't waste their money on all those books!

And life with the Fortune 500 isn't all bad. His clients do things "first class," an attitude that spills over to the way they treat hired talent.

"They treat you just like Johnny Carson or Jay Leno." Not a bad life if you can handle the travel.

Over thousands of appearances, Alan has developed the instincts of the seasoned performer. He knows audiences, and has advice for those who are serious about playing in public.

"Showmanship is," here he pauses, surprised at the question. "It's a little flair, a little savoir-faire, a little letting your personality show in a larger way."

There, he finally rested on a definition that seemed a comfortable fit, "Letting your personality show in a larger way."

"The key words are 'personality' and 'larger.' Not just putting your personality into the business, but doing it in a way that seems a little bit bigger than life. Better put would be to say 'a little bit bigger than expected or usual.'

"People like to be a part of things that stand out and amplify their vision of life in the slow lane. That's what Hollywood has to sell; the look and feel of lives and conversations lived above the context of schedules and responsibilities; the thrill of just touching, if only for an instant. People need energy and they will hungrily suck it from those who offer it for the taking."

To Alan, Houdini was a hero. Surprised?

"Houdini did everything larger-than-life."

Alan claims to know why Houdini never drove a car, a secret waiting to be spilled in a book authored by Alan, his magician-admirer. But Alan will tell you that being bigger-than-life is a sure way to stand out—a fact that has brought formerly staid IBM out of its starched white shirts and dark blue sincere suits.

We shared a laugh over audiences who look into their laps when the performer calls for a volunteer. "I like it when they do the 'Amazing Shrinking Person Trick'," laughs Alan, referring to the way audiences will shrink deep into their seats in the hope of becoming invisible when it's time to select a volunteer.

But that is only a symptom, not of silly audiences, but of poor performers.

"Rule number one is to never embarrass an audience.

"My best trait is to be able to watch the audience and decide who will play well. Audiences don't realize that it's a two-way street. They don't realize that you can see them. I'm always watching to see who is going to be a good performer—not to take over the show—but who I can bring up on stage and make the star for a moment."

The concept that we have used is the idea of being "in fun," psychologically ready to play. It turns out that all performers employ the concept, whether or not they have coined a phrase to describe the phenomenon.

For Alan, and for all of us who wish to invite the customer to play, audience members who are smiling, laughing at the right time, and applauding at the right time are excellent candidates for play. There are good audiences and...others. But the best are what Alan calls "theatrically, socially intelligent."

Theatrically, socially intelligent audiences know when to laugh and when to applaud. They know when and how to give a standing ovation. These are skills that young people must actually be taught through experience.

And it turns out that great performers are great audiences. They appreciate the performer's art and are able to enhance the experience through their own participation.

"One time at a trade show for the trucking industry, I spotted an older gentleman who was really being a good audience. All through the show, I appreciated how he laughed and applauded, always at just the right moment.

"After the show, he came up to say 'thank you', when I thought I recognized the face.

"I told him that I would be honored if he would allow a picture to be taken with me. We found the photographer and just before the shot was to be taken, he said, 'Why don't we do something that I sometimes do for special occasions? Let's turn our backs to the camera and when the photographer counts to three, let's just look back over our shoulders and smile.' "

Well, that pose turned out to be from the opening scenes of the television classic, "Love That Bob!" and, of course, Alan's admiring visitor was none other than Bob Cummings himself.

Great performers make great audiences. Perhaps it is that attentiveness to the needs of others, that ability to meet their needs...first, that makes for great performances either on the stage or from behind the counter.

Alan has worked the White House four times, and enjoys telling about his engagement to entertain the Gerald Ford family and guests.

When he asked where he should park, he was told, "Pull right through the gate and park right out front."

"What more could you want of life than a front space at the White House?" jokes Alan, who has definite opinions about how to treat an audience.

Wayne Alan thinks that showmanship begins with the willingness to simply be yourself, saying, "I like to think of myself as being a nice guy. My folks were that way. So when I walk onto the stage, I just try to emulate my dad and let the audience know first that I'm just a nice guy and you're going to have some fun. Then if their socks get blown off, well, that's all the better." But first just be a nice guy.

Then, of course, their socks are blown away. When Alan tears and restores a small flag right before the eyes of a stunned audience, it's easy to see why he is both a friend and consultant to the famous David Copperfield.

From close-up magic, prestidigitation some would say, to large prop-and-theme illusions, Alan manages to amaze, amuse, and mystify while deftly weaving the product at hand into the fabric of the unfolding act.

Alan recalls a series of four shows that he did for CBS affiliates and clients to help introduce the new fall season. A car buff, Alan drove a vintage Rolls Royce to the Four Seasons Hotel in Georgetown on the first day of the program. On the second day of the program, the

Rolls was left at home in favor of the family Chevy.

There are two glaring differences between arriving in a Rolls and a Chevy. First, the valet expects a ten dollar tip from anyone driving a Rolls Silver Don. Second, there isn't nearly as much respect accorded to the guy in the Chevy. Even if it's the same guy who only yesterday had managed to turn heads simply by arriving in an automobile too beautiful to be called a car.

That, says Alan, is only natural. But it is wrong.

Great servers understand. They will tell you in so many words, that every customer or member of an audience deserves to be loved.

Put in other words, great performers—great servers—are nice people, and showmanship is more than pizazz, although pizazz has its place.

Alan illustrates by telling about an encounter in Cincinnati.

Exercising a reconstructed knee, Alan happened by a gentleman walking an Irish Spaniel. It was the day before Mother's Day, a fact that may have made the already talkative Alan even more eager for conversation.

"I wish I had that Irish Spaniel of yours to give to my wife for Mother's Day," he offered as a conversation starter. "She would really be thrilled."

So started one of those exchanges between two people that rarely escalates beyond a comment on the weather. But with Wayne Alan, weather just isn't the issue.

"People think that showmanship means P.T. Barnum and Liberace. It doesn't."

"We talked for just a while. He asked me if I lived nearby and when I said no, he took time to tell me the best route to continue my walk.

"He brightened my life and I brightened his. That's the whole point of this business. You want people to walk away a little happier than you found them."

That's showmanship.

"When people realize that their personalities can shine...they can be showmen, too.

"Last week I got a fortune cookie that said something like 'the harder you work, the more more successful you will be.' I liked that, and couldn't help thinking that maybe I should turn my own life up a notch. Then I went into a little restaurant and saw a sign on the counter that put it into perspective. It said, 'It's nice to be important but it's more important to be nice.'

"And I remembered that someone had written that same saying in my high school yearbook. It must be true."

Call Betty at (800) 635-7524, Monday–Friday between the hours of 9 AM– 4 PM (Central) for information on how you can be invited to our ranch-based Positively Outrageous Service seminars.

CHAPTER TWENTY

Southwest Airlines, the Airline that Luv Built

How do customers come to feel close to a company? After all, the company that does their dry cleaning or repairs their car is really nothing more than an organized group of people in business to make a profit. When it comes to airlines, any way you slice it, convenience of schedule and price are the deciding factors.

Yet millions of frequent fliers have a special feeling for the stubby 737's of Southwest Airlines and the people that make them fly, in spite of the fact that Southwest is known for herding customers off and on planes with little more organization than a Chinese fire drill. And food service aboard a Southwest flight...isn't.

"Good morning! Are you still serving the breakfast peanuts or have you switched to the lunch peanuts?"

"Oh, you'll like these. We have the new filet mignon peanuts!"

A big meal on Southwest consists of an assortment of cookies and cracker snacks. Mmmmm!

If you fly to eat, then Southwest may not be the choice for you. On the other hand, if you want to get where you are going without spending a fortune, it may be a good idea to eat lunch at home and fly Southwest. Besides, even good airline food is rare.

What makes Southwest Airlines special is not the food service and open seating. That may help explain why Southwest is profitable, but has little to do with what makes Southwest special.

The people at Southwest are the secret ingredient.

Southwest has attracted a peculiar breed of customer-loving employees...and then they have managed to allow and encourage them to be themselves. At Southwest, fun is serious business.

To the public, Herb Kelleher, a self-described recovering attorney, embodies what has come to be known as the Southwest spirit. But there is no way on God's green earth that a single man could honcho the daily activities of a company that is spread over thousands of miles, and more than 12,000 flight attendants, pilots, mechanics and others.

The suggestion that Southwest Airlines revolves around the charisma of Kelleher is more than unfair. It's uncalled for.

"Honestly," sighs Southwest's Colleen Barrett. "In a way, it's almost offensive. I've been here for 22 years, a lot of us have. It's a team effort. Herb has a crew of officers who are fantastic.

"Herb has hired people who are like him. He's got all kinds of ambassadors."

No, there is a magic spell at Southwest that frees the human spirit of its employees to play with the customers and make them feel special while eating peanuts.

If you sneaked up on Kelleher, he would probably spill his scotch, but he'd admit that—like the wizard in the Land of Oz—he really is only the man behind the curtain. Lots of smoke and plenty of mirrors. It's not Herb, as employees and customers alike call him; it is a team effort that makes Southwest Airlines the most fun airline in the world.

Anyone who doubts that showmanship and profitability go hand in hand hasn't flown Southwest.

For my money, Southwest Airlines is run by a dynamo of a woman, Colleen Barrett, executive vice president, customers and corporate secretary. I know her to be Herb Kelleher's anti-matter. While he is a wild and crazy kind of guy, Colleen Barrett is the last person you would expect to lace on the party shoes. (Yet Barrett, like almost all Southwest employees, can boogie with the best.)

Barrett has a handle on what makes Southwest special, and not a lot of patience for those who ask for the secret and then fail to "get it" when it is handed to them on a platter. The phrase about not tolerating fools lightly comes to mind. But for those who ask, Barrett will talk, hoping that lightning will strike and finally someone will not try to make having fun a matter of scientific debate.

Asked for her definition of showmanship, Barrett responds quickly with, "We just call it fun. We aren't technical. You know that."

But they are technical. When it comes to issues of safety and quality customer service, Southwest people are pretty particular about keeping those planes shiny side up. They may paint them to look like Shamu the Killer whale or the Lone Star flag of Texas, but safety is never taken lightly. Then again, neither are Southwest's cultural values.

"We spend a disproportionate time on hiring...we do some very unique things...and we let people go...a lot."

There was the series of employment ads that showed Kelleher dressed as Elvis and captioned, "Work for the airline where Elvis has been spotted."

Then there is the story of the recruiters who told a group of applicants, "We understand how nervous you can get talking in front of a group of strangers. An old speaker's trick is to imagine that they are dressed only in their underwear. So...we thought we'd make it easy on you."

With that, they dropped their pants and stood before the group in SWA boxer shorts!

The same group required other applicants to wear Snootie, floaties or crazy sunglasses to the interview. The reasoning was that anyone not comfortable with a little pre-hire foolishness wouldn't last long at Southwest anyway.

Flight Attendants must complete nearly six weeks of intensive technical training. They can still be fired for not fitting the Southwest spirit, an idea that is protected as though it were the Holy Grail. For Southwest, being the only airline that will fire a pilot, the techie equivalent of God, for failing to fit the culture is nearly a badge of honor. Treat a ramp agent or skycap rudely and you'll be wearing wings sporting some other outfit's logo.

"Fit" is the operating word in a company where corporate culture is more carefully guarded than the checkbook. Kelleher and Barrett make it a point to visit each and every training class to personally impart the concepts of mutual respect, teamwork, fun and, here's an oddity...love.

They may spell it LUV in honor of the downtown Dallas Love Field that in the early days gave SWA its lift (pun intended.) Regardless of spelling, they mean it to be interpreted as a capital LOVE.

Hanging onto a corporate culture as touchy-feely as Southwest's is no easy matter in an age of high-tech, dog-eat-dog corporate behavior. But it is the culture that makes Southwest what it is, and everyone on the inside knows it.

And as might be expected, not everyone can operate in a work environment with such a loose-tight structure, where the reality of the corporate organization chart places everyone on the same line, just above Kelleher and his top execs.

Could an executive who is rigid and stand-offish survive at Southwest? Barrett thinks not.

"If he (Herb) didn't get rid of you, you'd probably leave on your own."

Barrett talks of advising close friends to seek employment elsewhere simply over the issue of fit. "We're very serious about fun and we hire people that fit that profile. Herb would say, 'Why do you think that business has to be a frown and ultra, ultra serious?' "

But it doesn't mean that Southwest has created the ultimate "Improv in the Sky."

"I'm not asking you to be a comedienne," Barrett tells graduating flight attendants. "I'm just asking you to be you."

"If you have a caring personality, a good sense of humor and you don't take yourself too seriously...if you have a spark of creativity...we bring out the best in you (because) we let you be you."

Respect for one another is a theme that, to insiders, probably speaks loudest.

Even the unions treat Southwest with respect and they get respect in return.

Walking through the modern corporate digs snugged against the runway at modest Love Field, a union representative was spotted trading laughs with two of Southwest's typically wholesome flight attendants. That's just the way the game is played at Southwest. From corporate to gatehouse, from hanger to flight deck, it is get along or get along.

To make the point, Barrett is vice-president of customers. And we're not talking just the ones who fly in the back of the plane. At Southwest, everyone is considered a customer, some just happen to be on the payroll. It is her job to look out for Southwest's largest and, thanks to Barrett, most vocal special interest.

If it's not good for Southwest customers and employee-customers, Barrett will be on hand to make certain it won't fly.

At the annual awards banquet, you can count on a full-scale celebration of Southwest Spirit, interpreted as "customer service with Luv."

Chutzpah

There doesn't seem to be an English word that adequately describes the scrappy style of marketing that has become nearly a Southwest trademark. When it comes to a fight, Southwest seems to be ready to mix it up with the big boys, taking their story straight to the traveling public.

And when it is only a matter of trumpeting low fares and frequent schedules, you can expect Southwest to hit the airwaves trumpet in hand.

Southwest has never settled for marketing campaigns that spilled syrupy slogans. Nope, their style of marketing is, like the airline itself, direct and fun.

In the early days, ads featuring flight attendants in hot pants and boots invited the business traveler to enjoy the airline that Luv built. To say it wasn't at least a tad bit sexist would be avoiding the issue. But for the times and for the Southwest, the ads were not much more than a reflection of the youthful spirit, the Southwest spirit, that even today is obvious the moment you step on board.

Southwest people have always had that girl...and guy next door, just scrubbed, but ever-so-flirty attitude that makes it feel like you are flying with friends.

Today's marketing is perhaps more reflective of the times but certainly not more sophisticated. Southwest is still positioning itself as that underdog, in-your-face airline just struggling to get along in a world threatened by monolithic corporate bullies.

Waltz along a jetway at any Southwest city and you may encounter an ad campaign that typifies the Southwest show-boatin' style. "We came, we saw, we kicked tail," is the copy that challenges the traveler to read further and discover that Southwest, little old Southwest, has done it, winning the coveted triple crown of the airline industry...again. Best in the business for on-time arrivals, lowest customer complaints and fewest lost baggage claims per mile, Southwest only looks like the "little guy."

Barrett said that, yes, there had been some complaints over the scrappy tone of the copy. Just enough to make her certain that the campaign was right on target!

Asked whether she believed that showmanship had ever cost the company a customer or two, she answered without hesitation that no doubt a few had slipped away. Most likely, these were first-time customers who didn't yet understand Southwest. Some people just aren't ready to have fun on a 7 AM flight. And while flight attendants are cautioned to use good judgment, Southwest just isn't the kind of airline that would put an employee in charge of a plane full of customers and then attempt to micro-manage their behavior with an overload of policy and procedure.

And a few customers can't accept that a "girl in sneakers, making jokes, can take care of safety."

While every customer counts with Southwest, Barrett is equally concerned about the impact of poorly targeted customer complaints. Every complaint is brought to the attention of the employee involved and Barrett worries that such a complaint could be very intimidating if the employee is new.

To graduating flight attendants, Barrett is careful to remind that, "This *will* happen to you. So you'll just have to be able to handle this kind of criticism," and roll with the punches.

Malice in Dallas

Southwest has always had a fun style, a fact brought home to this writer one day in Phoenix. Walking across the baggage area, I heard music. Real music. Live with lots of brass (a good description of SWA!)

It was coming from outside and it seemed to be moving. Never one to miss an opportunity to listen to great music, I hurried along, encouraged by the idea that the music just might be the product of a marching band.

The music was bright and bouncy and, doggone it, they were playing "Joy to the World!" What a great welcome for a tired traveler!

I stepped outside just in time to witness a parade that could have only been marshalled by the wacko brains of a Southwest-trained marketing grunt. There marched a local high school band, led by the Southwest mascot, a costumed figure that resembles the pudgy planes of Southwest. Close behind strutted the Sun City Pomms, a phalanx of octogenarian gals...what would you call them?... in sequined spandex and go-go boots.

There weren't 76 trombones, but there was a gaggle of Southwest employees decked out in Southwest formal attire, half tuxedo, half beach wear, you pick the half! Come to think of it, the schizo outfits pretty much tell it all. Southwest is serious about fun and serious about running a first-class, customer-focused airline. The heck of it all is that they manage to do both.

All this to set the stage for the most phenomenal marketing event in history, an event that came to be known as Malice...in Dallas!

It seems that the marketing gurus at SWA aren't the only folks willing to turn a phrase in the interest of sales. When they selected the phrase "Just Plane Smart" to point out that flying Southwest is a budget-sensible choice, little did they know that an aircraft supply company in Ohio had already staked out the territory with the slogan, "Plane Smart."

Naturally, Kelleher received a phone call advising him of the oversight. More than likely, language of the "Cease and Desist" variety came up in the conversation.

Now, Kelleher, attorney that he is, probably smelled a "My-attorney-can-whip-your-attorney!" situation just over the horizon. So he offered a simple solution.

"Why don't we settle this man to man? Why, we could arm wrestle for the right to use the slogan.   Say, a best two-out-of-three-match, winner-take-all?"

If the truth were known, it is more likely that Kelleher smelled more than a potential legal battle. He knows how to milk the press when the opportunity arises.

So it came to be that Herb Kelleher, 62-years-old and a picture of health thanks to his habit of "smoking two packs a day and bench pressing nearly a quart of scotch on a regular basis," came to meet a 35-year-old former college wrestler. The two squared off at Dallas' Reunion Arena, surrounded by a bevy of Southwest cheerleaders and a contingent of pro wrestlers hired to hype the occasion.

From the stands, thousands of pompoms waved, cheering on the two media gladiators, both already winners, thanks to the national media who had arrived with a battery of cameras to report this bout of the century.

The kid won the first round. Kelleher fought hard, but it looked like a few more reps with the scotch bottle would have been helpful. He cheated on round two, in a move that was about as spontaneous as the usual wrestling featured on late-night television. But the interloper wouldn't be caught unaware when Kelleher lined up for the third and deciding round.

What is really important is that there was no way that either contestant could emerge a loser. With media coverage from all three major networks, ESPN and even the BBC, getting to play was a win.

Okay. So who do you think won round three? Well, the kid, of course. (Kelleher let him.)

But in a touch, worthy of a mega-media mogul, the kid offered to allow Southwest to continue using the slogan. Not a bad day's work for a couple of guys who were able to turn a potential courtroom conflict into a masterpiece of media manipulation.

That is showmanship and that is Southwest Airlines.

CHAPTER TWENTY-ONE

Show-Off!

She could be a public speaker, an author, or even a television talk-show host. Her ideas about showmanship would serve any corporate executive well. Her philosophy is not unique but her occupation is.

She is Cynthia Morgan, a graduate student at a prestigious law school where she boasts an excellent grade-point average. In a year or two, she will take what she has learned into the courtroom, where she will play to a much different audience.

For now, she holds court before an all-male jury, dancing in a gentlemen's club in San Antonio.

Looking for a job with hours flexible enough to bend around her class schedule and provide an income that would allow her to keep her horses and enter the occasional rodeo, Morgan fell into dancing. A fellow law student, also a dancer, offered to get her what Morgan thinks is the perfect job.

Whatever you think of her occupation, there is plenty to learn from this six-foot, blonde entertainer.

"You have to have a lot of confidence. You can't go out there worrying about your appearance. This is your moment in the center of attention, so you just go out there and do your best. It takes a lot of smiling and eye contact.

"Whatever you do, don't just stand there and wiggle. Cover the entire audience and relate to the audience as individuals.

"Customers want to be treated like persons, not objects."

In spite of public perception, the women who make the best tips are the ones who have something to say.

"I make it a point to be up on current affairs. Believe-it-or-not, these guys want to talk about sports, business...even their wives. Our job is a transition between a hard day at the office and going home. They just want to go blank."

"It's almost 100 percent personality. Some girls never figure that out. They get nose jobs or breast enlargements and they still don't make any more money because they can't communicate.

"To be really successful, you've got to express yourself artistically and relate on a one-to-one basis. It's charisma, projecting a certain magnetism. The girls that do the best, establish eye contact. It really is a personality thing."

According to Morgan, arrogance has no place in showmanship, because "it's too easy to intimidate an audience. You have to make your audience think that you really care about them, that they are special."

Couldn't have said it better myself.

CHAPTER TWENTY-TWO

Clown!

I thought I had the wrong Emmett Kelly. Off by perhaps a generation, the Emmett Kelly I had on the phone was not the grandson of the world's most famous clown as I had been led to expect.

This was even better...it was his son, Emmett Kelly, Jr., and a world-famous clown in his own right.

Also on the line, I had managed to catch Kelly's biggest fan, his wife, Shawna.

Showmanship grew up in the circus. It was under the big top that the world found P.T. Barnum...or was it the other way around? Barnum did more than assemble a truly spectacular (would he have said "colossal?") array of wild animals and even wilder performers.

Barnum recognized the old saw about a tree falling in the forest. He knew that having a great circus wouldn't count unless the public got the word.

So it came to be that through Barnum and his wonderful circus, showmanship—call it self-promotion—was elevated to an art form.

Remnants of Barnum still may be seen and heard in the circus of today, although the flair for the grand and truly outrageous has dimmed somewhat.

We slipped under the big top when a five-ring circus blew into the town of Fredericksburg, Texas.

The smell of sawdust and fresh popping corn met us in the parking lot. But it was from the center ring that we heard echos of the past.

"Ladies and Gentlemen. Children of all ages. Prepare yourself for the world's most prodigious parade of ponderous pachyderms."

Perfect!

That's the environment where Emmett Kelly, Jr., meets his people, those children of all ages who for some reason fall in love with clowns.

Kelly's circle of friends has always been a fairly ordinary group, as long as you consider Tony the Wonder Horse, Gentle Ben, and the Blue Streak Roller Skaters ordinary. Maybe that explains why Kelly struggles with the definition of showmanship. He'd much rather explain what it is that motivates him to spend an hour painting on a sad face, draping himself in baggy rags, and then confining himself to a role where he cannot speak.

For Kelly, that ten minutes of applause does it all. Tired or hot or just road weary, the world of Emmett Kelly turns instantly bright and fresh with the roar of the crowd. "Once on stage, even on a bad day, I'm alive!"

Weary Willie, the character created first as a comic strip by his dad, the original Emmett Kelly, is known as a silent clown.

Here's an interesting point. We spend so much time worrying about saying just the right things to our customers and here is a fellow who has helped make history by being quiet!

Kelly and wife Shawna insist that it's all in the eyes.

At the World's Fair in New York, Weary Willie wandered into the African pavilion where he immediately found himself surrounded by a tribe of Watusi warriors in full paint, armed with spears, and pointing at this strange looking creature wearing warpaint like they had never seen.

"I didn't know whether to shit or wind my watch!" (Kelly, in person, has a much wider vocabulary than Weary Willie.)

"They had never been out of the Kingdom of Barundi. They were speaking Swahili. I was scared that they might think that I was making fun of them. And, hell, I don't speak no Swahili...I didn't speak at all!

"So I did monkey faces, figuring that they could associate with the idea of a monkey. Well, they started laughing and it wound up that after that incident, they came by nearly every day. We had learned to talk in our own way. They were a great group of guys!"

Ask Shawna what Emmett does for a living and she is quick to reply that "He makes people happy."

Not everyone. Kelly recalls playing a state fair on a scorching hot summer's day. A woman walked by with her young daughter in tow.

"Spit on the clown, honey," she instructed her kid.

"And she did! Right in the middle of my tie! It was a real oyster!"

That Kelly! He's such a wordsmith!

Even the great Emmett Kelly, Jr., understands that some folks just aren't open to play. He has the scars on both shins to prove the point. But just because some folks have no sense of humor doesn't mean that you shouldn't make the effort.

Most of the time his instincts serve him well. "I can pick out a good target. Most of the time it's women. I rarely make the wrong choice but when I do, you might as well play to a plate."

Shawna adds, "Women hug him. He's their hero. But I never get jealous, because I'm going home with the man; they're seeing just a clown."

Kelly warns that, while having a naturally responsive audience is nice, the audience is never to blame. It's his job to generate the fun and the fun begins with him.

"I have a good time. When people ask, 'Who are you playing to?' I tell them, 'myself.' Because if you are enjoying yourself, they enjoy you!"

"Everyday I get up and think, 'Here's another day that the Lord has given to me.' I try to make every day a fun day and a happy day for everyone around me."

Not bad advice for us all.

CHAPTER
TWENTY-THREE

Selling Sizzle

What do most corporate marketing departments do? Think of an endless variety of ways to give away product.

What do smart marketers do? Think of an endless variety of ways to add value to product and build relationships with the customer.

Advertising touts features, advantages, benefits, and price points.

Marketing builds relationships between the product and the customer, and helps add value.

Which strategy would you rather live by, advertising or marketing?

Which strategy do you think is the easiest to adopt?

There you have it, almost everything you really need to know about advertising and marketing. Certainly there are wonderful concepts such as "reach" and "throw weight." Don't forget all the science that revolves around such ideas as gross rating points and audience share. Throw in a healthy understanding of demographic analysis, and you'll be ready to write your own book.

But...make that, BUT! The single most important thing to understand is that the most effective marketing that ever occurs is done inside the four walls that you call the store, office, shop, or whatever.

And...make that, AND! Whether or not your marketing is effective depends entirely on how the customer, and your individual employee who loves on 'em one-at-a-time, feels when she walks out the door.

The best marketers are those who understand that everything they do which impacts their relationship with the customer is marketing. And before they run fancy ad campaigns, they make absolutely certain that the experience they are about to provide the customer is one which will make them feel good about their buying decision.

A Word from Our Sponsor

Madison Avenue only makes two kinds of commercials. The kind of commercial that the little guys make are "awareness" commercials. You know the kind. Those things that car dealers run late at night, where they run through about two dozen car deals so fast that you remember nothing. Ma and Pa businesses are the greatest users of awareness commercials. "Come see us for the best deal in town on..." whatever. As if we really believe that they could possibly out-discount Sam Walton!

The other kind of commercial is a relationship-extension commercial. I like to call it a "feel-good" commercial. Feel-goods promise only that the customer will feel good about her buying decision. Nothing much fancier than that.

The really sharp marketers realize that if you ride into town on the price train, you have to ride out of town on the price train. And trust me, the price train is not what you would call comfortable. The margins are just too darn tight for comfort.

So the big guys promise feel-good. Think about these commercials and try to guess whether they are awareness or feel-good productions.

First, the Delta Airline theme, "We love to fly and it shows." Awareness or feel-good?

Or how about my favorite? At the end of a long piano are three willowy women, dancing and making what we knew as kids as hand jive. Do you know it? Uh Huh? Of course! It's the Diet Pepsi commercial featuring Ray Charles. And it definitely is of the feel-good persuasion! You got the right one, baby!

Another favorite of mine—because we see it early in the morning—is the generic commercial that touts "The touch, the feel of cotton. The fabric of our lives." Makes you feel so good, you want to jump straight into those Jockeys!

Almost all of the really great, really memorable commercials are feel-good commercials. Do you want to know why? Because, believe it or not, while people want to *know* that they are paying a fair price, they want to *feel* good about the product they select.

Now, this feel-good feeling must extend to the entire circumstance surrounding the purchase. It is just as important that customers feel good about the seller as they feel about the product itself.

Customers will, and do, pay more for the sake of feeling good about a product.

There are limited exceptions.

Take pizza. Please.

Let's see a show of hands of all of you who have paid full retail price for pizza in the past 30 days. Look around. You don't see too many hands, do you? There is the guy from corporate, the one on the unaudited expense account. He doesn't count. It wasn't his money. Everybody else knows better than to pay full price for pizza.

Pizza guys should hang a big banner over their menu boards that says, "just kidding!"

The point is simple. Products that are overly discounted or indistinguishable from the competition, become commodities. And nobody with a brain pays full pop for something you can get on every corner in town.

There's an old saying that I use to make my son crazy. It goes, "If it was easy, everybody would do it." That's why everybody discounts, and only the hustling few are willing to put enough brainpower into their marketing to build the value through relationships. It is the power of relationships that allows you to sell at, or at least near, full price.

The downside of discounting is the irreparable damage that it can do to the integrity of your standard prices.

2+2 for $2.22

We had this dumbhead promotion that offered two pieces of chicken and two side items for the great big price of $2.22. Not a problem for the franchisor. They get their money right off the top, so whatever they do to build short term sales doesn't matter so long as the franchisees pay their bills.

Like all businesses, we have our share of regular customers. These are the folks who are so stuck in a habit that when you see them coming, you just put their order together because it never changes. Oh, they read the menu all right, as if they expect their tastes to have changed overnight, or in case you changed from a fried chicken joint to an upscale chinese restaurant without telling them.

Then they order the exact same thing as always.

One day a regular customer was straining to reread our menu. No problem. We already had his lunch in the bag, the order rung on the register, and the change in hand for the five dollar bill Mr. Three-Piece Dinner Pack always spent at lunch.

But this day was diferent.

He couldn't quite see around the humongous poster we had hung announcing the fabulous two-plus-two promo. In frustration, he just waved his hand and said, "Oh, hell, just give me one of these," and pointed to the poster.

Great! We had, in our infinite wisdom, managed to talk a customer into spending about half of normal.

Admitting to being slow but not stupid, it took me about half the drive home to figure out that there was something dreadfully wrong with that picture. I could concede a small discount to get a customer to try our food and service, but there was something goofy about offering a discount to a customer who was already standing flatfooted in my store.

I nearly flipped the Jeep turning into the payphone where I called the store and said breathlessly, "Tear down that poster!"

Worse than trading down is the prospect of destroying the integrity of your published prices.

Our franchisor decided that a great special would be eight pieces of dark chicken, no biscuit and all, for only $4.99. Worse than the fact that the total sale was much lower than our average, the special had, as a side effect, the possibility of positioning us as rip-off artists.

We had worked for months to educate the public about our delicious honey-butter biscuits. We exceeded company spec and made ours bigger, drenched them in honey butter and cooked them until the tops were a beautiful golden brown. This was a great product.

Now, the problem with the special is that it did not include biscuits, even though all of our regular menu offerings included them. Imagine sitting at home at just about our closing time when you catch one of our commercials. You've had our product a jillion times before and always loved reaching into the box and fishing out a hot, flaky honey-butter biscuit.

You see the commercial and assume "a great deal." You see chicken and a low, low price. But you probably don't catch the part that there will be only legs and thighs, and biscuits are not included.

How do you feel when you get home and discover that your deal isn't so much of a deal?

And having bought eight pieces for nearly dirt, what do you think about our regular menu prices? Never mind that they include biscuits, and that you are looking at the more expensive mixed chicken combination than you usually purchase.

We had a very high-tech system for taking orders, a small marker board mounted on the front window. Okay, so it wasn't all that high-tech, but it never broke down in mid-rush. And it could be replaced for about one percent of what its electronic equivalent would cost.

One Sunday morning, Christian was working the dining room register. We were just recovering from a $300 surprise order and were just a tad behind on bird, when the local churches let out. We were getting hammered and Christian had orders backed up on his marker board—about $80 worth—when a customer walked in, shouldered his way to the front and said, "Do ya'll have that $4.99 special I saw on TV?"

Now, this was after we had learned not to put up discounting point of purchase materials.

"Yes, sir. We do."

"Well, let me have three of those puppies."

Within seconds, nearly every waiting order had to be changed to the special. Before you could say "Hot bird, up," 40 of the 80 dollars in orders had evaporated.

Another time we had a serious craving for a chicken sandwich from a well known, quick-service restaurant chain. We were miles from the place, but the sandwich is sooo good that we thought it worth the drive. Now these sandwiches sell for right at three bucks each and we wanted two. (Do you need help with the math on this?)

As we pulled onto the lot, we looked up at the marquee and what do you think we saw? A sign that announced that any two sandwiches could be bought for all of $2.99!

Here we were...having driven miles out of our way to spend six bucks. And there they were...saying, "No. Three bucks should be plenty."

What's wrong with this picture?

Everyday low prices has been the most recent battle cry to be heard in the grocery business...in an attempt to get away from the responsibility to market creatively. Just lower all the prices and wait for customers to start streaming through the door!

Great idea. Too bad it doesn't really work.

Just as some items become commodities when they are overly or too frequently discounted, other items are not nearly so price sensitive. People don't buy more dish detergent when it's on sale because they wash more dishes, but simply because discounted detergent is cheaper. They *will* consume more snack foods when they are offered on special.

But the surprise is what constitutes a special. Shoppers like specials because they seem so...special. Price doesn't make a special special. Whatever we feature on our marquee sells. That's why suppliers fight so hard for endcap space. Those displays at the end of aisles are goldmines! Shoppers gravitate, or sometimes just bump against those end of the aisle displays, where it's so easy for product to be noticed and fall into the cart.

What stands out sells out.

Deal Versus Decision

Discounting can make you look dishonest, ruin the price-value perception of your product, and cost unnecessary dollars from the top and bottom line.

The problem is how to add sufficient value to the product so that, when everyone around is discounting, your sales remain strong.

Is It Worth It?

Earlier we looked at the trends that are shaping buying habits and discovered that consumers evaluate nearly every purchase decision, saying to themselves, these four deal-maker or heart-breaker words. "Is it worth it?"

A Mercedes won't get you to the ballgame any faster than a Chevy. Yet many apparently intelligent people find a way to justify the extra expense to purchase what is in reality just another automobile. Ask them why they made, what on the surface appears to be a foolish decision, and the best response you are likely to get is a simple, "It was worth it."

Well, what makes any purchase "worth it?"

Why will people pay far in excess to acquire one brand, and haggle for days over the purchase of another?

Simple. Some purchases are just, "worth it."

Value can be added by:

- Improving the product.
- Improving the service or support provided.
- Improving the relationship between the customer and the product.

New Improved!

Improving the product can be as simple as giving the product more value, not by adding value, but by making obvious the value that already exists. (See "Tangible," Chapter Eleven.)

If the product is physically improved by creating another model, then it is necessary to make certain that the customer is fully aware of the added features, and that those features are both desirable and meet the "is it worth it?" qualifier. Too often a salesperson throws out a pitch for features that are nice, but not seen by the customer as being anywhere near worth the increase in price.

When you pitch to the "is it worth it?" standard, better to be thought of as being just a bit too pricy than to earn a response of "so what."

Recently, we considered switching our database management software. The saleperson for the competing brand faxed us a long list comparing the features and benefits of both our current and the potential new software products. We were buying the proposal, beginning to see a real need. But as we got further down the list, the features that were touted became more and more esoteric, until we finally started reacting to each new feature by saying, "So what?"

What started out to be a professional and highly effective sales pitch turned into a confirmation for our original choice of software.

Make absolutely certain that you answer the "is it worth it?" challenge with real features and benefits, real and relevant to the customer at hand.

But Not on Price

Recently, a friend of ours told us a story about how his brother, the owner of a small building contractor's supply business, employed a surprising technique to counter heavy pressure from a very large, deep discounting competitor.

His tactic was simple to the point of elegance. He went to his customers and potential customers and said, "Tell me what I can do to earn your business besides being the lowest price in town."

Right up front, he verbalized what everyone already knew...that there was no way that he could compete on price alone. Once the truth was on the table, everyone was able to relax and concentrate on what turned out to be bigger issues.

His customers wanted service. You know, things like special hours, delivery, and the ability to special order without hassle. And what do you suppose happened? Sales went up in double, sometimes triple digits! Sure, there were some customers who had to make price the main issue. But who on this planet thinks they can satisfy 100 percent of the market 100 percent of the time?

At lunch today, I buried myself in the Lands' End catalogue and, in addition to great merchandise at reasonable prices, I was rewarded with this little gem: "We price our products fairly and honestly. We do not, have not, and will not participate in the common retailing practice of inflating mark-ups to set up a future phony 'sale.' "

Lands' End is telling us that we can rely on them to price their merchandise consistently throughout the season. We never have to worry that we paid too much for an item that would be half price in the next catalogue. I like that and I bet you do, too.

More importantly, I bet your customers appreciate not having to outthink another retailer. They can see quality merchandise and order it anytime, thinking only about the goodie that will soon be theirs to claim, without the worry of whether or not their timing was right.

The customers you lose over a few cents on the price tag must sometimes be considered as not-your-target-market in the first place.

If You Can't Beat 'Em

If you can't beat 'em, then, why in the devil would you want to join 'em? Decide right now whether or not you are in the commodity business.

If you are, decide to be nice to your customers but read no further. *Positively Outrageous Service and Showmanship* have not much place in your business.

If you are still reading, then decide this: "Price is never going to be the main issue in our business."

You can't outdiscount Sam Walton when it comes to selling commodity items. He can buy toilet paper and detergent cheaper than you if you were a 100 times larger than you are.

So stop trying to beat the discounters at discounting. Beat them at service. There you still have a chance.

If you need something to worry over, then worry that the big discounters will figure a way to provide the service and selection that right now only you can provide.

Not long ago I heard a story about a small girl who was scheduled for surgery. Her dad wanted to make the experience less intimidating. When he asked his daughter what she would like to take with her to the hospital, she mentioned a popular stuffed toy.

Unfortunately, the hour was late and the only place that he knew carried the toy was a nearby Sam's Club. Hoping against hope, he called the store and was surprised when a cheerful voice answered.

It turned out to be part of the night stocking crew. He explained his situation, and asked if there was any way they could save him one of the toys for pickup first thing in the morning.

"If you want to come right now, we'll have it for you."

When he arrived at the store, not only were they waiting with the toy, but he was told that it was a gift. The crew had chipped in to purchase the toy as a little encouragement for their unseen friend.

If you want something to worry about, worry about that.

The world of discounters operates on K-Mart time. K-Mart makes it a point to be open when customers have time to shop. Did I miss something or is this just so elementary that it should be obvious? If you want the world to beat a path to your door, make certain that it is open when they get there. Operate on K-Mart time.

While you are worrying about the discounters waking to the customers' non-price needs, consider this, please.

In the do-it-yourself business, one of the key reasons that people do not buy is that they don't know how to complete their do-it-yourself project. So projects either get done by a contractor or they don't get done at all.

The thinkers in the home center industry discovered that if they offered clinics to show people how to confidently use the products they sell, they would sell more of them. When was the last time you heard of a small hardware store owner giving a clinic to teach customers confidence building tips on home improvement projects?

When was the last time you saw any small business present a clinic? The best and least obvious example of a business using clinics to build both confidence and sales has to be Avon. They show women how to look and feel better by using Avon products. They make it easy. They make it fun.

What can you do to make it easier, more fun, or less threatening to purchase and use your products?

More

Ask your customers what you could do to make it easier to do business with you. Maybe longer hours are the answer. Maybe your return policy is a problem. How are you at delivering the product? Is your product in stock, available in the right quantities, and with just the right features to do the job without going overboard?

Are the directions easy to read? Is the color right, the weight appropriate, and is maintenance simple and not messy?

Does someone answer the phone promptly and is it the right person? Why does an untrained receptionist answer the line to the parts department other than to irritate us? Do you have a voice mail system that frustrates potential customers with long lists of options and endless commercial messages?

In the end, there is no point in giving more than passing consideration to the questions posed here. There is only one way to find out how to improve your service. Ask your customer.

But be careful. Asking your customers is dangerous because they are the ones who have chosen to endure your product and service for their own peculiar reasons. Be certain to ask people who are not your customers. Ask them to tell you why they choose not to do business with you. Just remember that there is no hope of being all things to all people.

Positively Outrageous Service as a Marketing Strategy

When we discovered the value of surprising our guests by delivering just a little more than they expected, we began to look for more ways to make them say WOW! Then we surprised ourselves at the many ways it could be done.

Surprises are not only fun, there seems to be no end to the creative ways you can pull them off.

Remember, please, that the purpose of Positively Outrageous Service is to create memorable customer service stories that are so special to the customer that she will be compelled to tell others. We're talking about nothing more than the reverse of negative word-of-mouth.

"Random and unexpected, out-of-proportion to the circumstance and the customer is highly involved," defines service that could be Positively Outrageous Service or merely outrageously awful service. The difference lies in whether the customer's expectations were exceeded or not met at all.

We know that people will talk about customer service, but only if what they get is different than what they expect.

The focus of Positively Outrageous Service is to surprise the customer just every now and then.

Our printer, Wally, at So Fast Printing has the concept down pat. Not only does he print our quarterly IdeaLetter, he reads them. Last month we asked Wally to print another batch of letterhead for the office. The job came back as usual. On time, neat and professional. Just what we expected.

A couple of weeks later, Mom came in with a new batch of Wally's work, and more. On the bottom of the stack were four bundles of beautiful note pads, neatly emblazoned with our logo. Everyone said, "WOW!" and wondered who had had the great idea and commissioned Wally to print the pads.

You're getting ahead of me!

It turned out that Wally had botched the first run when he printed our new letterhead a couple of weeks earlier. There had been a very small ink smear near the bottom of the sheet. Most printers would have said, "Good enough," and let things go at that. But not Wally.

Wally reprinted the job and, rather than toss the ruined pieces, he saved them until he had time to cut them down to note paper size, pad and shrink-wrap them, and slip them into our regular order as a surprise. Do you think we nickel-and-dime Wally on every order? Of course not.

Improving the Relationship

There are four simple tactics to improving your relationship with your customers through marketing.

- Have fun.
- Get people to your property.
- Involve the product.
- Do something good for others.

Just for the Fun of It!

Fun is a serious business tactic? You bet! In fact, fun is the number one way to get the customer involved with the product and the servers. If you want to create a relationship, then fun is the way to go.

If you are tired of Southwest Airlines stories, don't blame me! Get out and have some fun with your customers and I'll write about you! In the meantime, check out these fun ideas:

To inaugurate four new flights between Los Angeles and Las Vegas, Southwest hosted a dozen or so Elvis wanna-be's to a trip to the Golden Nugget casino. At the gate, the Elvi (that's plural for you know what) treated a huge crowd of the curious to crooning and posturing. The youngest Elvis was barely seven years old, and an elderly version of the departed hero rounded out the pack.

On the flight, customers were treated to pre-flight announcements performed to the tune of "All Shook Up," plus a few spontaneous renditions by the "real" impersonators.

Now, that's not what you would expect on a typical airline. But then, there is nothing typical about Southwest, not even the planes. Southwest has a plane painted to look like Shamu the killer whale and another decked out like the flag of Texas.

As long as we're traveling, how about M. E. Valdez, a bus operator for the VIA Metropolitan Transit System in San Antonio? Board Valdez's bus and you'll be treated to a running commentary describing the local sights. You could pay big bucks for this kind of showmanship, but get on the right bus in San Antonio and admission to the show is only 40 cents!

Remember, the best way to know if your marketing is Positively Outrageous is to ask yourself this question: "Is it newsworthy?" As surely as you want your customers to have stories to tell, if a reporter were presented with your idea, the first question out of the box would be whether or not the story was "man bites dog" or just another ho hum, "dog bites man."

The media are a cinch to attract and work with, as long as you keep their needs in mind. They want an interesting story and they want to get it as easily as possible. If you have an interesting story, the media folks appreciate your call or news release. If you don't have a truly newsworthy piece, then don't call the media. First of all, that's not the way to cultivate trust and friendship. Second, if you become a pest you may find yourself getting coverage that you don't want.

To make certain that the coverage you get is the coverage you want, help out by providing a clear and complete factsheet for your event. If you can write an interesting news release, do it. But if writing is not your strong suit, leave it to the pros.

Media people are just like the rest of us, they are over-worked and under-appreciated. If you want to write the entire story and hand it to them labeled as a press release, do it. You may be surprised to see it printed word for word. And best of all, they will be your words.

When you are interviewed, be certain to answer the questions that the public needs answered or that you want to answer. Just because a reporter fails to ask the right questions doesn't mean that you shouldn't go ahead and answer them anyway! Remember, reporters may be covering a dozen other stories and may not always share your enthusiasm for telling your story.

Any use of the media is a form of marketing. Any form of marketing contributes to your image. So be careful that even your commercial advertising reflects your corporate values and corporate personality.

Our commercials have always been carefully tailored to express our intention to run a fun kind of place where quality and service add value to the product. We had dozens of comments over the following radio commercials:

Fishin' Fun

Hi! This is Scott from Church's Chicken. Ah...I know you haven't heard from me in a while. I, ah, went to Europe. Yeh, that's right...uh to have lunch with...Princess Diana. I came back on the Queen Mary...nice boat. And she's a nice girl, too. Now, while I was on the Queen Mary, I was fishing—from the stern— and I caught the most wonderful fish. And I brought some back for you! You know, I don't really *like* fish but *this* is good stuff. We only serve the very best up at Church's. It's light and flaky and white and moist on the inside and kind of crisp on the outside with a wonderful, wonderful lemon seasoning. It's really, really good stuff. I mean you're gonna love it...even if you don't like fish, you're gonna love it. And if you do like fish...Whoa! This stuff is gonna send you to the moon.

All right, so I was kind of fibbing about the Queen Mary and all. I actually went over on the...Concorde. Yeah, that's right. They let me pilot it and we caught the fish with nets. They were flying fish.

This is Scott at Church's Chicken. Don't forget to love one another!

More Fish

Hi! This is Scott at Church's Chicken. See? I told you our new fish was some kind of wonderful. And now you've tried it and realize that maybe fish isn't so bad after all. So, just to make things interesting, I have another deal for you.

Order any of our terrific fish specials and you can add an ear of corn for the great, big bank-bustin' price of a quarter. Now I know that corn is a vegetable, but it isn't like I was trying to feed you broccoli or some other green stuff that tastes like weeds.

No, this is corn on the cob. Big, juicy, sweet and delicious. You liked the fish so trust me on the corn. Heck, I think corn is really some kind of fruit that some high school science teacher mis-classified as a vegetable. Plus, the corn you get at Church's isn't that little weenie stuff they sell at other places.

Now you just ride on over to Church's and have yourself some more of that delicious fish and add in a big juicy ear of corn for a quarter. For a measly quarter, you can throw it out if it doesn't suit you and at least you'll be able to look your Mama straight in the eye when she asks if you've been eating your vegetables.

See you at Church's...and don't forget to love one another!

Add fun to your daily routine and watch productivity soar. I know, on the face of it, when people are having fun, they're not working. Not true. When people are not having fun, they are thinking about anything but work. Fun, and a little competition, makes the day go fast as well as putting a little spring in everyone's step.

A grocer that I know installed a window between the produce

department and the back room cooler where fresh produce is prepped for display.

"I want our produce manager to be able to see our customers and be available if they have questions," was his explanation.

"Why don't you answer their questions before they ask?"

"How could we do that?"

"Well, I always see people squeezing the tomatoes and such to see if they are fresh. You could visit the local Radio Shack and get a small speaker that would hide easily in the tomatoes. Then when you look through the window and see a shopper squeezing the tomatoes you could talk through a microphone in a falsetto voice and say, 'Ooh! ooh! Careful, please! I'm as fresh as fresh can be!"

"Then you could make direct contact when you pick them off the floor!"

I have no idea why I put that story right here. I just like it.

Come Hither

The second tactic of POS Marketing is to get people to your property. Too often we are tempted to sponsor events that take place somewhere besides our store. Bad idea!

There are thousands of events that need to be sponsored, so our suggestion is to limit your participation to those events that get people to your property.

When the March of Dimes asked us to help sponsor their annual walk by providing T-shirts, we said a quick and final "No!"

"Gee, we didn't expect that you would say 'no.' You have a reputation for saying 'yes' to almost anything that helps the community."

That may be true, but we only say "yes" to things that help both the community and our business as well.

"We'll be happy to sponsor the March of Dimes, just not with T-shirts. Why don't you let us help you lay out the route? It can start here and we'll give everyone a hot honey-butter biscuit to start. It can end here and we'll give a piece of hot, delicious chicken to each finisher."

Our attitude is that if we can get our product into your mouth, you will be a customer. So, the goal of any promotion is to get you to our property and have you sample our product. Notice please how well our offer served both our needs and the needs of others. There is no way that we will sponsor anything that doesn't move folks onto our property.

Involve the Product

Okay, so your property just doesn't lend itself to a customer visit. Before you dismiss the idea out of hand, at least give another thought to having an event at your place. Just make sure that your place represents you well.

But here is an absolute...never do any promotion that does not involve your product.

At our restaurant, we don't do any promotion that doesn't in some way involve the product. We have had our customers eat our product, wear it, swim in it, push it, and spit it, but always the product is involved.

My favorite promotion had to be our crowing for biscuits promo.

Our franchisor decided to offer a nine-piece combo with side goodies for $9.99. It did not include biscuits, so we decided to throw in the biscuits for another dollar or make them free to anyone who was willing to crow.

Now, this was not a particularly pretty promotion. It turned out that the people in Kerrville are closet crowers.

Judging by the response that we got, folks must have had one heck of a pent-up desire to crow. We would say, "Would you like to add the biscuits? They're four for a dollar or free if you would like to crow."

"You mean crow like a chicken?"

"Yes ma'am, unless you have special training in crowing like a rabbit, a rooster version will be just fine."

Well, they would start to scratching at the floor with their feet, flappin' their little wings and bobbin' their heads like they had been preparing for this moment for years. Then they would rear back and let loose with a sometimes blood-curdling crow followed by a slightly embarrassed look that begged for an ovation.

One lady crowed in her car while sitting at the drive through. First she looked into her back seat, probably to check that none of her neighbors had stowed away. Then she let loose a crow that rattled windows for blocks. Actually it was more of a shriek, kind of air-raid quality with overtones of machinery in severe distress.

When she began to calm down and her breathing transitioned from a husky gasp to a heaving, though teary-eyed, rhythm, she looked up and as calmly as she could manage said, "Was that crow enough for you?"

The crew was in shock. Most had been unprepared for this perform-ance. Jesse had been cooking and by the time the crow had begun to decay, he was covered head to toe with flour. That's the impact this woman had. Finally, traffic out on the four lane began to move, although we could hear the faint wail of emergency vehicles n the background.

"Yes, Ma'am. I'd have to say that was one of the finest we've heard and we've heard our share."

"Well, where are my biscuits then?" she smiled weakly.

"Ma'am, I'm not certain, but I think they are on the seat of your car. I do believe you've done laid your own biscuits!"

If there was one problem with the great crow for biscuits promo, it was that the folks who participated seemed to have discovered some sort of lost human craving to feel close to their animal cousins. For months after the promo ended, customers would come into the store and very sheep-ishly say, "Can I crow?"

"Sure. It's okay. We're all friends."

There are other less dramatic examples.

The folks at Butterball have one of those products that doesn't really lend itself to an on-premise visit. Would you really want to show off a few thousand dead, naked turkeys in various stages of slaughter? Not me!

But Butterball still gets into the act by sponsoring dinners for their grocer-clients. And of course, turkey is the main course. What makes the evening special is that a whole turkey is delivered to each table. A chef is appointed for each table and it is the chef's duty to carve the turkey.

The chefs are given a commemorative carving set and chef's hat. As they carve the turkey, Butterball employees take instamatic pic-tures as a further memento of the occasion. Nice touch and definitely showmanship!

The Subway sandwich people have been both good friends and great clients. One favorite story comes from Troy, Alabama, where Bob and Patti Dinsmore have captured both the hearts and business of their neighbors through creative marketing.

Subway sandwiches just happen to be shaped like little tasty footballs. Not only can you eat them, they throw pretty well, too! The Dinsmores appear at local football games with a cooler of fresh Subway sandwiches. Whenever the local team scores, the band plays a hot rendition of "Subway My Way," while the cheerleaders throw Subway sandwiches into the crowd.

We've heard that when the team is behind and in need of scoring, the crowd chants, "Subway! Subway!"

Now that's showmanship in marketing. And while the Dinsmores won't take all the credit, attendance at the games has increased dramatically since they began this spirited promo.

Another way to look at this idea of involving your product is to keep in mind that you can also leverage your expertise. Always try to avoid donating money, no matter what the cause. Donate your time and talent. Donate your services. These have residual value, to both the public that you serve and your company as well.

As an additional benefit, donating of yourself is a much more tangible expression of your concern for the community than the donation of dollars. Dollars are soon melted into the general fund account and their source becomes obscured, a fact that does not serve your need nearly as well as leveraging product and service.

Do Something...Good

The neatest marketing tactic is doing something good for others. Call it the Law of Harvest, call it heads-up marketing. Whatever your orientation, doing something good for others comes right back to you. If you are the nicest person on the planet, you'll want your marketing to do something good for others. If you are the scum of the universe, you'll want to market the same way, simply because it's darned good business.

Muriel Siebert & Company has made 'charity marketing' a way of business and a way of life. Siebert sells new issues of securities in underwritings, which by itself is nothing out of the ordinary. What is special about Siebert is her promise to donate part of her profits on each sale to a charity of choice.

Typically, Siebert donates one-half of the commissions received, less clearing costs. To date, Siebert and her clients have sent generous checks to such causes as Habitat for Humanity, Citymeals-On-Wheels, Los Angeles Philharmonic, and the University of Pittsburgh.

Other companies have found that charity marketing is as good for the soul and the team as it is for the bottom line. We don't know any company that is involved with charity marketing with the intention of increasing sales, although increased sales are the inevitable result.

Southwest Airlines, there we go again, doesn't seem to have a policy on charity marketing. They are simply nice people.

A few years ago, a Southwest pilot discovered that an acquaintance was involved with the Ronald McDonald House, a home away from home where families of seriously ill children can stay and find comfort when they are in town for their children's treatment.

The pilot had lost a daughter to leukemia a few years earlier and said that, although he was emotionally unable to help at the time, he would help in the future.

A few months later, the pilot called and asked if he and a few other pilots, flight attendants, and other Southwest employees could cook and serve a family-style meal to the folks at the Dallas Ronald McDonald House.

The rest, they say, is history. Today, the Southwest family serves the dinner meal once or twice a month at Ronald McDonald Houses all along the Southwest route system. As Herb Kelleher said in a wonderful commercial created by Southwest on behalf of Ronald McDonald House, "We came over to fix dinner for friends and ended up falling in love."

You'll fall in love, too, when you put the corporate heart and pocketbook to work for good causes. Our only reminder is that since it is physically and fiscally impossible to say "yes" to everyone, say "yes" to those organizations that may in some way help your organization... because only a healthy business will be around to serve others.

Huntington National Bank of Columbus, Ohio, has taken charity marketing to new heights. Wishing to promote its lending program to inner-city residents, the bank enlisted the cooperation of inner-city churches. Because parishioners had little trust in financial institutions, the bank decided that a boost from the pulpit would be just the thing.

Under the Community Reinvestment Act, the bank was required to actively promote its services in lower-income neighborhoods. And because traditional advertising wasn't working, the bank came up with the idea to target the minority market in a less traditional way.

Today, marketing is done by and through the churches with the church receiving a $15 to $250 referral fee for new accounts.

Ben and Jerry's, the ice cream guys, must have a million ideas for charity-centered marketing. They have a free franchise program for non-profit organizations that will agree to operate a Ben and Jerry's shop and donate a percentage to charity. They sponsor concerts and a traveling circus. Those guys *are* a traveling circus!

But listen to what Heidi O'Conner of their marketing department says about this style of marketing.

"This way we give our customers the opportunity to make a decision based on personal experiences, as opposed to giving them an image that we want them to believe in."

Stop for just a moment and think about what giving your customers an opportunity to make up their own minds through personal experience could mean for your business. Now think that this is how you already operate! It is precisely through personal experience that customers decide whether or not to do business with you.

Our point is that, instead of letting advertising drive new fodder into the cannon of poor service, we should control the customer's experience from the beginning. If you must advertise, then market (and train), too. This is the only way to control the experience.

Have fun, get people to your property, involve the product, and do something good for others...that's the recipe for marketing that gets attention and builds relationships.

I walked into the restaurant and immediately noticed a woman reading our "Pride Wall," a small bulletin board where we post newspaper clippings and other evidence of community involvement.

"Excuse me. I'm the owner of this chicken outfit and it makes me nervous to see my customers waiting."

"Oh, I know you," she interrupted. "You're Scott Gross and I'm waiting for my okra to cook. They told me that you don't like to have it up in the afternoon because it gets cold. They promised me that it would be worth the wait, so I don't mind waiting at all."

"Well, they told you the truth but I still apologize for the wait."

"I don't mind, and I want to tell you how happy I am that you have great fried chicken."

"I'm glad we have good product, too. Why are you so happy?"

"I'm happy because of all the good things that you do in this community. I'd have to eat here even if it wasn't."

'Nuff said?

Grabbers

Everything that happens, that contributes to the customer's experience of your service or product, is marketing. Everything.

Smart marketers manipulate the environment to create mini-events or experiences with the idea in mind that customers will tell stories about their visit. We call these mini-events "Grabbers."

Grabbers are unusual, often out-of-context, experiences. They may be purely visual or they can involve the server. Whatever the case, grabbers arrest attention and make you think.

Grabbers can be as simple as choosing an unusual name for a product. We had trouble moving dark pieces of chicken, so we ran a special on "three-legged" chickens.

Grabbers are helped if you make up a little story to give the customer a verbal framework for the story you want them to tell.

"How's a three-legged chicken taste?"

"Well, we really don't know. They're so fast that this is the first time we've been able to catch one!"

Michael Hurst, a Florida restauranteur, added a seafood item to his menu, simply because he discovered that the fishermen who caught them referred to them as "bugs." Hurst knew instinctively that, while people may not like the idea of bugs in a restaurant, they no doubt would order them by the ton if properly presented.

And speaking of bugs in restaurants, Dick Chase of the University of Southern California, tells of visiting a Mexican restaurant in Boston and seeing a mouse repeatedly run out from a stack of Dos XX's beer to nibble crumbs on the floor. When Chase mentioned the mouse to the manager, the response was a surprising, "Mouse? Oh, you must mean Harry. Everybody knows Harry. Do you know what the good news is?" (Chase was at a loss.) "The good news is that mice and rats don't co-exist!"

So whatever you name it, even if it is a potential liability, have a little fun and you'll turn it into a story that will be told again and again.

As long as we're out to lunch, here are a few out to lunch restaurant names that single-handedly lasso customers:

Aunt Chovy's Pizza, Mar Vista, CA

Thai Me Up Cafe, Los Angeles, CA

Bermuda Schwartz, Winnipeg, Canada

Mei Luck, San Antonio, TX

Grabbers can come in any form. The Piggly Wiggly Supermarket in St. Charles, LA borrowed football jerseys from the local high school team and wore them the day before the opening game to show their support and team spirit.

If you show up at the Western Heritage Credit Union in Alliance, NE on your birthday, the computer will alert the employees and you will find yourself serenaded by an impromptu all-kazoo band. Now that will get you talking!

Thrifty Car Rental has made a science of Grabbers. System-wide, they throw what they call "Theme Days" that turn out to be fun, not just for the customer, but for the employees as well. Rent from Thrifty on a Theme Day, and you'll leave with both a car and a story.

First there was Smile Day, a day where every employee had as their primary mission to make the customer smile by doing whatever it takes. In Las Vegas, customers were greeted by a costumed showgirl and invited to pose for an instant photo. The reaction seemed to depend on whether or not the customer was alone or with golfing buddies.

Single men tended to be shy, but men in packs were the animals they are made out to be.

One Thrifty Theme Day was called "Secret Word" because customers who said the secret word were treated to a turn at a large wheel of fortune where they could win Thrifty Bucks, good for discounts on future Thrifty rentals.

Of course, the van drivers discretely let the secret word out of the bag, and customers across the country were contriving to work the word "smile" into everyday conversation. Everybody turned out to be a winner because the smallest prize on the wheel was a free upgrade. Now that would put a smile on a road warrior's face!

Another Theme Day, centered around golf, had customers putting for upgrades and also just for the fun of it. Who wouldn't rather be golfing than dragging through yet another airport?

And best of all, everyone gets to play. Whether it's the van driver who dresses for Halloween or the customer service representative who participates at the, yes, dunking booth, Thrifty has made dealing with Thrifty and working for Thrifty...F-U-N!

Karen Stickle, of Thrifty Las Vegas, said it all when she reminded us that, "We also do things for our employees...we surprise them, too!"

Call Betty at (800) 635-7524, Monday–Friday between the hours of 9 AM – 4 PM (Central) to order a videotape of Scott's keynote, Positively Outrageous Service.

CHAPTER TWENTY-FOUR

Bigger than Life

It's 32-feet long, 15 1/2-feet high. Blood runs from its steel teeth and flames shoot a blinding 20 feet into the air. It's a car. Sort of.

It's also a rolling broadcast booth that seats 20 on plush couches, designed to be "awesome and terrifying, yet fun; unique, yet ultimately cool."

Rick Hensler of Universal Studios of Florida is its master and because it is larger-than-life, it was easier to fund than a new fax machine!

Larger-than-life may be the operating phrase that guides the fun at Universal Studios. There, an unusual combination of talent, ride-techies, and movie people has created an experience worthy of the larger-than-life label.

When Universal Studios started to think about a marketing vehicle to promote their new and definitely larger-than-life attraction—Jaws, The Ride—a real vehicle was exactly what the inhouse dreamers dreamed.

The Jaws machine, called The Land Shark, is a Mad Max meets Spielberg publicity stunt-on-wheels. It gets a mention here only because it is indicative of the thought processes that put showmanship to work on a daily basis at the world's largest movie studio and theme park.

Some people have all the fun. They work in a business where customers specifically pay to play. But while the circumstances at Universal Studios may not closely resemble those at the average service company or retail store, the lessons we can learn will apply just about anywhere.

The first lesson must surely be that larger-than-life gets attention. Hensler is much smoother than his background with Barnum and Bailey might suggest. He defines showmanship in terms that would make a yuppie marketer feel right at home. But according to Hensler, the definition of showmanship may legitimately vary depending on the industry.

At Barnum and Bailey it was "excess. Do it big. Do it loud and in your face."

Showmanship gets a fancy definition at Universal Studios. Says Hensler, it is "a combination of planned attractions, activities, entertainment elements and street surprises."

A secret of Universal Studios must be the unusual gene pool of its creators. While most theme parks have a decidedly cartoon look, Universal Studios looks like the operating film and video production studio that it is. When movie set designers get together with designers of high-tech amusement rides, something magic happens. The high-tech experience is heightened by the meticulous attention to detail of the sets.

Hensler is amazed that customer surveys rank Universal Studios as the best of the best when it comes to cleanliness, yet, for example, the New York set comes complete with cracked sidewalks, discarded chewing gum, even realistic pigeon droppings. (Apparently Bob and Edith from Waterloo, Iowa know fake dirt from real dirt and appreciate the difference.)

Fun begins with people. Think you have problems finding good help? Try hiring quality people in a market where there are more hotel rooms than in any city on earth. The secret, if there is one, is in sticking to your standards and hiring only the best of the best, even when it may be tempting to "settle."

Hensler says that hiring is the most important step in the process of creating the showmanship at Universal Studios. "You can't train people to like people."

You can train people to act like Bullwinkle or his pal Rocky, but only after you have people who are naturally "nice, who just want to make people happy."

As for the Rocky and Bullwinkle training, after you have someone of the right height to fit the rather size-specific costumes, there is plenty to know about how costumed characters move and react.

But one major difference in the people department sets Universal Studios apart. Rather than ask people to stick to carefully prescribed scripts, Universal Studios "doesn't strip people of their personalities. We don't want all of our people to act the same. We want them to be themselves. It's more legitimate."

Once in the park, guests naturally expect to be entertained, but it is the unexpected that makes the difference. Universal is careful not to put all of the planned activities on the daily program guide.

Think about it! Here is the old saw that advises us to underpromise and overdeliver. That, and the very concept of Positively Outrageous Service, is to surprise the customer on a random, unexpected basis.

Surprise is a key element of showmanship and universal Studios delivers in a big way. From the street performers who pop up unexpectedly to the thrill of discovery in the new Jaws ride that you are under attack, Universal Studios has cooked up a surprise for every turn.

Probably the best surprise of all comes from how Universal Studios handles lines. In Positively Outrageous Service, we talked about waiting as an opportunity to make the guest say, WOW!

Waiting is one of the surest ways to diminish the perceived value of a product or service...unless you can figure a way to make the wait part of the product.

Lines at Universal Studios have been incorporated into the ride itself. For example, while waiting to ride the skies with E.T., the guest enjoys spectacular scenery and is reminded of E.T.'s dilemma, his need to get back home.

By the time guests reach the mechanical portion of the ride, they are already part of the show.

If there is one thing that the average business could learn from theme parks in general, it is the idea that waiting need not be a distraction. It can be part of the fun.

One other easy-to-overlook lesson begging to be learned from Universal Studios is the idea that Spielberg calls, "Riding the Movies." Because the guests have, for the most part, seen the movies upon which the rides are based, something more emotionally is at work than simply enjoying the ride. Guests bring with them to the experience, all of the feelings that they felt while watching the movie—sort of a double emotional whammy.

The same is true for any business. They say that you are only as good as your customer's last visit. What you do for the customer today colors expectations for the next visit.

But at Universal Studios, "We try to go so far beyond what anybody anticipates. And once you get beyond 'very good' to WOW, it leads to word of mouth."

Couldn't have said it better myself!

CHAPTER TWENTY-FIVE

Last Call

I've never seen a sprite. But I have talked with one. She was my last call and honestly, I was just too tired of writing to really want to talk to anyone else. True, the people interviewed for this book have all been delightful, the kind of folks that you would like to invite over for dinner.

Most were strangers, friends of friends, or people who had a reputation for being the best in their business. When you get involved with a subject like showmanship or Positively Outrageous Service, a funny thing happens. You find yourself spoiled by being around such nice people. The subject just doesn't attract people who aren't 100 percent wonderful.

We had done all the interviews and everyone had been grand. They were fun, interesting and I was pleased that some universal truths had emerged. We only passed on one interview, because the person we had thought would be a neat guy didn't pass the "Mom test." When Mom called to try to set up the interview, she had said that this person had been sort of arrogant and although not rude, not at-all like the others.

I didn't bother to make the call. Besides we had plenty of interviews already completed or scheduled. So one more or less wouldn't have made all that much difference.

I had hoped that Sherry Moreau would be out of town and I could call it quits.

When she picked up the receiver, I knew in an instant that my luck was better than my attitude.

Moreau has one of those jobs that most people don't consider a job at all. They just don't realize how much raw talent and sometimes gut-busting work is required to be a professional actor. This actor is different because she specializes in corporate productions. About half of her work is at tradeshows. The other half is sales meetings.

Few Americans realize just how elaborate corporate productions can be. But think about it. If you're putting on a program for 10,000 or more, you want it to be BIG.

Asked what she thinks is showmanship, Moreau said, "Being able to to sell an idea with pizazz."

Of course, selling a company and its products to an audience that is far from captive, such as at a trade show, is no small talent.

Almost by definition, Moreau's audiences are sophisticated. They are the buyers of usually big-ticket merchandise, or franchisees of large corporations. So if you can move this kind of audience you are a pro. Sherry Moreau is just that.

"I want them to leave knowing that they have had a nice time, and with a good feeling about what the company is."

"So, you're kind of like a salesperson?"

"I've often wondered about what is the difference."

What is the difference? Sell an idea, sell an emotion? There doesn't seem to be much disparity between the two. And the techniques are pretty much the same as well.

When Moreau first started, she worked with a client that manufactured modems. Twenty-five years ago, modem was hardly a household name. So Moreau was recruited to create a character who would help take the mystery out of the curious black boxes that, to the customer, worked exactly like the ones offered by the competition.

That year, Moreau appeared as a parody of herself, a character named Sherry. She played the devil's advocate, attempting to show that she had an idea that would do the job just as well at half the cost. Dragging elaborate props onto the stage she would inevitably run into, in the end her invention would explode, proving once again that her client's product was the best choice.

Today, the Sherry character is still dragging out ever-more elaborate props, always leading to the same disastrous end. Showmanship pays. Her client has created Sherry dolls, Sherry alarm clocks, Sherry you-name-its.

Knowing your audience is key. Sound familiar?

"This is good," Moreau warmed to the question about how to read an audience. "The same way that any performer...a salesperson, for that matter, would do it. If you feel you've made a mistake, you leave quickly but nicely. Use your sixth sense.

"I've thought about it. I'm always watching the audience. If I see someone who is a good audience participant, I know there is a good candidate. When there are women in the audience, I know it will be a good audience."

We stopped for a laugh, wondering if we had just agreed to a sexist statement. But I agreed that, no, women really do make a better audience. They laugh more easily than macho-thinking men.

"Women are great laughers and if you can get one woman laughing, the rest of the audience will follow."

We agreed that audiences in Las Vegas at eight-thirty in the morning are not "in fun." Nor are audiences of franchisees who are meeting in Orlando, a mile from Disney World on a sunny, winter afternoon.

And there are audiences that you expect to be great that turn out to be awful. Like the show she did in Belgium, secure that the script had been slowed enough to take into account for an international audience. Too bad they all were wearing headphones so they could hear the translation! So much for timing!

Are there universal truths that may apply to business as well as the stage? Moreau says, try these on for size:

"To imitate someone else's style is always wrong."

"To find out what you are comfortable with and go with that, is always right."

"People like to laugh. The most serious people in the most serious industry like to laugh. And laughing helps remembering."

"Here's a basic. If it's script, learn your lines before you begin to ad lib. You can't make a script your own until you know the original."

"Three-inch heels really hurt."

CHAPTER
TWENTY-SIX

Fiesta!

There are days that stick in your memory. Something special that made the time spent stand out over other days that would be forgotten, passed into personal history as ordinary. One day—a short visit, really—to Fiesta, Texas stands out for me.

I got to look showmanship in the eye. I was invited to play...a switch, since it is usually me that does the inviting.

What I learned is that I've been right all along. Showmanship is a universal concept, applicable to absolutely every endeavor. But I had never really met someone who I regarded as an artist, a practitioner of showmanship, a master of theater.

In high school, I was what my friend and neighbor, Grady Fort, calls a "band weenie." I was easy to spot, tall and skinny, tootin' my clarinet as we marched at half time. So I missed all the stuff that you learn from the drama teacher. Besides, I've never thought a great deal of drama teachers or their students. Sorry, but we produce video, and it's nothing more than a fact that if you want someone to overact and sound about as natural as a Bubba sipping chardonnay, then hire a local thespian for hockey results.

So, here comes an apology to all of you who may have actually learned something of value in high school drama. And here's an invitation to everyone to visit Fiesta, Texas, where you will have the pleasure of seeing some of the finest performers on either side of the Pecos.

They call it "Streetmosphere." Herb Henson is its writer and director. I forget his official title, but Creative One will do in a pinch. In 1972, Henson developed the concept of Streetmosphere for Renaissance Faires.

In a few words, Streetmosphere is the art of taking the show to the audience. It is theater performed in the artificial streets of fairs and theme parks.

The goal of Streetmosphere is to involve the audience and make *them* the stars of the show.

Not everyone who has ever aspired to act can be successful playing a role on the street. Most would need the support of elaborate props and even more elaborate scripts. With Streetmosphere, you are on your own in a continuous game of improv. Of course, there are pre-scripted bits and routines but, in the heat of the street, you are at the mercy of the crowd.

We often see street performers who have been hired to entertain at special events. Henson says that too often these performers are no different than a poorly trained salesperson. "The character will intimidate the audience and the audience will walk on the other side of the curb to avoid them. You see that a lot with mimes and clowns.

"The reverse happens as well, when the actor becomes too intimidated to approach the guest."

Quick! Pay attention! This applies to you!

"The solution," says Henson, "is to find the happy medium by learning to read your audience and know how far to go, who to go to, and how to approach them. It's a sales job.

"You need to be able to read the customer and know how much they'll go along with you, trying to include them in the improv with your character."

It turns out that, not only are the concepts of acting applicable nearly one on one with the business world, few of the terms need much translation.

Henson is a former restauranteur who observes that, "Everyone's in show business. When a customer sits down to eat, what do they watch?"

They watch the waitstaff, the cooks, even the person cleaning tables. "So make it fun to watch."

Close your eyes. Are you hearing an acting coach, an airline executive, or a restauranteur? You can't tell from the words, that's for certain.

So what makes a good "show-off?"

"It's less a matter of being quick-witted than just listening and making eye contact. It's genuinely caring about your guest.

"I tell my people that when guests leave the park, I want them to say, 'Boy! I met some wonderful people today...and...oh!...by the way, weren't they entertaining?'

"The objective isn't that we are so entertaining or that we are so witty...it's that we were so...gregarious (willing to share who we are).

"In improv, the objective is to make the other person look good."

Auditions are a way of life in the acting profession. But as Henson is quick to point out, "This applies to any job. You can make it mechanical and boring or you can make it full of life and fun for the customer."

When he auditions for new actors, the process is rigorous. He wants to be absolutely certain that the actor he hires is perfect for the role. Not bad advice for the rest of the business world.

The hiring decision is roughly weighted 60 percent on personality, 30 percent on talent, and 10 percent on plain, old gut feeling. Notice please, that while Henson's Streetmosphere performers are among the finest to be found anywhere, only 30 percent of the decision is attributed to talent.

Henson asks auditioners to read a one-minute monologue and, on follow-up auditions—there are always more than one—the performers are required to show their stuff in improvisation exercises.

The "games," as Henson calls them, "are to see how willing they are to take risks."

Playing with customers is risky business. If you are not willing to risk your own embarrassment, it's not likely that anyone will have much fun.

We asked a Streetmosphere performer, a young woman with a basket for a hat, what it takes to be successful playing with customers. In spite of the ridiculous costume, she is a very talented actress and insightful as well.

"You've got to take risks, have fun, love your audience and be yourself."

Sounds like a Henson student to me.

Henson's rules are simple and few. But the greatest rule we learned from Henson himself. "Rule number one is to love your audience. Whether or not they love you is immaterial. You love them. And when that happens, it's real hard not to love somebody who loves you."

Call Betty at (800) 635-7524, Monday–Friday between the hours of 9 AM – 4 PM (Central) to order an audio tape of Scott's Positively Outrageous Service and Showmanship.

CHAPTER TWENTY-SEVEN

Bug Management

So how does a guy who writes and speaks about managing customer service organize his own company?

Easy! Bug Management!

It looks a little like a bug, our disorganization chart, that is. Only this bug has no head, just several. Five to be exact, odd-looking appendages that loosely represent the major divisions of skill and labor in the group.

Based on five key principles, our bug management concept is the very hallmark of democracy and empowerment. First, the principles:

Have Fun

Intelligent Risk

Ownership and Incentive

Consensus Management

Love One Another

And at the center of it all, Customers First! We decided right up front that if something isn't right for our customers, it isn't right for us. In fact, in the early stages of creating our management model, one of our associates leaped to the board and corrected a drawing that showed our mission statement at the center of a set of concentric rings.

He put "Customers" in their place, before mission or anything else, for that matter.

We want to always be the first to ask our customers how we can better serve their needs. And we darned sure don't want to be in the position of cutting corners, if the result is a product less than the customer deserves...our customers deserve the best value we can produce.

After years of working at jobs, we are all ready to have an avocation, something that you do because you want to do it. Of course, we believe that "If you are not willing to sweat, you're not cut out for our team." Overall, if it's not going to be fun, what's the point?

Too many people think of their work as the dues you pay to have fun when it's over. Well, life's too short and work is too long for work not to be fun and rewarding.

We once heard mental health defined as the ability to take intelligent risk. Certainly that describes the climate at healthy, growing, innovative companies. Intelligent risk isn't a matter of spending foolishly, but it is a practice of investing in new ideas and giving people an opportunity to grow. The moment a company gets addicted to ever-increasing returns, innovation is dead in the water.

The best way to encourage team spirit: Make team goals and individual reward inseparable. We want everyone on our team to have measurable goals and then be rewarded on the basis of their performance. Small salaries, big bonuses for outstanding performance will be the rule.

And wouldn't it be nice to be able to use the words "my company" and really own a piece of that rock? Ownership is where we're headed.

Consensus management may sound easy, but when new directions require unanimous votes of the managing group, only well-thought out ideas are likely to be approved. Since it takes a 100 percent effort to make a new idea fly, we decided it should require a 100 percent vote of support before the first dime is spent.

Love one another. That's been said before, but it never happens too often. Why not create a company that truly is for the people who get things done? Why should there be unnecessary layers of management, when politics can cost a company its very existence?

We've seen companies destroyed by politics and have learned the hard lesson that politics kill.

A bird's-eye-view of our organization consists of a series of concentric rings. In the center is the customer, our reason for existing. We're here to serve, and that requires that the customer be placed right at the middle of it all.

Surrounding our customers is our mission. The mission comes out of our focus on the customer. It is simply stated as "Have fun and make the world a better place, while becoming number one in customer service management."

The next ring out represents those five founding principles discussed earlier. The principles support the mission.

And finally, we have the organization itself represented by the five members of what we call our "Peer Council." There is no president, titles are only assigned for the comfort of our customers, but internally they are meaningless.

While we are small, every employee is welcomed to attend our peer council meetings, although voting is limited to the five peers after they consult with their staffs.

From the beginning, we had three "business imperatives" that have served us well:

Take fun, challenging projects.

Work only with honest, enthusiastic clients.

Get paid commensurate to our contribution.

These principles brought us to the party. They have helped our hard work pay off. And we think that they will continue to serve our "disorganization" as long as we never try to work the "bugs" out!

Call Betty at (800) 635-7524, Monday–Friday between the hours of 9 AM – 4 PM (Central) for a free copy of our IdeaLetter.

CHAPTER
TWENTY-EIGHT

Accolades of POS

Yogi!

His name is Yogi. And if you ask him, he is the best cabbie in all of Chicago.

I haven't had the opportunity to ride in Yogi's cab, but if my mail is any indication, he must be one heck of a marketer. Several folks have sent me copies of a newspaper article describing a ride with this fantastic, freeway flyer.

Yogi decorates his cab to suit the season. At Christmas, he wears a Santa hat and manages to string lights throughout the interior of what would otherwise be nothing more than another cab.

Once he has you inside, Yogi takes it upon himself to see to your entertainment. He makes full use of the tape deck acting as a driving DJ and taking care that you hear at least one commercial message that reminds you that you have been fortunate to have been selected for the "best cab ride in Chicago."

Signs hanging in the cab echo the same slogan, and Yogi does his level best to keep the promise.

Now, if that isn't showmanship at its basic best, I don't know what is. It also proves that in any business, it is the details that make the difference.

Bon Jour

Bon jour! This is Pierre, the chef.

I've just finished the last two days baking. You must try my fresh French bagettes. They're waiting for you either through room service or at Chez Colette.

Bon appetit!

So goes the French-accented recording that serves as a wake-up greeting for guests at the Hotel Sofitel in Minneapolis.

Now that's showmanship! Any ideas what it does for the sale of pastries?

Carl's Clown

Jeff Haring sent an article from the Thousand Oaks (California), *News Chronicle,* saying that it "reminded me of your book."

The article is a half-page spread on a fellow by the name of John Campbell who, according to the paper, is "...the David Letterman of the fast food drive-in...serving up laughs along with every hamburger that's ordered."

John works the drive-through precisely because it is an extra difficult position from which to reach out and make people feel good, an area in which John is apparently an expert. Because he can't see his customers, he has to wait for their response to decide if they are 'in fun.'

"If they start laughing, then I know that I can go further with them."

John calls artificial sweetener "chemical additive," and house dressing becomes "condo dressing" in keeping with the local economy.

Okay. So he's not all that funny. But he does add pizazz where it is seldom seen, and he does have a loyal following of customers who come in to watch the show, even if it's not what you would call prime-time material.

And perhaps that's the point. You don't have to be a polished performer to play. All you need is a little chutzpah, the willingness to step out of the box and take a chance.

Thank You

Shopping by catalogue may be convenient, but people like Melanie and I miss the relationships that develop more naturally when you become a regular shopper at a local store. So it is doubly important for catalogue companies to work on establishing a relationship that develops customer loyalty.

Smart catalogue merchants use the same models issue, after issue and many include folksy messages that give insider information about the company. Lands' End includes a small insert for first-time shoppers that tells the Lands' End story of life and business in rural America. Such efforts to make tangible the company usually pay off in customer loyalty.

Bedford Fair is one of Melanie's regular catalogues. Maybe the small card that was enclosed in a recent order, helps explain why. It said, "So that you may enjoy your purchase more quickly, this shipment to you has been upgraded to Priority Mail or Airborne Express at our expense. It's our way of saying 'Thank You' for your business."

Line Drawing

The Subway franchisee in Selma, Alabama has discovered an interesting way to make waiting in line desirable. Once each week, on a random basis, customers who are waiting in line for their Subway sandwich are given a number. A drawing is held to determine the lucky number, with the winner receiving a Subway T-shirt or some other prize.

A little creativity has made waiting in line fun...and sometimes rewarding!

Play Ball!

One facet of Positively Outrageous Service is that it is so out-of-proportion to the circumstance that it stands out, creating compelling, positive word-of-mouth. Doing something just a little bigger and bolder is the key to standing out.

CIT Group takes this idea seriously. To help attract corporate accounts, they send a baseball autographed by sports legend Willie Mays to the chief financial officers of a carefully targeted group of potential client companies. Their simple request is that the recipients keep CIT in mind for future financing needs.

Also mentioned is that an additional baseball, this one autographed by Stan Musial, is available in exchange for completing an enclosed reply card. And a third baseball, autographed by Mickey Mantle, will be hand-delivered if a sales representative is granted an appointment.

According to the *Wall Street Journal,* CIT's investment of $17,000 resulted in all three balls being delivered to 89 of the 96 targeted CFOs. The results? A whopping $60-million dollars in new loan business!

Unexpected Crunch

In Kentucky, we called it a "sussy." Others call it serendipity. Whatever you call an unexpected gift or pleasure, it's almost as much fun to send one as it is to be on the receiving end.

We purchase all of the music used in our video production business from a first-class outfit named Omni Music. Early on, we decided to only do business with nice people. And were we ever right-on-target to choose Omni Music!

In addition to delivering top-notch production music, the folks at Omni are always good for a pleasant conversation or even a surprise.

When we opened the carton containing the latest music update, out fell a note and a candy bar called "Rainforest Crunch," made entirely with Brazil nuts harvested from the rainforests, sort of a save-the-planet and eat it, too, proposition. The note read that if we were 'feeling the crunch,' it might be a good idea to take a few minutes to enjoy a snack and listen to the latest from Omni Music.

I tossed the note but saved the bar until I could share the idea with you. Mmmm! That's delicious!

Adopt-a-Child

Friends at Piggly Wiggly decided to put up an adopt-a-child Christmas tree in their supermarket. The tree was decorated with dozens of small envelopes, each with the first name of a child in need of a little help from Santa.

Inside was a card listing the child's age and two gifts, one that the child needed, like a sweater or such, and a second that the kiddo wanted.

Customers were encouraged to select a child and return the presents a week before Christmas.

Within six hours, the tree had been picked clean by shoppers thrilled with the opportunity to do something good.

A second tree was soon erected.

Merry Christmas!

Waffle Hello!

Walk into the Waffle House restaurant in downtown Covington, Kentucky and discover what they mean by southern hospitality. Every customer, and I mean every customer, is greeted by the friendly folks on duty.

Most customers are known by name, but even strangers don't remain strangers for long. Someone has either done a first-class job of hiring or a first-class job of training. It takes a special crew to have everyone on duty greet every customer. It made me say WOW!

American Greeting

Flight 227, 1-18-93, SAT-DFW.

"Hey, it's me again. The temperature at this altitude is right at 61 degrees below zero. So we ask that you keep your hands and arms inside.

"At takeoff, we weighed just over 300,000 pounds. Forty-eight thousand pounds was fuel, 4,000 was baggage and, between you and me, we weighed in at about 22,000 pounds which probably indicates that it's time for me to go on a diet!

"We took off at 173-miles-per-hour and are doing about 521-miles-per-hour at the moment. That's not any record, but it sure beats the old Volkswagon."

Thrifty Miami

Linda Korbel of Howard Johnson had an important meeting scheduled in the Florida Keys. More than important—she was to lead the meeting. When she arrived at Thrifty Car Rental in Miami, she was ready to hit the road. Too bad she had everything but her driver's license.

Unable to rent her a car but concerned that the teacher would miss the class, the rental agent offered the next best solution, a personal driver all the way to Islamorada. Now that's Positively Outrageous Service!

Really Big Limo

San Antonio has a tourist attraction that is rarely listed by the Chamber of Commerce, but should be. The local public transit system, VIA, is an award-winning operation, due mainly to the quality of its bus operators.

One story involves two gentlemen who decided to use the Park 'n Ride service to attend a San Antonio Spurs game. They parked their car at a lot on the northwest side of town, took the VIA special to the game, after which they hopped back on board for the return ride to their car.

Boy, were they surprised to discover that they had taken the wrong bus to the opposite side of town! Instead of a short drive back to their hotel, they were now faced with the prospect of a late-night cab ride, if they could find one.

"No problem," said operator C.H. Solis, who promptly radioed that he would be a taking a "long cut" back to the garage. Talk about happy customers!

What Do You Want? Blood?

We often complain that getting good service is like getting blood out of a turnip. Well, at Dane County Credit Union, you get more than just good service, you can even get a pint of blood. At least that's what happened when Lisa Smith, a member service rep, found out that one of the members had suffered considerable blood loss during an operation and needed donors.

Smith, on her afternoon off, literally rolled up her sleeve and went to work!

Says President Linda Wilkenson, "These employees never cease to amaze me!"

Me, too!

Get Along, Little Meter

In Texas, we rope steers just for the fun of it. But what do you rope if you are living in New York City? A cab? Well, at the Cowgirl Hall of Fame Restaurant in Greenwich Village, they rope parking meters.

Looking for an interesting way to involve customers in the experience of the old west, restaurant owners held a roping contest curbside.

"We're a struggling little place, and we don't have a promotion and advertising budget like the big chains do," reported co-owner Sherry Delamarter.

Okay, Sherry. But what do you do with a parking meter once you've caught it?

Fresh!

Just to prove their point that the food is always fresh at Chevys, a west coast Mexican restaurant chain, an advertising campaign was rolled out that was fresh as the food itself. Chevys prides itself on the fact that, to make certain that everything they serve is fresh, fresh, fresh, and to make good on the promise, they have banned anything that is canned or frozen from their kitchens.

Now they have a fresh ad campaign that really makes the point that at Chevys, absolutely everything is fresh. Chevys commercials are aired the same day that they are shot. To prove it, they include a shot of the headlines from the morning newspaper!

Delta Was Ready *Before* I Was!

The good folks at Delta Airlines helped to sponsor a seminar put on by my friends at the Orlando/Orange County Convention and Visitors

Bureau. Part of Delta's contribution was to provide my air travel.

After I presented Positively Outrageous Service to nearly 800 enthusiastic folks, Delta decided to try out the concept...on me!

As the seminar was about to end, my associate, Cindy Harris, came in with the news that Delta had called to say that my flight had been changed.

They had found room for me on a flight that left later but arrived in New York, my next stop, earlier than the previously scheduled flight. Nice surprise! But the real surprise came when handing in my old boarding passes for reissue.

The new ones put me in first class! They love to fly...and it really shows!

New Friends

Racing to the airport at the end of a pleasant vacation in the Bahamas, Trudy Sanders and her husband realized that they needed a quick lunch to tide them over until they could be fed on the plane. They are not your typical fast-food customers at home and they wanted to avoid starting the habit if at all possible.

Unfortunately, they had managed to pass all of the acceptable candidates before a Subway sandwich shop became their last option.

Inside they were greeted by a pleasant young woman, who seemed to go out of her way to introduce herself and her product to these first-time visitors. Much to their surprise, the food was as fresh and pleasant as the conversation. The deciding moment came just as they were about to leave. The franchise owner marched proudly to their table and presented them with two fresh from the oven, gourmet cookies.

"We'd like to have our two new friends remember us kindly."

That's Positively Outrageous Service and not surprisingly, guess who are now Subway's biggest fans?

As an associate of mine put it, "One franchisee somewhere got a whole lot of business for franchisees everywhere!"

Southwest Airlines Donated Over 600 Tickets Last Christmas to Financially-Strapped Senior Citizens

"I want to thank you for a wonderful trip. I won the 'Home for the Holidays' promotion that your company has every year. I was able to see my sister who has cancer.

"I want to thank you again, because without this opportunity I would not have been able to see her."

—Frances Prichard,
Dallas, TX

And POS Works for Internal Customers as Well

Here's a sample from...Surprise! Southwest Airlines!

"In August, our plane was in Reno and our crew had 40 minutes of groundtime. We three flight attendants went about cleaning the plane and folding seatbelts. Two RNO ramp agents, Scott Fowler and Roy Beatrice, came up and said, 'You girls quit cleaning and go and get yourselves something to eat and relax a little.' When we returned, Scott and Roy had not only folded every single seatbelt on the plane, they also cleaned it as if it were a terminator. They even went so far as to vacuum.

"This was definitely above and beyond the call of duty. They had a busy day on the ramp, but then to come up and clean our plane was definitely not their required job duty. They took a real concern for our feelings and an understanding of our lifestyles as flight attendants."

— Genie Cunningham,
PHX Flight Attendant

Smooch!

"Recently, I had an experience with Southwest Airlines that I would like to share with you because it really made quite a wonderful impression on me.

"It was May 20, 1992, and I was dropping off my boyfriend. His flight left Indianapolis at 2:30 PM.

"As we approached the counter, the lady greeted my friend, checked him in, and informed him that the plane was ready to leave, and to please hurry. Our good-bye was sad because we knew we wouldn't see each other again until school started again in the fall, but it was also very hurried, which really bothered me. But as I tearfully watched him walk down the jetway, a man tapped me on the shoulder, and told me to 'go and say good-bye to your man!' It turned out to be the Captain of this flight, who then escorted me to the front of my friend's airplane. He told me that he would allow me to say goodbye to my 'man' as long as I repeated what he said.

"The Captain then got on the PA system (and mind you the plane is completely full and ready to go) and asked for everyone's attention. I saw my friend finding his seat in the middle of the plane. The Captain then handed the receiver to me and said, 'Say goodbye, Chad. I love you,' which I did with tears running down my beet-red cheeks! Chad looked to the front of the plane and saw me and ran up and gave me a hug. In the meantime, the whole plane has said in unison, 'AAAHW,' and then broke out in a loud round of applause!

"I then had to say goodbye to Chad because the plane was ready to leave. I thanked the captain and flight attendants who were there. This experience makes up one of my fondest memories, and I won't ever forget it."

—A.C.,
Barrington Hills, IL

Play Ball!

August 16, 1992, Mr. Sheerer came out to the Tulsa Airport to inquire about a flight to Houston, so he could go and see his grandson play softball. Sheerer required the use of a wet cell battery-operated wheelchair. Southwest Airlines Customer Service agent, Sandra Buckley, told him Southwest Airlines could transport him and his wheelchair. He was so excited when Sandra gave him the news, that he left our counter thrilled about the trip and happy with the service that Sandra had provided. He could not wait to get home, share his excitement with his wife, and call his grandson.

Thinking about his trip, Sheerer got in his van and drove off, failing to reposition his wheelchair lift in his van. As he drove away, the extended lift hit the car in front of him, causing that car to hit another car in front of it.

Once Sandra realized that Sheerer was the gentleman involved in the accident, she immediately went outside to see if he was all right and to offer her assistance. Sandra got very involved at that point.

It seems that after the accident, Sheerer told Buckley that he would have to refund the ticket because he could no longer afford to go to Houston. The cost of repairing the lift on the van would be approximately $5,000. The van had to be fixed because his wife was ill and had to go to the doctor's office for medical treatments. Her reliance on a wheelchair made repairing the van a necessity.

With much regret and tears in her eyes, Buckley voided the ticket, but did not give up hope of figuring out a way to make Mr. Sheerer's trip possible. After long deliberation, Buckley pulled out that "Positively Outrageous Customer Service" — this time it was her own credit card — and purchased Mr. Sheerer a roundtrip ticket. She then called him and told him that he WAS going to see his grandson play that softball game after all!

Southwest Airlines Comments:

"Why, we even ran an employment ad once that stated, 'Work at a Place Where Wearing Pants Is Optional.' "

Perhaps Vice-President of People, Ann Rhodes, said it best, "We look for people who color outside the lines." When people are hired at Southwest Airlines, they are not expected to check in their individuality at the door. It's just the opposite—they are strongly encouraged to use it in whatever way makes them feel comfortable. And wasn't it that zany CEO Herb Kelleher who said, "We take the competition seriously, but not ourselves."?

Customers Tell Us...

"Yes, we occasionally receive complaints from customers who feel that joking over the PA system and/or playing/having fun with our Customers is in poor taste—that such activities have no place in an airline environment. But we get very, very few of these letters. We do, however, receive literally hundreds of letters each month commending us for making flying fun again!"

— *Colleen Barrett,*
Southwest Airlines

"...the flight was scheduled to leave at 9:10 PM, we boarded at 11:15...needless to say we all were anxious, tired, and frustrated. When your crew sensed the tension of the passengers they responded. In all my years flying, I rarely paid attention to the takeoff instructions—they are boring. However, the German accents of Hanz & Franz (from Saturday Night Live) captured the attention of all. The tension was soon replaced with laughter. We want to thank your crew.... Please keep up the good work and we will be back!"

"As a corporate-travel manager, I am in the habit of ignoring the routine flight instructions, but, in this case, I was immediately attracted by (your) presentation and delivery. This was great entertainment for which the other passengers applauded. And, I am convinced that everyone who applauded her humor also knew what to do for their personal safety."

Going the Extra Mile

One of the many ways to providing "Outrageous Service" is by turning negatives into positives. Here's a story from the Richmond Savings Credit Union, Steveston branch, where Lee Edwards did just that.

A member who had received business checks with no holes punched in them came into the branch and spoke to Edwards. He could have just apologized for the error (printer's fault) and returned the checks to Intercheque, but the member would have had to wait (more time) for the checks to arrive again.

So instead...Edwards drove over to Steveston Printers, had them punch the holes, and then personally delivered them to the business client.

Would You Like a Pizza with Those U.S. Drafts, Sir?

A Broadmoor member (Richmond Savings Credit Union) recently came into the branch during his lunch break to purchase four U.S. drafts. He needed them mailed to Houston, Texas, ASAP. Jo-Ann Kwantes discovered that only three U.S. drafts remained in the whole branch. Needless to say, the member was not very pleased.

Kwantes immediately offered to make a fast trip to Steveston Service Centre for more drafts, and to have the drafts ready for sometime later on in the afternoon. Unfortunately, the member would not be able to get back to the branch before closing time. No problem. Kwantes then offered to drop the completed drafts off at the member's house on her way home from work!

This potentially irate member ended up extremely impressed with the service he received, and left with a very positive view of Richmond Savings! Way to go, Jo-Ann Kwantes!

For the Positively Outrageous Service Record Book

"Here is a story straight from the dog-eat-dog world of Southwest Airline's our front-line Customer Service agents. During the summer of 1989 (you might say, the dog days of that long summer), Ontario Customer Service Agent Joni Hallmark was working the ticket counter when a customer checked in with his pet. A dog. A big dog. A big, mean dog. Hallmark does not remember what kind of dog it was, just that it was a 'killer dog.'

"Well, the customer wanted to take his dog with him on vacation. When she told him that Southwest does not transport animals, the customer's fangs began to show; both the man's and the dog's. In short, neither customer was very happy. It seems that our human passenger had to make a connection, using non-refundable tickets, with another carrier down line. He *had* to get on his planned flight. He could not rebook, nor did he have the time to make arrangements for his dog. As Hallmark said, 'What was the guy to do?'

"She graciously offered to take the man's dog home and care for it over the length of our customer's entire two-week vacation! Since the mongrel's name has been long forgotten, let us call him 'Bagtag.' Naturally, Bagtag's owner did not provide a dog cage, because he expected the airlines to do so. Consequently, Bagtag spent the rest of the day chained to a baggage cart. A cart no one could go near except Hallmark. Needless to say, the ramp agents were greatly relieved when she took Bagtag home at the end of her shift.

"For half a month she fed and entertained Bagtag, who repaid her kindness by tearing up the grass in her new backyard. The cost of Bagtag's upkeep came directly from her own pocket.

"Eventually our customer returned from his vacation; a truly restful experience, because it had been a vacation from Bagtag as well. He retrieved his dog and went on his way, never fully realizing what Hallmark had done for both of them. Without a doubt, this is a story of Positively Outrageous Service that leads the pack."
—*Submitted by Mark James Boyter, Phoenix Captain*

A Builder's Square customer came to Karen Schwenk in Mishawaka, Indiana asking to purchase a grill as a gift for a friend. She said that she wanted to bring the friend into the store later that day to receive it.

By the time the customer and her friend came back into the store, Schwenk had decorated the box. Nice touch!

Sandy Hensley at Builder's Square in Canton, Ohio has a real sense of ownership.

When a customer asked her if this was her department, she told him, "If I can help you in *any way,* that *will* be my department."

A customer came into Builder's Square in Peoria, Illinois and asked Mark Grimshaw to order some parts for a lamp that had been broken. Upon investigation, Grimshaw learned that the lamp had been discontinued. So he found a display model, but it was dented and scratched...so he had the customer bring the broken lamp into the store so that the parts could be swapped.

The customer was extremely impressed with Grimshaw's ingenuity and great customer service...and so are we!

Chris Rempe at Builder's Square in Kansas City, Missouri was asked to leave the service desk and help cover plumbing, because they were short-handed. A customer called to see when her faucet—which she had a rain-check for—would come in.

Rempe found out that no order had been placed for the customer's faucet, but that there were four faucets on hand.

When he returned to the phone, the customer had hung up. Rempe went to the courtesy desk and looked through all of the rain checks on file and found the one for the customer. He then called the customer with the information needed.

Now that's POS!

Positively Outrageous Service is a matter of surprising the customer. But this story is a first because it surprised the *author!*

Corporate executives at Morris Air were pleased but not surprised when they received a call from a mother who said there weren't enough words to adequately compliment the flight crew on her family's flight to Orange County. They were taking their son, Tommy, to Disneyland for his 6th birthday, and that was exciting in and of itself. But, to add to the moment, once the plane had gained altitude, the flight attendants summoned Tommy to the front of the plane and then the entire plane, led by the enthusiastic crew, serenaded him with a rousing rendition of "Happy Birthday." Then, to put the "icing on the cake," at the end of the flight the pilot, Sam Parks, took Tommy to the cockpit, sat him in his seat and took a picture of "Captain Tommy." Needless to say, this was a birthday Tommy and his family will never forget, thanks to a Captain and flight crew that demonstrated Positively Outrageous Service!

"Captain"

The surprise for me was that Sam Parks used to fly corporate aircraft for Church's Chicken. Back in the "old days," Sam and I put in plenty of hours rattling around the country in a twin engine prop job, and later in a jazzy Lear jet. He pulled some stunts then that definitely wouldn't win friends from commercial passengers, but he was practicing POS long before I gave it a name. (Also, he always managed to be low on fuel near Jacksonville, Florida, where Sam knew a place that sold "fried" ice cream.)

A friend at Morris Air, based in Salt Lake City, writes:

"There are times we 'mess up'—and then it's scramble time to make amends and, at the same time, take advantage of a golden opportunity to demonstrate Positively Outrageous Service. The following is just one example:

"Last spring, a couple planning to honeymoon at one of our Getaway destinations in Mexico, found themselves without their tickets and necessary vouchers and time was running out. Needless to say, the customers were very stressed so, in the spirit of POS, Brandon and Josh from our Ticketing Department, saved the honeymoon by driving 200 miles roundtrip to personally hand-deliver the tickets to the eager newlyweds."

Now that's POS!

Thrifty

The Thrifty crew in Detroit really got into the Smile Day fun and won our National Smile Day contest. Their winning entry featured a dunk tank set up on the Thrifty lot. Thrifty customers were encouraged to "Dunk the Competition" and win prizes ranging from frisbees to discounts on their rental or free upgrades. Detroit customers were also treated to a special souvenir caricature of themselves, professionally drawn as they completed their rental transaction.

Football-n-Fun Day was held in conjunction with the announcement of the Thrify Car Rental Holiday Bowl Sweepstakes contest. Many locations for Football-n-Fun Day served hot dogs and soda. Footballs were thrown through hoops or at targets for free upgrades and discounts. Other rental centers had their local high school band perform.

In October, 1992, two days of scary fun were held in celebration of Halloween at Thrifty rental centers nationwide. Rental agents wore costumes of all sorts. One rental agent came dressed as a safety dummy while others sported gangster outfits, cheerleader togs, and other creative costumes. Our San Francisco location held a "Scariest Face Contest." Customers were asked to make their scariest face and a rental agent then snapped a Polaroid of the customer. Each participant was given a free upgrade at the time of rental as well as a followup letter thanking them for participating in the fun.

The one day set aside for lovers, February 14th, was a big hit at Thrifty locations throughout the U.S., except we celebrated for a week. A "Show Us Your Kisser" contest was held in several locations, with participants receiving discounts and upgrades on the spot.

La-keen-Ta!

If there is an award for showmanship in marketing, then it has to go to La Quinta Motor Inns, a friend of value-minded travelers for years. Their new management has decided to add a bit of personality to the chain and solidly target what has been their bread-and-butter all along, the business traveler.

The hundreds of thousands of road warriors, who drag to their rented cars every business morning, heading out for another cup of coffee and yet another sales call, have known for years that if you want a clean, safe room at a pocket-friendly price, La Quinta is just the place.

Now La Quinta has them in the bulls-eye of target marketing.

We were blown away to discover that an audio tape came as part of the monthly update of our La Quinta Returns program. In addition to a jazzy newsletter, the tape included travel tips and even an interview with the one and only Zig Ziglar. We preach the importance of talking to your customers but now, La Quinta actually does it!

How many road warriors must tool along the highways listening to one Jimmy Buffett tape after another? Then here comes a tape from La

Quinta. Oh, sure, throw it in the briefcase. There will be plenty of time to listen on the long stretch between Fort Worth and El Paso. The bonus comes when it's discovered that the tape is really well done; it's interesting, professionally produced, and out-right useful. It's an invitation to stop at the end of another rough day.

We called La Quinta to get the full scoop and, in the process, cajoled a few secrets. Sorry, we can't tell what's coming up next. But, trust us, it's really different, almost cost-free, but will do more to establish a relationship with regular guests than pajamas with feet!

Call Betty at (800) 635-7524, Monday–Friday between the hours of 9 AM – 4 PM (Central) to order an audio tape of Scott's Positively Outrageous Service and Showmanship.

CHAPTER
TWENTY-NINE

Hi! This is Scott

Maybe I'm just not all that creative, but since the beginning of this grand adventure, "Hi! This is Scott," has been an opening line that has served me well.

Nineteen years ago, I used that line to introduce myself to a cute, brown-eyed PBX operator at the company where I worked.

She was in Santa Monica, California and I was somewhere on the road in New England. I was a road warrior then, and still am today. Then it didn't matter when I got home, since there was no one at home to make being home important.

But that was then, and today there is nowhere on earth quite as nice as being home in beautiful Center Point, Texas. And if you haven't guessed, that brown-eyed operator is waiting at the door everytime I come dragging in. She's still cute, too!

We have a son who looks amazingly like me and the cutest "daughter-ette" a Dad-in-law could want. The kiddo is a super salesman, honest and customer-service minded like no one I know.

We have worked hard—first trying to make a go of a restaurant business—before we finally figured the combination that later was christened Positively Outrageous Service. Then came the arduous process of building a service-training company to allow us to share the ideas that made the difference for us. Twelve and fourteen hour days have been the rule, not the exception.

But when you are working with someone you love, doing things that seem to matter, the hours don't seem to be that much of a problem. So maybe the day 19 or so years ago, when I transferred my call to the marketing department to find out if that operator was as cute as she sounded, was not such a bad idea after all. Hey! Opening lines are only dumb if they don't work.

Now that we are looking for ranch property so we can invite our friends (clients) to visit and experience Positively Outrageous Service in person, we're going to close a long, tough, and fruitful chapter to give us a better focus on what is just over the horizon.

94.3 on your FM dial, Hot Country KRVL
June 10, 1993

Copy: Hi! This is Scott, formerly of Church's Chicken. You heard me right, I said formerly. Melanie and I have decided to turn our attention to other projects and leave the chicken to someone who can give it the attention that you, our valued friends and customers, deserve.

The past eight years have at times been difficult. In the beginning, we ate more chicken than our customers. But we also had fun, and maybe that's the biggest lesson that we have learned. Business, whatever it is, should be fun.

With your help, we've taken a little chicken store and made it grow. We enjoyed country western music on the old patio. We dropped ping pong balls on the parking lot, and we enjoyed seeing customers crow for free biscuits. Mostly we've enjoyed working with some of the nicest young people ever.

We've made a lot of friends and we hope to continue seeing them at Church's, where we know you will always get the very best chicken in town and our idea of Positively Outrageous Service.

Over the years, we had several opportunities to sell, but resisted until we could find just the right buyer who would be best for our community and our crew, who we think of as our family. The new owners are Ronnie and Janice Bowen. Not only are they good operators, they are good people, too.

Melanie and I say thank you very much for your kind support. See you at Church's...and don't forget to love one another.

CHAPTER THIRTY

Manager's Tool Box

Foreword

Serve well
Have fun
Make a difference
Love one another

Positively Outrageous Service

Random and unexpected
Out-of-proportion to the circumstance
Invites the customer to play
Creates compelling, positive-word-of-mouth

Outrageous Service

Random and unexpected
Out-of-proportion to the circumstance
Customer is highly involved
Creates compelling, negative word-of-mouth

"In Fun"

Psychologically ready to play

Controlling Trends

Aging population
Declining leisure
High-tech requiring high-touch to balance *
Polarized buying habits
  *John Naisbett

To Give POS

Suspend anonymity—"Flirting"

Scott's Law of Expansion

Business will expand in direct proportion to the number of winning employees that can be found. Hire all the winners—get all the business!

Three Marketing Mindsets

Believable
Convenient
Desirable/exclusive

Auditions

Simultaneous
Top management involved
Employee input
Customer input

Audition Techniques

Monologue
Echo
Simultaneous story
Phone call
Mirror

Leadership Principles

Passion-charisma
Flexibility
Risk-taking
Servant leadership

Opening Lines

Develop a standard patter as a guide.
Watch for trigger words.
Encourage experimentation.
Provide masks and costumes, real or imaginary.
Best encouragement is a good example.
Start by playing on the phone...it's easier!
Watch for opportunities to play.
Watch for customers who are "in fun."

How to Flirt

Look, listen, test.

A Few Good Lines

Hi! It's great to see you again.
That's what I got.
I'm Gladys Knight. These are the Pips.
Introduce yourself with an amusing way to remember *your* name.

Creating Ownership

Invest in individual employees.
Make sure the company works for the employee (benefits).
Resist titles and too much policy (suspend estrangement).
Invite everyone to share their ideas.
Adopt great ideas and give plenty of credit.
Make first mistakes risk-free.
Serve "sacred cows" for lunch.
Provide plenty of support: Time, tools, training, and
    encouragement.

Elements of Signature Showmanship

Surprise
Theme
Do-able
Non-topical
Careful about core values
Participation—optional
Included in the price
Impromptu
Make decor part of the show
Decorate the employees (costumes!)
Consider group showmanship
Make showmanship a department

Retail Theater

Listen to the customer.
Dare to be different.
Take good ideas and run.
Commit to be the best.

"E's" of the '90s

Entertain
Educate
Environment

Nike Values

Customers first
Authenticity (deliver *your* personal best and make a customer,
    not a sale)
Risk
Innovation
Commitment
Team value

Creating Fixation

Cadence
Imagery
Pitch
Tone
Body language

Tangible Value

Share insider's details.
Tell about the obvious.
Create a myth.
Add a label.
Brag about the exception.
Name it.

What's In, What's Out

In	*Out*
Nike	Reebok
Leadership	Management
Teams	Organizational charts
Stories	Policies
Training	Winging it
Sharing	Hoarding
Respect	Egos
Communication	Indispensability
Quality	Getting by
Relationships	Overreaching
Innovation	Habit
Listening	Commanding
Dreaming	Dozing
Pro-act	React
Profit	Perks
Preparation	Gut reaction
Caring	Taking for granted
Professionalism	Profanity
Future	Past

Non-Rules for Showmanship

Do everything bigger.

Do what hasn't been done.

Do old things in a new way.

Ignore nay-sayers.

Management by Walking Around (MBWA) Questions for Customers

What did you think of our service today?

What could we do to make your visit more enjoyable?

Where else do you shop for...?

Who do you think is our biggest competitor? Why?

What could we do to get you to come in more often?

What other stops are on your list today?

Do you know anyone who is unhappy with us? Why?

How did you hear about us?

How often do you do business with us?

Why did you decide to shop with us today?

Tell me how we're doing!

MBWA Questions for Our Internal Customers

What could we do better?

Why did you decide to apply here?

What are we doing that is really stupid?

Tell me what may be getting in your way.

What do you hear from our customers?

What are we doing that really bothers you?

How could we improve our product or service?

Do you have the tools and training that you need?

About the Author

T. Scott Gross is a master at removing mystery. His ability to communicate complex ideas simply comes from years of hands-on training, primarily in the hospitality industry.

When not speaking at conferences and conventions, Scott handles the day-to-day operations of one of the nation's most unique service training companies.

Scott is best known for his high energy platform skills. His gentle humor keeps audiences laughing while they learn handfuls of practical ideas. Whether speaking to a corporation or a national association, Scott is a storyteller extraordinaire, comfortable with audiences of any size. He is most at home with professionals who have high customer contact.

Scott has helped some of America's best-run organizations design video-based training programs, intended mostly for employees with direct customer contact. He has discovered how to be the low-cost provider of quality video training and marketing programs.

Scott has turned his skills as a script writer and platform performer into three fun-to-read books: *Positively Outrageous Service—New and Easy Ways to Win Customers for Life, How to Get What You Want from Almost Anybody,* and his latest, *Positively Outrageous Service and Showmanship—Industrial Strength Fun Makes Sales Sizzle.*

Additional copies of *Positively Outrageous Service and Showmanship* may be ordered by sending a check for $12.95 (please add for postage and handling $2 for the first book, $1 for each extra copy) to:

MasterMedia Limited
17 East 89th Street
New York, NY 10128
(212) 260-5600
(800) 334-8232
(212) 348-2020 (fax)

Scott Gross is available for speeches and workshops. Please contact MasterMedia's Speaker's Bureau for availability and fee arrangements. Call Tony Colao at (800) 4-LECTUR.

Other MasterMedia Books

To order MasterMedia books, either go to your local bookstore or call (800) 334-8232.

POSITIVELY OUTRAGEOUS SERVICE: New and Easy Ways to Win Customers for Life, by T. Scott Gross, identifies what the consumers of the nineties really want and how businesses can develop effective marketing strategies to answer those needs. ($14.95 paper)

HOW TO GET WHAT YOU WANT FROM ALMOST ANYBODY, by T. Scott Gross, shows how to get great service, negotiate better prices, and always get what you pay for. ($9.95 paper)

OUT THE ORGANIZATION: New Career Opportunities for the 1990's, by Robert and Madeleine Swain, is written for the millions of Americans whose jobs are no longer safe, whose companies are not loyal, and who face futures of uncertainty. It gives advice on finding a new job or starting your own business. ($12.95 paper)

TAKING CONTROL OF YOUR LIFE: The Secrets of Successful Enterprising Women, by Gail Blanke and Kathleen Walas, is based on the author's experience with Avon Products' Women of Enterprise Awards, given each year to outstanding women entrepreneurs. The authors offer a specific plan to help you gain control over your life, and they include business tips and quizzes as well as beauty and lifestyle information. ($17.95 cloth)

SIDE-BY-SIDE STRATEGIES: How Two-Career Couples Can Thrive in the Nineties, by Jane Hershey Cuozzo and S. Diane Graham, describes how two-career couples can learn the difference between competing with a spouse and becoming a supportive power partner. Published in hardcover as *Power Partners*. ($10.95 paper, $19.95 cloth)

WORK WITH ME! How to Make the Most of Office Support Staff, by Betsy Lazary, shows you how to find, train, and nurture the "perfect" assistant and how to best utilize your support staff professionals. ($9.95 paper)

THE LOYALTY FACTOR: Building Trust in Today's Workplace, by Carol Kinsey Goman, Ph.D., offers techniques for restoring commitment and loyalty in the workplace. ($9.95 paper)

DARE TO CHANGE YOUR JOB—AND YOUR LIFE, by Carole Kanchier, Ph.D., provides a look at career growth and development throughout the life cycle. ($9.95 paper)

TWENTYSOMETHING: Managing and Motivating Today's New Work Force, by Lawrence J. Bradford, Ph.D., and Claire Raines, M.A., examines the work orientation of the younger generation, offering managers in businesses of all kinds a practical guide to better understand and supervise their young employees. ($22.95 cloth)

STEP FORWARD: Sexual Harassment in the Workplace, What You Need to Know, by Susan L. Webb, presents the facts for identifying the tell-tale signs of sexual harassment on the job, and how to deal with it. ($9.95 paper)

TEAMBUILT: Making Teamwork Work, by Mark Sanborn, teaches businesses how to improve productivity, without increasing resources or expenses, by building teamwork among employees. ($19.95 cloth)

FINANCIAL SAVVY FOR WOMEN: A Money Book for Women of All Ages, by Dr. Judith Briles, provides a critical and in-depth look at financial structures and tools any woman wanting to achieve total independence can use. ($14.95 paper)

MIND YOUR OWN BUSINESS: And Keep It in the Family, by Marcy Syms, COO of Syms Corporation, is an effective guide for any organization, small or large, facing what is documented to be the toughest step in managing a family business—making the transition to the new generation. ($18.95 cloth)

OFFICE BIOLOGY: Why Tuesday Is the Most Productive Day and Other Relevant Facts for Survival in the Workplace, by Edith Weiner and Arnold Brown, teaches how in the nineties and beyond we will be expected to work smarter, take better control of our health, adapt to advancing technology, and improve our lives in ways that are not too costly or resource-intensive. ($21.95 cloth)

ON TARGET: Enhance Your Life and Ensure Your Success, by Jeri Sedlar and Rick Miners, is a neatly woven tapestry of insights on career and life issues gathered from audiences across the country. This feedback has been crystallized into a highly readable guidebook for exploring who you are and how to go about getting what you want from your career and your life. ($11.95 paper)

HOT HEALTH CARE CAREERS, by Margaret T. McNally, M.A.,R.N., and Phyllis Schneider, provides readers everything they need to know about training for and getting jobs in a rewarding field where professionals are always in demand. ($10.95 paper; $17.95 cloth)

SELLING YOURSELF, by Kathy Thebo and Joyce Newman, is an inspirational primer for anyone seeking to project a competent, confident image. Drawing on experience, their own and others', these entrepreneurs offer lessons in simple techniques that can add up to big successes. ($9.95 paper)

Order Form

If you would like to order *Positively Outrageous Service and Showmanship* or Scott's other books, just fill out and send a copy of this form to:

MasterMedia Limited
17 East 89th Street
New York, NY 10128
(212) 260-5600
(800) 334-8232
(212) 348-2020 (fax)

Name _____

Address _____

_____

City _____ State _____ Zip _____

Please send me the book(s) indicated below:

_____copy(s) of *POSITIVELY OUTRAGEOUS SERVICE
        AND SHOWMANSHIP* at $12.95 each = $_____

_____copy(s) of *HOW TO GET WHAT YOU WANT
        FROM ALMOST ANYBODY* at $9.95 each = $_____

_____copy(s) of *POSITIVELY OUTRAGEOUS SERVICE*
                    at $14.95 each = $_____

Add $2.00 for postage and handling for the first book
    and $1.00 for each additional book. Total enclosed = $_____

Make payment by check or money order, to MasterMedia Ltd. Sorry, we do not accept credit card payments.